Networks of Mind: Learning, Culture, Neuroscience

Kathy Hall, Alicia Curtin
and Vanessa Rutherford

Routledge
Taylor & Francis Group

LONDON AND NEW YORK

First published 2014
by Routledge
2 Park Square, Milton Park, Abingdon, Oxon OX14 4RN

and by Routledge
711 Third Avenue, New York, NY 10017

Routledge is an imprint of the Taylor & Francis Group, an informa business

© 2014 Kathy Hall, Alicia Curtin and Vanessa Rutherford

The right of Kathy Hall, Alicia Curtin and Vanessa Rutherford to
be identified as authors of this work has been asserted by them in
accordance with sections 77 and 78 of the Copyright, Designs and
Patents Act 1988.

British Library Cataloguing in Publication Data
A catalogue record for this book is available from the British
Library

Library of Congress Cataloging in Publication Data
A catalogue record for this book has been requested

ISBN: 978-0-415-68374-6 (hbk)
ISBN: 978-0-415-68375-3 (pbk)
ISBN: 978-1-315-85079-5 (ebk)

Typeset in Bembo
by RefineCatch Limited, Bungay, Suffolk

MIX
Paper from
responsible sources
FSC
www.fsc.org   FSC® C013604

Printed and bound by CPI Group (UK) Ltd, Croydon, CR0 4YY

We dedicate this book to Rita, Emmet, Joan, Willie John, April, Johannah, William, Breege, Camille and all the members of our families, past, present and to come.

Contents

Acknowledgements

We acknowledge the neuroscientists who generously participated in open-ended interviews with us about their work, its possible implications for learning and development, and about their visions for the future of their discipline. We also thank artist April Curtin, who produced the illustrations on the brain included in Appendix A. We acknowledge the interest and support of our academic and administrative colleagues in the School of Education, UCC, especially the following: Paul Conway, Anita Cronin, Maura Cunneen, Angela Desmond, Claire Dooley, Siobhan Dowling, Mary Horgan, Karl Kitching, Stephanie Larkin, Fiachra Long, Brian Murphy, Rosaleen Murphy and Stephen O'Brien. Kathy Hall would like to acknowledge the many helpful meetings and conversations she had about sociocultural theory with Professor Patricia Murphy who was leader of the Masters in Education Programme (E846) at the Faculty of Education and Language Studies at the Open University. Chapter Four of this book is informed by Kathy's writing for that course. Special thanks to Bruce Roberts at Routledge who commissioned the book and thanks too to Hamish Baxter – their patience allowed us to devote the necessary time to completing the manuscript.

This book could not have been completed without the support of loved ones; we especially thank Tom, Barry and Ronan.

Chapter 1

Introduction

Making the case for examining sociocultural theory and neuroscience

Rationale and orientation

This introductory chapter sets the scene for the book. It highlights the main themes and messages that will be developed throughout the chapters. It provides a rationale for the focus of the work and gives a flavour of some of the big ideas that will be fleshed out more comprehensively and critically later. It explains the background to the writing of the book and introduces the author team.

Some socioculturalists claim that sociocultural theorizing is on the rise and that culture is cutting edge, frontier thinking (Roth and Tobin, 2007). More recently, other researchers have made similar claims for neuroscience and for 'cultural neuroscience' in particular (Kitayama and Park, 2010). It is appropriate and timely, therefore, to open up such claims for scrutiny and to question their significance in the context of learning, teaching and human flourishing generally. How can we make use of culture as an analytic tool for our work as teachers, researchers, policy makers? How is culture understood by sociocultural and neuroscientific researchers? What are the assumptions and grounds underlying the sociocultural and neuroscientific perspectives and how, if at all, are they complementary? We hope this book will contribute to thinking and practice on such questions. It will examine ways of thinking about culture that can pay dividends for how we foster learning, for how we frame success, competence, failure, and so on, and for how we research learning.

As we write this introduction (17 February 2013), an article in the science section of the *New York Times* announces that President Obama's administration is planning a ten-year scientific project to examine the brain and 'build a comprehensive map of its activity'. The project, to be called 'The Brain Activity Map', is expected to trigger some three billion dollars over the next ten years. In his State of the Union address, the President cited brain research as an example of how the government should 'invest in the best ideas'. The designation by a previous USA President of the 1990s as the 'decade of the brain' had already greatly expanded research opportunities and funding streams in neuroscience, with media attention spiralling as a consequence. It is clear that the neurosciences and their sub-disciplines are growing in popularity, status and visibility. Witness the level of interaction on the Internet, *TED Talks*, TV programmes (e.g. Charlie Rose's *Brain Series* on Bloomberg TV and Susan Greenfield's *Brain Story* on the BBC). Because of the recent and rapid expansion of work in neuroscience and its claims about learning and development, as well as its popularity and uptake by educators, it is important to explore its permeation into understandings relevant to education. We set out, therefore, to review the emerging insights from this line of inquiry, explore its fit with established concepts and theories which have emanated from sociocultural science, and consider its utility for education.

Sociocultural ideas like identity, power and culture have salience for many researchers and practitioners but they are not dominant or taken for granted by educators, policy makers and researchers interested in learning. Why sociocultural theory has not enjoyed greater status and application among those seeking to understand and enable development is worth pondering briefly at the outset. There are, we believe, some possible explanations for this state of affairs. First, the ideas are complex, complicated and contentious and they draw on a range of disciplines and theories, including psychology, philosophy, sociology, education, history, semiotics and structuralism, phenomenology and hermeneutics, and cultural and discourse studies. Like all theoretical perspectives, sociocultural theorizing has evolved its own concepts, language and vocabulary which challenge dominant and powerful ways of thinking about and facilitating learning.

However, complexity and interdisciplinarity are inadequate explanations for the slow, if not absent, uptake of sociocultural themes in education policy making and practices. The second explanation, we suggest, is much more relevant. The distributed nature of human thinking, action and meaning-making which is the hallmark of sociocultural thinking conflicts in various ways with Western individualism, intellectualism and rationality. The pre-eminence of the individual divorced from context, structure and institution, as the source and focus of development, has proved highly resilient and resistant to other ways of conceptualizing learning, ability and mind. Thus, an important explanation for the delay in uptake is historical and structural.

Our institutions of learning—schools, colleges and universities—are structured and organized in a manner that privileges personal responsibility and individual achievement. This applies as much to matters of curriculum, pedagogy and assessment as to the physical structure of spaces like rows of tables/desks and lecture theatres. A sociocultural perspective challenges a system that unproblematically attributes successes and failures to individuals and, as such, challenges the way schools function to categorize, select, differentiate and credentialize students without appropriate reference to opportunities to learn. The aspects of schooling that are deeply entrenched and accepted, and power dimensions associated with them, work to ensure the status quo endures. Yet, we know from sociocultural theory itself how practice is never entirely determined but is always open to revision and change.

A further explanation for the limited attention to sociocultural perspectives in learning is the role of traditional psychology in education, with its emphasis on systematically examining phenomena such as personality and self-esteem as if they are variables independent of the social world. Linked to this is another inhibitor–the dominant discourse of quality and effectiveness besieging pedagogy, together with the desire on the part of education policy makers and researchers for 'scientific respectability' based on objectivist notions of knowledge and evidence, and 'what works', orientations that deny the complexity of people's experiences. Indeed, psychologists themselves (Kirschner and Martin, 2010) have recently called for greater attention within the discipline to the 'sociocultural turn' lamenting the overly simplistic, reductive, excessively instrumental and market-driven approaches to concepts such as 'self', 'mind', 'emotion' and 'identity'.

An argument of the book is that sociocultural theory has significant explanatory power: it offers a rich and fruitful set of theoretical resources for understanding and supporting learning, and if acknowledged by educators, could extend opportunities to learn across the lifespan and do so in more equitable and inclusive ways.

We draw on neuroscience in two key respects. First, we are interested in the way some ideas in neuroscience, though coming from a very different theoretical perspective and set of assumptions, appear to align with fundamental ideas in sociocultural theorizing: for example, the notion of opportunity to learn, lifelong learning and the role of emotions in learning. Neuroscience's emphasis on neuroplasticity and the environment are especially relevant and will be examined in some detail. The neuroscientific idea of how the brain regulates and produces a self, challenges the sociocultural notions of agency and intentionality, and we examine this from both perspectives. Additionally, emerging ideas from neuroscience on the 'social mind' and within its own frame of reference, on the social dimension of learning, will be compared and contrasted with sociocultural ideas about mind as distributed.

We are interested in how some aspects of brain science appear to endorse what sociocultural theory has promoted for some time. In particular, we examine the significance of experience and opportunity to learn arising from both perspectives. This is an important focus of the book. We are very aware of the allure of neuroscience, not just for educators and different professional groups, but for members of the public in general. As we prepare this book, a well-known sports broadcaster, Colm Murray, on the Irish national television station, is talking with neuroscientists about his recent diagnosis of motor neuron disease and the fact that he is participating in a drugs trial in search of a cure. As he talks (23 January 2012, RTE1) he refers to his brain as his 'quintessential essence', 'soul' and 'identity'. Technologies such as brain imaging capture the public's imagination in their intimation that the mysteries and secrets of human consciousness could finally be revealed.

The second prong of our engagement with neuroscience, then, is more critical and can be illustrated with what might seem an unremarkable vignette from a 'knowledge exchange' project that two of us are currently leading. In one of its many discussions (on inclusion and learners designated as having 'special education needs') involving a group of teachers and project leaders, one particularly confident, senior teacher, who works in an Autistic Unit attached to a school, argued that children with autism are 'hard-wired differently'. She argued that they are more creative than non-autistic people and that those closely associated with the technological advances of the computer industry, especially in Silicon Valley in California, exhibit a very high incidence of autism. As an example of the neuromyths which have not gone unchallenged from within the neuroscientific community itself (e.g. Dekker *et al.*, 2012), this vignette is an illustration of how the language of neuroscience has permeated the thinking and undoubtedly the practices of teachers, with inevitable consequences for learners, communities and institutional practices. Because neuroscience has begun to transform understandings of ourselves as teachers it merits critical analysis and review. While we acknowledge and discuss in the chapters that follow the neuroscientific insights that enrich our sociocultural understanding of learning, we think it is also important to attend to how neuro-discourses are infiltrating and shaping the way learning, disability, selfhood, mind, environment, and so on, are talked and written about. In doing this, the book tries to explain why neuroscience is so seductive.

Our line of analysis involves elaboration of how education has appropriated neuro-discourses and how neuroscientists have appropriated educational and even sociocultural discourses. In this regard, we will show how neuroscientists position learning, the learner, knowledge, the teacher and learning contexts. How are the messages and concepts from neuroscience shaping teacher and learner identities and potential identities? We address this by offering an analysis of written and oral texts, performances and events of and for neuroscientists. We draw on published research and claims about neuroscience. As we explain in a moment, we draw on open-ended interviews conducted with neuroscientists, all of whom have published in peer-reviewed neuroscientific journals.

Whether the potential hybridity across the two different discourses proves productive for enhancing learning opportunities is debatable and awaits judgement. The different assumptions, often contradictory, underlying the two perspectives, suggest the need to exercise caution. The book will look closely at these assumptions and consider their implications.

In a recent doctoral seminar in which students were discussing the work of several socioculturalists, one student, keen to know if sociocultural theory 'works' in practice, asked the question: What evidence have you that the sociocultural theory works or is effective in practice? It is not an unreasonable question to address in this introduction. The question points to a number of pertinent issues about sociocultural theory that need to be acknowledged at the outset:

- it does not describe or enable some ideal practice and therefore is not the same as, say, 'critical pedagogy', whose ideal is social justice (although we believe that a sociocultural orientation on the part of the educator is likely to maximize inclusion and foster social justice in that it directs attention to how opportunities to learn are allocated and denied people);
- it tries to understand and explain human action and the social world, taking the person as an actor in the world and as inseparable from it;
- it offers a vocabulary and a perspective for the way the social world is;
- it provides a way of seeing and analysing social phenomena and has the potential to raise self-awareness and open up new possibilities for understanding and action in relation to the promotion of learning; and,
- it offers a framework for researching important questions and issues in education and in the social sciences more generally.

Context

Linking to our book title and the idea of networks and networking, one of our motivations, both for ourselves and for the reader, needs further elaboration. Not coming from a neuroscientific background, the body of neuroscientific research we draw on in this text derives from our critical study of relevant neuroscientific literature over the past several years and from our participation at the 2011 Wiring the Brain Neuroscientific Conference, during which we conducted interviews with eighteen neuroscientists.

Wiring the Brain is a biennial international neuroscientific conference, held in 2009 and 2011 in Wicklow, Ireland and held at Cold Spring Harbour Laboratory, New York in 2013. We attended and presented at Wiring the Brain: Making Connections from the 12th to 15th April 2011 at the Ritz-Carlton Hotel, Powerscourt, Wicklow, Ireland. The goal of that particular meeting was to stimulate cross talk between scientists approaching questions of brain connectivity from traditionally separate disciplines. In an online publicity blog post, organizer Kevin Mitchell, from Trinity College Dublin, writes:

> It will bring together world leaders in the fields of developmental neuro-biology, psychiatric genetics, molecular and cellular neuroscience, systems and computational neuroscience, cognitive science and psychology. A major goal is to break down traditional boundaries between these disciplines to enable links to be made between differing levels of observation and explanation. We will explore, for example, how mutations in genes controlling the formation of synaptic connections between neurons can alter local circuitry, changing the interactions between brain regions, thus altering the functions of large-scale neuronal networks, leading to specific cognitive dysfunction, which may ultimately manifest as the symptoms of schizophrenia or autism. Though the subjects dealt with will be much

broader than that, this example illustrates the kind of explanatory frame-work we hope to develop, level by level, from molecules to mind.

(Mitchell, 2010)

Over the four days, presentations from speakers were divided into six sessions: Making Connections, Circuit Dynamics, From Genotype to Phenotype, Activity Dependent Development and Plasticity, Connectivity and From Brain to Mind. Of particular interest to us were Circuit Dynamics (network-level and experience-dependent brain mechanisms), Connectivity (the structure and function of large-scale brain networks, their development and the development of new methods to visualize them) and From Brain to Mind (understanding how brain mediates perception, cognition and behaviour). Three keynote presentations were given by Christopher Walsh, Harvard Medical School (Genetics of Human Cognitive Disorders), Gyorgy Buzsaki, Rutgers University (Brain Rhythms and Cell Assembly Sequences in the Service of Cognition) and Carla Schatz, Stanford University (Releasing the Brakes on Synaptic Plasticity: PirB, MHCI and NgR).

The conference was held in association with Neuroscience Ireland and BioMed Central, and boasted a number of public institutions and large corpo-rate sponsors such as: Science Foundation Ireland, National Institute of Neurological Disorders and Stroke, Genentech, Institute of Neuroscience: Trinity College Dublin, Roche, Philips, Hussman Foundation, Novartis, irelandinspires.com, Health Research Board and Pfizer. Exhibitors (placed nicely in the tea/coffee area) included: LaVision BioTec, Brain Vision UK, Integrated DNA Technologies, Agilent Technologies and Molecular Devices. *Nature* and *Neuron* helped publicize the event, and a follow-up series of review articles based on the conference were to be published in several of BioMed Central's journal titles, including: *BMC Biology, Neural Development, Molecular Autism* and *Neural Systems & Circuits*.

New to this neuroscience world, we took this conference as an opportunity to learn more about neuroscience while at the same time networking with a number of national and international world leaders in the field. Like fish out of water, we studied carefully everything around us and were, at the beginning, reluctant to engage in dialogue with neuroscientific discourse at the level as presented at the conference. The plush surroundings of the Ritz-Carlton and Powerscourt, the executive suites and the gourmet lunches provided, served to remind us well that this was a conference unlike most others we had been to before. The opulence of the welcome reception with sparkling wine and mouth-watering canapés set in the splendour of the Ritz-Carlton is a moment we will not forget.

We participated in the conference by way of a poster-presentation session. We were also very privileged to be able to arrange interviews (prior to the conference) with all three keynote speakers and many of the other speakers at the event. In all, we interviewed eighteen neuroscientists, spoke informally with many more and are extremely grateful to them for their time and generosity, as we acknowledge elsewhere. Having read extensively about neuroscience, from the perspective of educational theorists, such as the work of Usha Goswami (who has also contributed to our understanding of neuroscience), and dabbled a little in the research of the conference attendees we had selected for interview, it was time to fish or cut bait, so to speak; cast our nets or get caught in them.

Fortunately for us, we decided on the former, and our experiences, interviews and poster presentation provided us with the solid ground and raw materials we needed to develop our understandings of neuroscience in this text. From the inside out, we now experienced what we had read about from the outside in, while we debated what it meant to say that we learn, from a neuroscientific perspective. Embraced as something of a curiosity, our questions were answered and our poster session provided us with some very interesting informal feedback in terms of our ideas. Aligning with the conference theme of 'making connections', our poster stood alongside others on genetic variation, diffusion tensor imaging, protein interaction studies; as our names now stand alongside the neuroscientists on the delegate list.

We believe it is important to share this experience with the reader as in this book we move on to interrogate neuroscientific practice and discourse, drawing some tentative conclusions about its importance to education and, specifically, learning. Essential to our text is credibility. It is important that the reader understands we do not do this blindly. While we are not neuroscientists, at this conference we entered a space where we could delve deeper into this world and engage with it, so if we did not walk a mile in the shoes of a neuroscientist, we at the very least tried them on for size, so to speak. Setting out on this project, our conference poster summarizes very well our foundational aims and provides further context for our text.

The beginning of our story: Wiring the Brain, 2011

Our focus at the outset was to interconnect sociocultural and neuroscientific discourse in an explanation of how our brains and our experiences make us who we are. In our presentation, we wanted to demonstrate to a neuroscientific audience how sociocultural ideas (such as the relevance of experience/opportunity to learn/environment, personal histories, meaning, participation, feelings of belonging, emotion and memory) bring meaning to new understandings and evidence emerging from neuroscience. Stationed at our poster, discussions of plasticity and sensitive periods, mirror neurons and common experiences, imitation and culture, mind and brain, turned into debates about the nature of making claims and what it really means to say that we 'learn'. Our poster invited feedback and critique as we also placed a book nearby where attendees could anonymously leave written responses on our project. Throughout the conference we received very positive feedback, and our interviewees and the people we chatted with were very interested in our

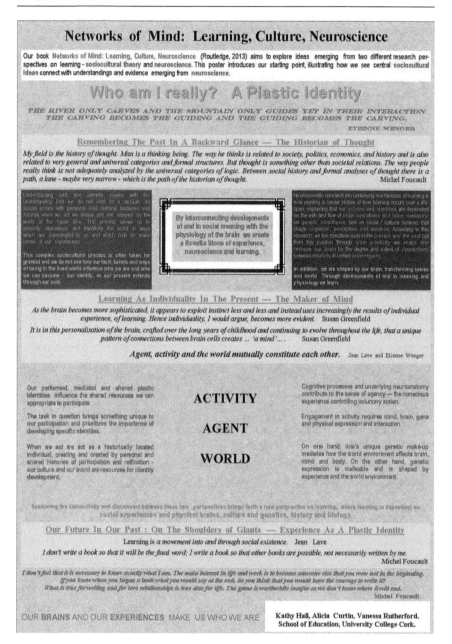

Figure 1.1 Poster at the International Neuroscience Conference (Wicklow, Ireland: April, 2011)

work. To date, sociocultural and neuroscientific perspectives had not (and still have not) been brought together in any clear or concise way, and our presentation and attendance at the conference aimed to inspire discussion on the:

- potential value of connecting these two perspectives;
- importance of filtering lessons from sociocultural and neuroscience perspectives into educational policy and practice; and,
- contemporary need for evidence-based approaches to education, nationally and internationally.

As time went on, however, and as you will see in the text, our experiences, interviews and research complicated our aim, as sociocultural and neuro-scientific discourses contrasted with as well as complemented each other. A story of learning connecting these two discourses through points of comparison and discord was to be much more intricate and multifaceted than we had originally imagined. Our title *Networks of Mind: Learning, Culture, Neuroscience* came to have many meanings as the richness of this particular understanding of learning began to develop in the clashes as well as the similarities between both discourses and practices.

'Networks of Mind' is also a term that perhaps requires a little unpacking at the outset. The word 'network' by definition refers to an interconnected group or system. In our text, it stands for the neural, social and cultural networks that interconnect and are a part of the learning process. More than this, however, it also stands for the networks of discourses and practice implicit within these spheres of modern life. These discourses can themselves at times be contradictory as they carry the lived experiences, past and present, of a particular community. They put forward a particular way of viewing learning and the world but, in so doing, each defines the word 'network' in its own particular way.

Neuroscientists study neural networks, mapping the solo brain into networks of neural activity dependent on what particular task an individual is engaged in. Social networks, by contrast, define the individual as always a part of the community, never alone in the process of learning. The term 'social network' has recently been appropriated to sites dubbed 'social-networking sites' such as Facebook or Twitter, and the form and function of these sites themselves provide very good examples of what the word 'network' means in this context. Here, the network exists outside rather than inside the individual as day by day we share our lives with those around us and invite shared discussion of our practice. Cultural networks we use to define the way in which everything we do as a species is based on our past. Those gone before us have left cultural tools through which we can communicate and mediate the world–language, mathematics, science.

Through this text, we move between and through these discourses and worlds, these networks and sub networks of learning and living. Inter-connecting and deepening our understanding of the opportunities and tensions inherent in these discourses we create our own network–a network of mind where learning becomes embedded in the networks themselves; where neurally, socially and culturally, learning emerges as a part of experience.

To see learning embedded in networks from a sociocultural perspective, defines knowledge not as a 'hand me down' but as a joint creation–shared and mediated on site reconstruction of experience. As social beings, we do this so well it becomes an implicit and tacit part of the learning process, but we must remember, as we stress throughout this text, our conversations, experiences and learning are all imbued with cultural and social meanings. This means we cannot use psychology, philosophy or even neuroscience alone to provide us with the answer to life and how we learn. As we search for meaning in our experience we develop theories, not facts; hypotheses, not truth. As you read this text, it is important to remember that neuroscience and sociocultural theory develop their own particular vocabulary and syntax to bring meaning to experience but that this is a human endeavour. We tell ourselves stories every day, and it is through these stories that we come to experience the world as meaningful; that we learn. This text provides one such story of learning, cautioning individuals not to accept without question the implications of what we say for our understanding of learning and living.

> Language, and the ways of knowing which it affords liberates; but it comes with snares of its own. Although it allows us to learn from the experience of others, and to segment and recombine our own knowledge in novel ways, it creates a different kind of rigidity. As Aldous Huxley said: 'Every individual is at once the beneficiary and the victim of the linguistic tradition into which he has been born–the beneficiary inasmuch as language gives access to the accumulated records of other people's experience; the victim insofar as it … bedevils his sense of reality, so that he is all too apt to take his concepts for data, his words for actual things.'
>
> (Claxton, 1997: 46)

With this understanding in mind, we present this text as one such story about learning. Thus far, we have defined the word 'network' in terms of interconnected groups or systems such as the 'systems' of neuroscientific and sociocultural discourses and practices. Here, we use the word 'network' as neuroscience often appropriates the term: as a noun to describe discrete and separate things–measurable and predefined entities or groups of entities.

However, as socioculturalists, we also prioritize another definition of the word 'network'. Using 'network' as a verb imbues our title and our project with deeper meaning. Just as we networked with neuroscientists at Wiring the Brain, 2011, our text invites its readers to bring their own experiences to bear and network with, engage with and interrogate discourses and assumptions just as we do. Understanding our text as both process and artefact, where each reader makes meaning anew from the stories collected, this text itself creates as well as presents 'networks of mind' as individuals make meaning, negotiate experiences and ultimately draw their own conclusions about what we mean when we say that we 'learn'.

Making the text: authors

The authors work in the School of Education, University College Cork. Collectively they have been exploring and discussing sociocultural and neuro-scientific literatures for several years, meeting regularly to share perspectives and debate particular studies and the plan for this text. Kathy Hall's interest in sociocultural perspectives spans decades, originating in her interest in language and literacy. A member of the British Psychological Society (BPS) she has maintained an interest in cultural psychology with particular reference to relational and cultural aspects of learning and pedagogy (e.g. Hall *et al.*, 2013). She is interested in interdisciplinary perspectives on learning (e.g. Hall *et al.*, 2010) where academics and professionals from a variety of backgrounds tease out and analyse the complexities of the reading process. Along with Alicia Curtin, she is currently investigating workplace learning, more particularly the professional learning of experienced teachers as they seek to better understand their own and others' practices. Alicia's research employs sociocultural theory to explore issues highly relevant to education and learning. These include: adolescent literacies and learning in and outside of the traditional classroom context; language and identity (Curtin, 2011, unpublished PhD thesis); and neuroscientific perspectives on literacy and learning (Curtin and Hall, 2013). With a background in psychology, Alicia is deeply interested in exploring concepts such as mind and consciousness from a variety of perspectives and is a member of the Educational Studies Association of Ireland (ESAI). She has presented recently (with Kathy Hall) on issues central to learning at the United Kingdom Literacy Association (UKLA) International Conference, the Association for Teacher Education in Europe (ATEE) and the European Conference on Educational Research (ECER). Vanessa Rutherford has a background in the history of medicine, specifically medical thought and practice in social, cultural and learning contexts (Rutherford, 2013). A member of the Royal Academy of Medicine in Ireland, she is currently a researcher on an Irish Research Council (IRC) funded project on mathematics student–teacher identity and school/university partnerships (Conway, Murphy and Rutherford, 2013). She is interested in emotions, embodiment and mathematics education. Vanessa has presented her work at the international Platform for a Cultural History of Children's Media, the International Research Society for Children's Literature, the Society for the History of Children and Youth, and Educational Studies Association of Ireland (ESAI).

Structure and sequence of chapters

The book is structured into fourteen chapters. Following this introductory chapter, four chapters offer a detailed analysis of key concepts in both sociocultural and neuroscientific research: brain, mind and culture. These concepts are foundational in both perspectives and will be defined, explained and debated in these early chapters. Chapter 2 explores complementary and contrasting definitions of the word 'brain', teasing out the different conceptions, including the view of brain circulating in popular neuroscientific discourse. Distinguishing brain from mind, Chapter 3 examines notions of mind, introducing, in particular, the idea of mind as distributed, and it signals the importance of this notion of mind for learning. Culture is pivotal to sociocultural theory and is a recent theme in neuroscience as well. Chapters 4 and 5 address this theme in detail. In offering a rich and useful take on culture, practice and identity, Chapter 5 sets up a framework for a detailed discussion of aspects of learning examined in subsequent chapters.

The next six chapters are about 'learning worlds'. Informed by the analyses of earlier chapters, these chapters extend, illuminate and exemplify the themes and issues already theorized in the book. Chapter 6 attends directly to learning and what it is from the gaze of the neuroscientist and socio-culturalist, identifying overlaps and discontinuities. From here, the focus narrows to particular dimensions of learning: ability, talent and creativity, language, emotion and memory. Of course, this is a selection from a long list of possibilities that could exemplify and deepen the more theoretical perspectives presented in the earlier chapters. While we chose these topics to illustrate and extend the earlier ideas, we also believe they merit examination in their own right as they are so pertinent to an understanding of learning and participation in the world, especially to schooling. Sociocultural rather than neuroscientific in orientation, Chapter 7 discusses success and failure, and explains how one implicates the other, in line with our analysis on culture in Chapters 4 and 5. Chapter 8 examines the performance of talent and seeks to understand what we can learn about talent and creativity from an exploration of both perspectives. Chapter 9 links language, culture, plasticity and experience, and here we explore how our practices, rather than our brains, are affected by changes in participation and reification. In view of the significance of feelings for living and learning, Chapter 10 considers emotion from both perspectives illustrating some of the points alluded to in earlier chapters. History and memory are central, in different ways, to both perspectives and Chapter 11 investigates definitions, understandings and applications of memory in both views by posing two key questions: what is memory and why do we remember and forget?

The last three chapters together return the reader to linkages, potential synergies and differences overall in the two perspectives in relation to the study and promotion of learning. Chapter 12 reconsiders metaphors, or identifies metaphors, that have relevance across the theories of learning and development—the chapter suggests heuristics that are both common and helpful in the two ways of looking at development. Chapter 13 is devoted to an explicit comparative study of both takes, with a view to understanding the allure of neuroscience. This chapter demonstrates the complexity of socio-cultural theory and discusses the possibility that neuroscience as a discipline may colonize the learning space. On the basis of the analyses offered throughout the book, the final chapter postulates sociocultural theory as a human and humanistic science that has enormous explanatory power in understanding and promoting learning.

This book does not seek to add another neuro-interdisciplinary area to the many that already exist. In critically examining both sociocultural and neuroscientific conceptualizations and research, we hope it makes a modest contribution to understanding on how humans transform themselves as they live and learn.

Chapter 2

Defining brain

Introduction

This chapter defines brain from a neuroscientific perspective. We draw on the 2007 OECD report, *Understanding the Brain: The Birth of a Learning Science*, a seven-year synthesis of brain-informed approaches to learning, grounding our discussion of neuroscientific research by first explaining a neuroscientific understanding of learning. Drawing on our interview data, we present a neuroscientific model of learning and discuss the implications of a neuroscientific understanding of learning. We explore the uptake of neuroscientific research in popular culture, revealing that in some instances neuroscientific research can be reported incorrectly, misunderstood or even completely wrong. We look at the language in these accounts, questioning what reading and following this advice might mean for our practice. Considering the ethical implications inherent in neuroscientific research, the chapter concludes with a warning against the take up, unquestioned, of neuroscientific discourses and practices. The words we use carry meanings for what we do and this understanding of the power of language is at the heart of this chapter.

Searching for a brain

The sum of the square roots of any two sides of an isosceles triangle is equal to the square root of the remaining side. Oh joy! Rapture! I got a brain! How can I ever thank you enough?

(Scarecrow in *The Wonderful Wizard of Oz*, 1939)

What is a brain? What is its function? Nestled inside the skull that shiny mound of being, that mouse gray parliament of cells, that dream factory, that petit tyrant inside a ball of bone, that huddle of neurons calling all the plays, that little everywhere, that fickle pleasure dome, that wrinkled wardrobe of selves stuffed into the skull like too many clothes in a gym bag.

(Ackerman, 2004: 3)

The brain is pruned and probed, explored and explained, graphed and photographed, our own unique and individual 'monstrous, beautiful mess' (Allman, 1990: 3). Philosophers, psychologists, neuroscientists and education theorists have spent their lives researching this evasive and mysterious organ looking for explanations of behaviour, learning, consciousness and, for many, the secret of life itself. While some may seem to have been more successful than others in their endeavours, the secrets of the brain remain elusive to universal definition. Claiming, however, that we do not have a definition, or more accurately contesting definitions, of the brain is to miss the point.

Regardless of our own particular perspective, our exploration of the brain shares one purpose—a definition of the brain that claims a particular understanding of learning, consciousness and self. Reading different texts, engaging in different conversations about brain function, we change for ourselves conceptually and literally our brains on a daily basis. It is in these processes that the brain becomes a contested site for competing discourses which urge us to live our lives in different ways. It is in these processes that definitions of the brain are produced and reproduced. These definitions do not culminate in a product, rather, they support multiple and mutating definitions which exist and co-exist in the processes and discourses we develop to capture them. This chapter examines brain-based research, and questions what it is really saying and the implications of this for our practice. Defining brain from a largely neuroscientific perspective, this chapter attempts to challenge the power and allure neuroscientific discourse holds over our understanding of learning.

Enter the brain

> Even though it is common knowledge, it never ceases to amaze me that all the richness of our mental life—all our feelings, our emotions, our thoughts, our ambitions, our lives, our religious sentiments and even what each of us regards as his or her own intimate private self—is simply the activity of these little specks of jelly in our heads, in our brains. There is nothing else.
>
> *Phantoms in the Brain* lecture, BBC Radio 4 (Ramachandran, 2003)

> I am often reminded of the image that one might just as well try to understand the sort of people that live in a city like Los Angeles by looking at the traffic patterns on the freeways, as to look at the transmission characteristics in the brain and expect to tell what sort of houses the people lived in, and whether they had Picassos on the walls or preferred the music of the Beatles.
>
> (Adey, 1968)

Understanding how we define contested words such as 'brain', 'mind' and 'consciousness' and accepting the power that these definitions hold has very specific and loaded implications for our everyday practice. What we think influences what we do and why we do it. The popular discourse of neuroscience is currently being picked up by individuals who want to 'learn better', the main problem being that no attention is given to the questioning of neuroscience as only one theory of learning and the implications for the beliefs associated with this discourse because of which people are currently changing their practices in dramatic and minute ways.

This chapter begins by exploring definitions of the word 'brain'. In doing this we are breaking ground for our own definition of brain, understanding the brain in later chapters as a place where learning occurs through neuroscientific and sociocultural processes, when, just like the infamous straw-stuffed man, having a brain is not the end but the beginning of the story. Aware that our own theorizing and conceptualizing of brain is itself a construction that makes its own implicit claims about learning, we question and make explicit throughout this text the implications our language and understanding has for how we live. Central to our understanding of brain science is that environment and experience are key.

'Can't you give me brains?' asked the Scarecrow.

'You don't need them. You are learning something every day. A baby has brains, but it doesn't know much. Experience is the only thing that brings knowledge, and the longer you are on earth the more experience you are sure to get.'

(*The Wonderful Wizard of Oz*, 1939)

Oh joy! Rapture! I got a brain!

Can neuroscience truly improve education? This report suggests a complex, but nonetheless definite answer: 'yes, but ...'

(OECD, 2007a: 21)

Returning once more to the overjoyed Scarecrow and his newly acquired brain begs the question: what will he do with it? While he may never learn fully the inner workings of this new prized possession, what he needs to realize is that the definitions of brain he appropriates from research or popular culture will impact him in every learning experience and interaction he finds himself in from that moment on. Trying to understand the central concepts of one perspective and define them in terms of another is a difficult task, but is central to our thesis. Pausing here to imagine the Scarecrow as neuroscientist or socioculturalist and considering his past and future thoughts and actions from this perspective might sound silly, but is in fact a fertile exercise in identifying for oneself similarities and differences between these two perspectives.

The OECD (2007a) *Understanding the Brain: The Birth of a Learning Science*–which is a seven-year synthesis of brain-informed approaches to learning–provides a very good overview of a neuroscientific understanding of the role of the brain in learning. Looking a little closer at this highly relevant and comprehensive report provides important context for our own publication. For our purpose here, which is to summarize the research relevant to our own thesis, we will also refer to the shorter paper *Understanding the Brain: The Birth of a Learning Science–New Insights on Learning Through Cognitive and Brain Science* (OECD, 2007a).

The OECD report begins with a brief explanation of the brain's architecture. We will summarize some of the main points from this discussion to provide a basis for the discussion that follows in the remainder of our text. The brain is made up of neurons and glial cells. There are approximately 100 billion neurons in the human brain. Neurons are the basic building-blocks of the nervous system. These nerve cells have electrical and chemical properties which allow for the transmission of information between these cells. Each neuron in the human brain exists as a part of various extensively interconnected networks. A connection between two neurons is called a synapse. Glial cells are interspersed between neurons and provide support and insulation. In neuroscientific research, various functional-imaging technologies such as fMRI, MEG, PET, OT, and so on, are used to visualize and study the activity of the changes of blood flow as a result of neuronal activities. Using these tools, neuroscientific studies try to temporally and spatially localize cerebral networks to develop our understanding of learning mechanisms.

Neuroscience understands learning and memory processes as embedded in networks of interconnecting neurons. This interconnection occurs when one neuron (termed a 'presynaptic neuron') transmits information to another neuron (termed a 'postsynaptic neuron') which receives the information. Often, many presynaptic neurons are involved in the activity. The activity level at each synaptic connection regulates its strength or weakness and ultimately its very existence. The OECD report understands this process as responsible for the 'structural encoding of learning and memory processes in the brain' (OECD, 2007a: 37).

Many factors influence this interconnection or communication between neurons, what neuroscientific researchers would understand as learning, including the increasing of connections (synaptogenesis) or the decreasing of connections (pruning) through use. Myelination also influences communica-tion between neurons in a maturing process where, over time, a substance called 'myelin' wraps around a part of the neuron which sends stimuli to other neurons, the axon. These sheaths of myelin act as insulation for the axon and the transmission of information. When an axon is insulated, just like a wire, the electric impulse sent from the neuron can 'jump down the axon in the gaps between the fatty sheaths. Myelinated axoms can transmit information 100 times faster than unmyelinated ones' (OECD, 2007a: 38).

These processes are understood as revealing the extreme plasticity of the human brain and the influence of experience on the brain as neuronal networks are shaped by experience. The degree of modification depends on the type of learning with long-term learning producing more profound results. Learners who learn a great deal in one subject area experience a large growth in neural connections in the related area of the brain. Plasticity is a feature of the brain throughout life, but there are also optimal or sensitive periods during which particular types of learning are most effective, though this sensitivity is currently being challenged in some neuroscientific studies. In infancy we experience an extraordinary growth in synapses; adolescence brings extensive structural changes along with further production of synapses; and, finally, in adulthood fluency or experience with a task can reduce brain activity levels so in later life due to greater processing efficiency we in fact use our brains less.

Describing the functional organization of the brain, the OECD report explains that the brain operates according to the principle of functional localization–that the brain is a highly specialized organ with different areas in the brain responsible for different tasks. Neurons serving similar functions are connected with each other in assemblies. Assemblies are also connected to each other linking brain areas directly and indirectly in complex networks. The brain itself is comprised of two hemispheres; the right and the left. The right hemisphere is understood to play a role in spatial abilities and face recognition, and the left hemisphere is understood to play a role in language development, maths and logic. Parts of the brain have been found to generate neurons throughout life (neurogenesis) and this along with the death of other neurons over a lifetime changes the structure of the brain as it processes information about environment.

Neuroscientific research on the importance of environment highlighted in the report reveals that nurturing is crucial to learning. The environment is seen as something to be modified and optimized so as to improve learning. Emotions have the power to re-sculpt neural tissue and the quality of the social environment and interactions, nutrition, physical exercise and sleep are all listed as environmental factors that impact learning. If we take this advice, and condition our minds and bodies accordingly, we can take advantage of the brain's plasticity and facilitate learning.

The report highlights many key messages and themes from neuroscience for the future of learning, including the following:

- Educational neuroscience is generating valuable new knowledge to inform educational policy and practice.
- Brain research provides important neuroscientific evidence to support the broad aim of life-long learning.
- Neuroscience provides powerful arguments for the wider benefits of learning, particularly for aging populations.
- There is a need for holistic approaches based on the interdependence of body and mind, the emotional and the cognitive.
- In adolescence, young people experience a well-developed cognitive capacity (high horse power) but emotional immaturity (poor steering).

- Curriculum and education's phases need to be informed with neuroscientific insights.
- Neuroscientific insights can be employed to contribute to our understanding of learning disorders such as dyslexia, dyscalculia and dementia.
- Neuroimaging can potentially identify individuals' learning characteristics and base personalization but because of this may also lead to more powerful devices for selection and inclusion.
- Key areas identified for further research include the 'better understanding of such matters as the optimal timing for different forms of learning, emotional development and regulation, how specific materials and environments shape learning, and the continued analysis of language and mathematics in the brain' (OECD, 2007a: 6) which 'would, if realised, be well on the way to the birth of a trans-disciplinary learning science' (OECD, 2007a: 6).

The report also highlights that much needs to be done to understand 'what type of learning requires the interaction of others and on the role of cultural differences' (OECD, 2007a: 12). As we will see in later chapters, and particularly in Chapter 4, this quote reveals the bounded and closed neuroscientific understanding of culture; one that we are trying to open up in this text. In this, we align in some way with the report, which states that:

> We by no means claim that neuroscience is a panacea—and that it will start a revolution in education, especially not immediately. The project leaders have time after time warned us that 'neuroscience alone is unlikely to solve every, if any, educational issue'. The answers to many educational questions are to be found elsewhere, whether within education itself or in other social science reference disciplines.... This report shows that a genuine trans-disciplinary approach drawing from many disciplines is required to respond to the increasingly complex questions with which our societies are confronted.
>
> (OECD, 2007a: 21)

Brain-based learning: a neuroscientific model

Moving from a neuroscientific definition of the brain to one of learning reveals a mechanistic and determined understanding of learning, as exemplified in the following excerpt from Interviewee H, at the (2011) International Neuroscience Conference in Wicklow:

> For me, learning means updating an internal model generated and maintained by the brain about the world. The brain is distant from the world. All it has are sensory inputs that are ambiguous, noisy and the brain has to make sense of them. Any given particular input obtained needs an

image encoded by neurons in the brain and then the brain has to interpret something causing it in the real world. In order to do that it has to have a model. That model is maintained and updated by the brain in light of prediction arrows and that updating is learning–changing of the parameters of the mathematical model by the physiological architecture of the brain.

In this neuroscientific definition of brain, the brain and the world are completely separate entities. Learning is understood simply as updating in a computational sense and the power lies in the brain to be all you can be. He continues:

> There is one overarching theory that may be interesting for learning which claims that the brain may have evolved for nothing other than to generate a model of the world–input, then predictions, what the world delivers. All your brain has to do is interpret these–if your predictions about the world are wrong either you change the way you interpret the world or change your actions where your predictions conform to what the world delivers.

From this perspective, rethinking the mind–brain connection is relatively straightforward as mind is understood as the firing of neurons in an effort to create an internal model of experience and the world. Using clinical language, the brain is explained in terms of a mechanism of learning that computes and calculates data to an internal model that then has to interpret and adapt based on past and future updating (learning). Within this definition, learning becomes a very solitary pursuit, the updating of one's internal models, without an understanding of societal or cultural values of experiences or any mention of social interaction. The agent and activity are locked together in a face-off that can result in perfection for the learner, but only if his or her internal models are good enough.

The pursuit of learning in this case means perfecting these internal models that are stored in the brain and there are a plethora of neuroscientific self-help popular texts on the market that claim to do exactly this. Popular bookstores now have display sections labelled 'Smart Thinking' alongside their 'Self Help' texts. Should you want to be more successful, think better, jump longer, be happier; it seems that a textbook exists with which you can actually improve your life. No other discourse has permeated, or perhaps infiltrated, our lives so completely as the language of neuroscience. Yet believing in this discourse also means believing that consciousness and selfhood exist only in moments where our internal model succeeds in arbitrary processes to bring meaning to experience. It begs the question: how exactly do we define mind, self and identity?

Defining the brain, as we have done here, has many implications for our understanding of learning. In his (2011) text *Mind, Brain and Education: The Impact of Educational Neuroscience on the Science of Teaching*, David A. Sousa explores some of these implications, which we reproduce in Table 2.1.

Table 2.1 A neuroscientific understanding of the brain: Implications for our understanding of learning

Finding	Implication
The human brain continually reorganizes itself on the basis of input through neuroplasticity.	Experiences the young brain has at home and school help shape the neural circuits that determine how and what the brain learns in later life.
Neurons regenerate in the brain and this process is stimulated by physical exercise.	Exercise is fuel for the brain and time for active breaks enhances learning.
Rather than multi tasks, the brain alternates tasks, meaning that the brain can really only focus on one activity at a time.	When learning, the brain should not shift between activities until the primary activity is adequately learned.
When young students learn a second language this does not interfere with their learning of their first language.	Instruction in new languages should be started as early as possible.
Good readers use different neural pathways than struggling readers (Shaywitz, 2003).	Computer programs can be created which help children with their reading by effectively rewiring the brains of struggling readers.
Working memory capacity is decreasing.	Depth rather than breadth is important in learning. Fewer items which are explored more deeply are more likely to be remembered.
Emotions influence learning, memory and recall.	Learning should be linked with activities that evoke emotions in a positive emotional climate.
Movement and exercise have critical roles in learning and memory.	Learning is not a static process— movement and breaks are important.
The emotional part of the teenage brain develops much faster than the rational part.	With knowledge we can better understand the unpredictability of adolescent behaviour. We should also be wary that choices made by adolescents are not final.
Circadian cycles affect focus. Because of this our ability to focus naturally wanes for 30 to 45 minutes just past the middle of the day.	Teaching and learning is most difficult at this time of the day.
Persistent sleep deprivation triggers stress which due to related increases in blood levels reduces ability to focus and impairs memory.	Working into the night or spending too much time on social media can impair focus and memory.
Intelligence and creativity are not genetically fixed and can be modified by environment or schooling.	Learners can raise or lower their own intelligence or creativity.
Exposure to the arts can increase one's attention, spatial skills and creativity.	The arts are important contributors to the development of cognitive processing.
Schools' social and cultural climates affect teaching and learning.	A learner's social growth impacts learning.

Source: Based on Sousa, 2011

Other educational insights assumed to be gleaned from a neuroscientific interrogation of the brain include the fact that the technology that shapes the world we live in, is now also rewiring and restructuring the brains of our children. While neuroscientists confirm the positive impact on the brain of Internet use through encouraging higher order thinking skills and engaging multiple brain areas, there are also drawbacks. In her (2011) paper *The Teenage Brain and Technology*, Feinstein states that it is speculated that the snap-decision making and multi-tasking demanded online and in computer games is resulting in individual's honing these skills to the point of fostering a reduced attention span. Even more worrying is the implication that our new dependence on technology and social media is actually stunting our social interactions and growth.

Making the news: brain headlines[1]

Investigating how these and other neuroscientific understandings of brain-based learning are filtered and transmitted through the media and popular culture to become a part of our everyday practice, is to begin to understand how neuroscientific discourse infiltrates our bodies and activities to simultaneously become a part of self, and deny the existence of self. Kevin Arscott, writer, educator and editor of *The New Journalist* has, in a recent online article (see www.thenewjournalist.co.uk/2012/02/12/just-one-copy-of-the-daily-mail-could-ruin-your-life/), highlighted how neuroscientific research can be misrepresented to the general public in newspaper and online articles. Looking at one popular tabloid newspaper website, declared at the time of writing 'the most read news website in the world', Arscott tells how it has twice won the Orwellian Prize for Journalistic Misrepresentation of a scientific paper in a national newspaper judged on the number of factual errors in the piece. Commenting on this, Oxford University neuroscientist, Dorothy Bishop, responsible for awarding the prize, stated that in relation to the article entitled 'Just one cannabis joint can bring on schizophrenia as well as damaging memory', 'the academic paper is not about cannabis, smoking or schizophrenia'.[2] While the authors of this text, who are not neuroscientists, do not claim to judge the accuracy of newspaper articles in terms of neuroscientific research, an Internet search reveals some very confusing, misleading and at times contradictory headlines in this area (see Table 2.2).

Taking these recent headlines and trying to make wise lifestyle choices is almost paralyzing. Anorexic, vampire bookworms who don't go outside during the day and sniff rosemary on occasion seem to do alright, but what about the rest of us? Statements such as 'chilling pictures reveal shocking effects of alcohol, cigarettes and even caffeine on the *mind*' equate brain and mind and assume that mind is captured, known and measured in fMRI scans. We are *made* intelligent, fat, racist, good mothers, criminals, rioters by our brains, which in the case of psychopaths is defined as *physically deformed* to *prevent* them feeling fear or guilt.

Table 2.2 Newspaper headlines

Date	Headline
26 June 2012	Racism is 'hardwired' into the human brain–and people can be prejudiced without knowing it
11 December 2012	Jogging outside could make you stupid–and more likely to suffer mental health problems
16 November 2012	Air pollution in towns and cities 'ages brains of over-50s by three years'
4 April 2012	The brain diet: Eating the right foods can improve your memory, lift your mood and help you concentrate for longer
21 April 2012	The God spots revealed: Scientists find areas of the brain responsible for spirituality
6 May 2011	The wrong amount of sleep 'can age your brain by up to SEVEN YEARS'
11 April 2012	New brain study shows what makes us intelligent (Hint: The answers are behind your forehead and your left ear)
17 October 2012	Could a transfusion of young blood REALLY rejuvenate old people's brains? Vampire-like treatment could stave off the effects of ageing, say researchers
15 October 2012	It's not all about calories and exercise–your BRAIN could also be making you fat
23 November 2011	Psychopaths aren't just mentally different–their brains are physically deformed to prevent them feeling fear or guilt
30 March 2010	Scientists discover moral compass in the brain which can be controlled by magnets
28 February 2012	How sniffing rosemary could boost your brain power
12 June 2012	Why meditation helps you focus: Mindfulness improves brain wiring in just a month
11 August 2011	Can't add up? We are either born with a mathematical brain or not
5 December 2011	Violent homes have the 'same effect on brains of children as combat does on soldiers'
20 December 2011	Eating less 'can boost your brain and help you remember more'
9 August 2011	Rioters may have 'lower levels' of brain chemical that keeps impulsive behaviour under control
25 August 2012	Getting lost in a good book can help keep you healthy
4 September 2012	Men and women really DO see things differently: Our brains process colours in different ways
4 May 2009	Are you wrecking your brain? Chilling pictures reveal shocking effects of alcohol, cigarettes and even caffeine on the mind
19 October 2012	Children who suffer brain injuries are more likely to become criminals later in life
28 November 2011	Boost your baby's brain power: Scientists say wait two years before having your second child
20 September 2011	Can't stop yawning? You might not just be tired … your brain could be over-heating
15 November 2011	Teenage video game players have brains 'like gambling addicts'
28 October 2012	Horrifying scans that show the real impact of love: Brain of neglected child is much smaller than that of a normal three year old
23 December 2011	'Baby brain' syndrome IS real … and it makes you a better mother

The key to our own spirituality is hidden in the brain, alongside a moral compass that can be externally controlled. Mindfulness and meditation *improves* brain wiring in just a month, while the wrong amount of sleep could be doing irreversible damage to our brains. Overheating and violent homes can do damage to your brain, but if you want to be a maths genius you are either born with it or not.

The language itself that is used in these headlines is disturbing and should be subject to further analysis. It is deterministic, damning–in the excuses made, all power is taken from the individual and placed on the text and the brain it represents. We are made by our brains, and our brains themselves may come previously hardwired so that even they are not in control of what follows. The line *Teenage video game players have brains 'like gambling addicts'* captures very little of what it means to be either a teenage child or a gambling addict, yet readers engage with this on a daily basis as if it all makes sense.

Taking as an example the *Daily Mail* article 'Psychopaths aren't just mentally different–their brains are physically deformed to prevent them feeling fear or guilt'[3] and looking at the implication behind the language used exemplifies our argument that popular neuroscience is making extreme claims of what it means to live and learn without providing readers with any actual evidence for these claims:

> Brains of psychopaths have 'broken links' between parts responsible for empathy and guilt.... MRI scan can determine if someone is a psychopath.... Research offers hope of a 'cure'.... Psychopaths such as Hannibal Lecter–Anthony Hopkins' character in Silence of the Lambs–have detectable, physical differences in their brains. The news could help 'screen' for psychopaths–and even help treat the formerly untreatable disorder.... New research has uncovered that manipulative, callous and sometimes violent behaviour could actually be hard-wired into psycho-paths from birth.... The disorder is untreatable–and this discovery could unlock new ways to understand, and perhaps even treat the disorder.... 'I hope our research will shed light on the source of psychopathy–and strategies for treating it'.[4]

Brain in brief: the Jennifer Aniston gene

Aligning itself with all that is bright and shiny, the ability of neuroscientific discourse to adapt and target different individuals and societies is very powerful. The title of this section alludes to the identification of the Jennifer Aniston neuron in a recent study by Rodrigo Quian Quiroga (building on the work of Itzhak Fried), where he identifies a single cell that fires in an individual's brain in response to the concept of Jennifer Aniston, a famous TV and film star (Quiroga and Panzeri, 2013). That is, in a specific patient he found that the same neuron fired every time the patient saw any image of Jennifer Aniston, heard her voice, or recognized her name, either written or spoken. This led to further neuroscientific research and the identification of other such celebrity genes such as the Bill Clinton gene and the Halle Berry gene. What followed was a series of Internet, news and magazine bulletins aimed at all and no levels of neuroscientific understanding, taking this finding as evidence for different meanings.

Those engaging with the debate came from many different backgrounds and disciplines hyping neuroscience as Godlike in its research and insights, yet never agreeing on what these insights were. Headlines such as *Neuroscientists battle furiously over Jennifer Aniston* and *Scientists discuss Jennifer Aniston gene: Fascinating or freaky?* touched a new audience, while the articles themselves had little to say. Other neuroscientists contested that rather than finding the Jennifer Aniston gene, what was actually observed was the summit of associated neurons; that when we think of Jennifer Aniston, we think of everything about her–hair colour, eye colour, tan–and the neuron that lights up in this study is actually receiving signals from thousands of lower down neurons responsible for associations such as colour, shape, etc. At the end of the debate what became clear was that nothing was clear, but that seemed to matter least of all. New theories of mind, memory and related concepts were being posited as a result of these findings while the findings themselves had nothing conclusive to say. Even more worrying is the forgotten question that, if it were possible that a Jennifer Aniston gene exists, what implications would this have for our understanding of self–can a single brain cell think?

It is because of incidents such as this that we believe neuroscientific discourse as it appears in the popular press (and where it is accessed by a very wide audience), lacks not only the critical but also the explanatory power to, alone, explain something as complex as its own subject matter, the human brain. Beyond this, we also believe that the whole of life's experience does not boil down to 1300 grams of grey matter. Linking back to the points we make in Chapter One, when neuroscientific research removes the experience from the investigation, there is simply no experience to explain.

Education, ethics and neuroscience

> The Brain does not think, we think the brain.
>
> Nietzsche (in OECD, 2007a: 21)

In its discussion of the ethics and organization of educational neuroscience, the OECD report previously discussed also highlights some important questions in relation to a neuroscientific definition of brain and learning. The report asks for what purposes and for whom is fMRI data being researched and used, suggesting the very possible abuse of brain imaging and research. It also states that the boundary between medical and non-medical use of products affecting the brain is not always clear cut, asking if parents should have the right to give their children substances to stimulate scholarly achievements, with inherent risks and parallels to doping in sport. Also central to the report's concern is the very pertinent question: where will all this knowledge take us? Advances made combining living tissue with machines could be used to control individual behaviour as well as help those with disabilities. Finally, the report highlights a question central to this book: is a neuroscientific approach to learning, alone, an overly scientistic approach to education?

> We cross our bridges when we come to them and burn them behind us, with nothing to show for our progress except a memory of the smell of smoke, and a presumption that once our eyes watered.
>
> (Stoppard, 2013)

As a discourse on the verge of changing how we live our lives, it is only natural that the phenomenon should be questioned and interrogated just as other perspectives that attempt to develop theories of mind are (psychology, philosophy, sociocultural theory). It is surprising, then, that this is not the case. Under the banner of science but without conclusive evidence or indeed a conclusive subject of study (brain, mind, consciousness . . .), the allure of neuroscience ensures it remains untouchable while other discourses such as sociocultural theory are dismissed without proper consideration of their value for education theory and practice. In their article 'Mind, brain and education: The birth of a new science', Ferrari and McBride (2011) summarize the power of neuroscience very well:

> Research shows that neuroimages such as MRIs are persuasive to both educators and to the public (Weisberg et al., 2008). Feigenson (2006) hypothesized that neuroimages reduce psychosocial complexities to features of the brain that can be directly viewed. When faced with complex, unfamiliar information, individuals tend to use a reductionist structure to reduce psychological phenomena to their lower level neuroscientific counterparts (Weisberg et al., 2008). In addition, neuroscience is associated with powerful visual imagery, which tends to render scientific claims more convincing.
>
> (Ferrari and McBride, 2011: 95)

We conclude this section with another example from what has now become an endless bank of sub-disciplines—the area of literary neuroscience—and a study completed by Natalie Phillips, professor of Eighteenth-Century Literature and Culture at Michigan State University. Professor Phillips asked participants to either read closely or scan Jane Austen's *Pride and Prejudice* while lying in an fMRI scanner (Phillips, 2013). Neuroscientists told Natalie that there would be few differences in brain function between these tasks but in what has been termed *a neuroscientific twist*[5] there were some interesting results.

Neuroscientists found that close reading activated parts of the brain usually involved in movement and touch, as though readers were themselves a part of the story. Identifying these activated areas in the brain, neuroscientists were surprised but happy with the results. In their fMRI slice of brain life, neuroscientists claim to have explained the process of reading. The problem remains, however, that they have not. All they have done is looked at the process of reading in another way. The fMRI scans themselves, and the neuroscientists that read them, both lack the explanatory power to provide a theory of learning. fMRI scans provide subject matter for analysis and explanation, but are not explanations in themselves. We ask readers to bear this *in mind* as we move forward with our sociocultural exploration of brain, mind and learning.

Conclusion

In this chapter, we have attempted to define the brain, and learning, from a neuroscientific perspective. In doing this, we divide neuroscience into the neuroscientific research and studies carried out in labs and universities around the world, and the neuroscience as distilled through popular culture and media. We also note, most importantly, that this is a distinction not always made as newspapers and popular texts literally tell us how we should live our lives.

Aligning with one of the central principles of the OECD (2007a) *Understanding the Brain: The Birth of a Learning Science*, we believe that neuroscience alone, in either context, cannot carry sufficient meaning and understanding through which we can usefully conceptualize or theorize about learning. We put forward sociocultural theory, an integration of social and cultural perspectives, measuring it in later chapters against neuroscience for its explanatory power. Writer and literary critic Ralph Ellison once said that 'Education is all a matter of building bridges' (Ellison, 2013). In our journey in writing this book we set out with a similar understanding, but have come to the conclusion that if we want to build bridges we first have to know how to draw a line.

Notes

1 From http://www.dailymail.co.uk
2 Article available at http://deevybee.blogspot.ie/2012/01/2011-orwellian-prize-for-journalistic.html–Bishops Orwellian prize.
3 Taken from http://www.dailymail.co.uk/sciencetech/article-2065161/Psychopaths-arent-just-mentally-different--brains-physically-deformed-prevent-feeling-fear-guilt.html
4 Taken from http://www.dailymail.co.uk/sciencetech/article-2065161/Psychopaths-arent-just-mentally-different--brains-physically-deformed-prevent-feeling-fear-guilt.html
5 http://www.npr.org/blogs/health/2012/10/09/162401053/a-lively-mind-your-brain-on-jane-austen

Chapter 3

The making of minds

Introduction

This chapter takes a broad-strokes approach to our central thesis: that the brain is an inherently social organ and learning occurs when an individual takes part in an activity within a particular community of practice, context, culture and world. Developing on the discussion within the last chapter, sociocultural theory and neuroscience take their places here as two vying explanations of learning, as the language and metaphors intrinsic in both are interrogated with reference to their respective understandings not of brain, but of mind and selfhood.

Defining mind

> I always thought of it like you said, that all the strings inside him broke. But there are a thousand ways to look at it: maybe the strings break, or maybe our ships sink, or maybe we're grass—our roots so interdependent that no one is dead as long as someone is alive. We don't suffer from a shortage of metaphors, is what I mean. But you have to be careful which metaphor you choose, because it matters. If you choose the strings, then you're imagining a world in which you can become irreparably broken. If you choose the grass, you're saying that we are all infinitely interconnected, that we can use these root systems not only to understand one another but to become one another. The metaphors have implications. Do you know what I mean?
> (Green, 2008: 301)

In this text, we explore the connectivity, to borrow a neuroscientific term, of neuroscience and sociocultural theory, but that is not to ignore the inherent tensions and disconnects between neuroscientific and sociocultural discourses and practices. Understanding this as a sociocultural process we cannot create an organic synthesis as both carry their own baggage in terms of their histories, language, communities of practice and ongoing tensions within their own respective fields. Despite this, we believe there to be real value in our endeavour as, for us, metaphors matter. What we believe about how we learn governs how we view and understand learning and impacts practice, policy and society itself.

The language we use to talk about learning has real-life effects for how we live. What is mind? Where is it located? Is mind an effect of the brain? Or is mind more relational, shared between communities and cultures over time in reifications (shared beliefs) of right and wrong, true and false? This chapter investigates in greater detail notions of selfhood and mind, asking what it means for our *selves* to understand learning and life in a particular way.

To do this, we turn neuroscientific and sociocultural discourses on themselves and each other in an attempt to uncover what both say about the concept of mind and what it means to learn; questioning ultimately what this says about them. Neuroscience and sociocultural theory can be understood as mirror images of mind, as they reflect through very different lenses the same subject–what it is that happens when one learns.

We will begin with a story.

> I remember I was eight years old when my grandmother died. There was a huge funeral and hundreds of people came. I cried for days. My mother told us we should not be too sad and even tried to get us to help at the funeral. My sister refused to go to school and we slept in my grandmother's room for a long time afterwards . . . Then when I was thirteen my mother died. We went to the funeral Mass and our friends and neighbors walked past us to shake our hands but I knew in my gut they were all thinking that they were glad they were not us and wondering what they would do in our situation. I remember that my sister could not stop shivering all day even though it was really hot. After the funeral only a few people came back to our house and my dad went to bed. I helped our neighbor Jenny serve the tea and sandwiches and then finally everyone went home. No one bothered to wash anything up. I went upstairs and then it suddenly struck me that we would have to wash them in the morning. Me, Elly and dad. My mother was dead. Elly was asleep when I opened the door so I did not bother with the light. I crawled into bed and closed my eyes. I could not sleep for hours but even then I did not cry. I could not believe that my mother was gone.
>
> (Samantha, age fifteen)

Samantha's story of the deaths of her grandmother and her mother in childhood and adolescence is a poignant and heartfelt remembrance of painful experience still very much a part of her everyday life. Though now fifteen years old, Samantha misses her mother and her grandmother every day. More than this, however, Samantha's story reveals in many ways a sociocultural and neuroscientific learning process; that mind and body are inextricably linked through neural, cultural and social networks that become apparent in a study of brain development, everyday experiences and social interaction. Samantha's experiences emphasize the physiological, neural *and* social factors that influence mind, learning and development in our day-to-day lives.

As a young child, Samantha's best response to her grief is to cry; a physiological response to the sadness felt at the death of her grandmother, most likely accompanied by chemical changes in the brain evident in behaviour as a lack of concentration and motivation, listlessness, appetite loss and despair. Her means of coping comes through her social interaction with her sister and others as well as crying and a more systematic physiological regulation of emotions. These physiological changes occur in Samantha's brain and shape her cognition and thought as the activation of different neurons alter mental states, which Samantha experiences as feeling and emotions and which, in turn, affect her thought and social behaviour in very different ways. At the same time, however, Samantha engages in social interaction with family and friends, talking to her sister and mother, and this also shapes her experience of her grandmother's death and activates certain other neurons in the brain that influence brain development, social behaviour and interaction. In this way, Samantha learns how to cope with the experience of her grandmother's death by employing the neural *and* social networks available to her at this time; and both influence Samantha's experience, thought, brain development, social interaction and learning.

At thirteen years of age, Samantha's experience of grief is very different. Her disbelief at her mother's death means that her body and mind cannot engage in an appropriate way with the emotions she is feeling and she is cut off from her grief and experience physiologically and socially. She cannot cry because her shock and disbelief at her mother's death block the activation of the part of her brain that regulates the feeling of sadness and crying. Despite this, because of her previous experience of death, Samantha also knows exactly what will come next. She has learnt through experience that, even after death, life goes on. Dishes must be washed and she and her sister must return to school.

Samantha's story emphasizes the importance of a life history and social interaction approach to a study of physical brain development. Brain plasticity–the ability of the brain to change as a result of experience and social interaction– connects sociocultural and neuroscientific perspectives. Samantha's experiences provide this book with a methodological framework, as her story reveals the social mind and physical brain in action, interaction and development.

Mirror images of mind

Each morning, we wake up and experience a rich explosion of consciousness–the bright morning sunlight, the smell of roast coffee and, for some of us, the warmth of the person lying next to us in bed. As the slumber recedes into the night, we awake to become who we are. The morning haze of dreams and oblivion disperses and lifts as recognition and recall bubble up in the content of our memories into consciousness. For the briefest of moments, we are not sure where we are and then suddenly 'I', the one that is aware, awakens. We gather our thoughts so that the 'I' who is conscious becomes the 'me'–the person with a past. The memories of the previous day return. The plans for the immediate future reformulate. The realization that we have things to get on with reminds us that it is a work day. We become a person whom we recognize ... We glance at the mirror. We take a moment to reflect. We look a little older, but we are still the same person who has looked in that same mirror every day since we moved in. We see our self in that mirror. This is who we are.

(Hood, 2012: viii)

Who am I? When I wake up in the morning, what does it mean to be 'me' and how do I know that I am 'me'? Defining a sense of self is central to our understanding of who we are and what we do. The concepts we appropriate to understand our selves, the language we employ to talk about 'me', 'I', 'self', all carry collected meanings and assumptions for our future practice. For many of us, recognizing who we *are* is often the first turn on the road to who we want to *become*. Neuroscientific discourse equates our sense of self with consciousness, claiming that consciousness can be understood as 'the appearance of a world' (Metzinger, 2010a: 15). The metaphor of the sleepwalker appears frequently in neuroscientific research to illustrate the nature of human consciousness. Presenting a sleepwalker as an unconscious human being, unaware of the world around them, we see very quickly what a difference consciousness makes. It is:

a certain fluidity, a flexibility, a context sensitivity ... We have the feeling of being present in the real world ... You could describe it as a specific illusion, but it is a major neurocomputational achievement of the human brain–the sense of presence as a self in a conscious scene.

(Metzinger, 2010a)

While the sleep-walking image does capture very nicely the experience of consciousness, it lacks the explanatory power to define it. It might be seen as a 'specific illusion', 'a major neurocomputational achievement of the human brain', but what does this actually mean? What does this add to our understanding of self? As a lens and a mirror, neuroscientific discourse is too narrow in focus alone to put real meaning on experience.

Mirrors provide us with an important metaphor as we explore symmetry and asymmetry between competing discourses. It is interpretation that is key. Mirrors do not reverse objects; rather, a mirror presents an image to an observer, who in the act of seeing, reverses parts of the image. It is in the experience of seeing itself that the reversal occurs. If I hold a sheet of paper which displays text that is written backwards up to a mirror, I will indeed be able to perceive it in the mirror the correct way around, but my right arm which holds up the piece of paper is still in the same relative position in the mirror (on the right). My head is still on top. My legs are at the bottom. Interpretation takes over, however, and suddenly I have an image that makes sense to me, as part of the image is manipulated so we can perceive it in a different way–seeing and believing.

Neuroscience acts as a mirror through which we can see what happens in the brain when learning occurs. Sociocultural theory acts as a mirror through which we can see what happens in our practice when learning occurs. Both can offer valuable insights for our understanding of learning but it is important to remember that both of these perspectives are developed discourses and do not represent universal truths–in plain terms, the glass can lie. Further, it is our belief that neuroscientific discourse, alone, does not provide us with adequate explanations of learning that can be usefully and gainfully employed in education theory development.

This issue has now become even more problematic as sophisticated and deterministic neuroscientific discourses fail to recognize that its brain-based studies offer us one way to investigate learning–visually through fMRI scans etc. Mapping the brain is a human endeavour and dependent on human instruments, tools, measures. Neuroscience is a person-made tool through which we, as a society, have decided it is valuable to study learning. However, somewhere along the way the tool has become the evidence. Using an introverted lens, neuroscience looks on itself to explain something that exists independent of neuroscientific research. A study of learning has become a study of the brain, and no one has stopped to ask why. Studying what happens in the brain when one learns can provide interesting insights into the process of learning and mind, as can a study of what happens in the world and in social interaction. But learning is more than just what happens in the brain or what happens in the world.

An example of the very intricate nature of the relationship between learning, culture and neuroscience can be found at the very outset of brain-based research, and traced through history. Before we had fMRI scans, new technology, etc., we had the physical brain. Scientists studied the physical matter, asking what role brain size played in learning and intelligence. Earlier than this, explanations of intelligence were sought in the skull. Even now, as recently as 2012, new pictures of Einstein's brain have caused a sensation in the neuroscientific world. Einstein's intelligence, in this most recent study, is *possibly* attributed to his prefrontal cortex, as the brain itself is, by comparison, quite small in size. There is also now an iPad app, where you can poke and prod the brain of the famous genius just in case you might find some secrets yourself that have eluded the scientists. This neuroscientific preoccupation with brain size and physicality, an organ five times larger than expected for a mammal of our size, rather than a study of learning is very interesting. In its focus on form, neuroscience has turned on its head and its subject of study becomes itself rather than what it means to say that we learn.

Since its inception, neuroscience has struggled to explain or even collate the relationship between the physical brain as an organ in the human body and the almost mystical processes it attributes to it. As a sociocultural contrast, Professor of Evolutionary Psychology and head of the Social and Evolutionary Neuroscience Research Group at Oxford University, Robin Dunbar, and his research in the animal world, exemplifies the explanatory power of sociocultural theory as he elucidates how larger brains facilitate social behaviour. His study of locusts reveals most interestingly that this solitary creature literally changes its brain when it enters the swarm phase of its life cycle as it migrates to a different location in a swarm. As each locust becomes aware that they are now a part of a group, the areas in the brain associated with learning and memory enlarge by one-third, evidencing the very social nature of the brain and its relationship with social interaction and environment.

This again aligns with our central thesis that, as a discourse, neuroscience lacks the explanatory power alone to explain or even explore issues such as mind, human learning and self, because it is a closed circular system that begins and ends in the brain, without a definite understanding of the role the brain itself or environment, for that matter, plays in learning. Who is to say that the lines and dots, colours and flashes when we hook a brain up to a man-made machine actually mean anything at all? They mean something because we say they do. Or perhaps because we tell them to.

Killer brains

It is very interesting here to remember the very disconcerting experience of neuroscientist Jim Fallon who, in his study of the brains of serial killers, unearthed a deep, dark secret in his own family and in his own brain. Having studied over seventy brains belonging to murderers, Jim found out that his own family line was home to eight possible murderers, including a famous distant cousin–Lizzie Borden. Correlating findings from family brain-scans with an analysis of genes thought to be associated with violence and aggression, Jim found that his own brain was not dissimilar to those of the murderers he had spent his life studying.

He found that areas in his own brain associated with social adjustment, aggression, impulsivity and the processing of emotional reactions were 'turned off' in comparison with most people, where not only are these areas 'turned on', but they are also roughly in balance. In Jim's brain and in the brains of the murderers he studied, these areas, believed to be involved with ethical behaviour, moral decision-making and impulse control, exhibit no or very low activity. Jim's story stands as a cautionary tale, a very modern Aesop's fable, suggesting, on the one hand, the danger of too much knowledge and, on the other, questioning what we should take as known from the story. Examining this story using a sociocultural lens reveals that we can no more know our brains than we can know our minds or our selves, as identity and selfhood, meaning and belonging are won and lost from moment to moment in social interactions and shared experiences. Jim's final word on the embarrassing and surprising series of events echoes this sociocultural sentiment:

> I had a charmed childhood. But if I had been mistreated as a child, who knows what might have happened? ... We will never know, but the way these patterns are looking in general population, had I been abused, we might not be sitting here today.
>
> (Jim Fallon, quoted in Naik, 2009)

A neuroscientific matter of mind

> The great topmost sheet of the mass, that where hardly a light had twinkled or moved, becomes now a sparkling field of rhythmic flashing points with trains of traveling sparks hurrying hither and thither. The brain is waking and with it the mind is returning. It is as if the Milky Way entered upon some cosmic dance. Swiftly the head mass becomes an enchanted loom where millions of flashing shuttles weave a dissolving pattern, always a meaningful pattern though never an abiding one; a shifting harmony of subpatterns.
>
> (Sherrington, 1942: 178)

The beginnings of neuroscience are often traced back to this quote, a rudimentary understanding of brain function that has been in recent times fleshed out in neurons and synapse. Here, the creativity of the brain is viewed as an enchanted loom, which whizzes and whirrs according to its own special and secret tune. The loom is enchanted, it moves by itself–it needs no weaver. There is no self or me, there is no other, there is just the magical loom. Here, again, just as with the sleepwalker, nothing is explained–it simply is in isolation and splendour.

Understanding mind from a neuroscientific perspective defines mind and self as simply an effect of the brain, and mental distress can be remedied by medication in the brain. Closed off from the outside world, the mind simply functions because of changes in neuron and synapse. A neuroscientific understanding of mind as movement and chemical processes in pathways and circuits creates a real sense of urgency around critical periods, windows of opportunity and milestones where in learning and selfhood all can be lost or gained according to neural function. Diagrams of neural networks show how cells wire and fire together through a language of determined connectedness, where optimization and improvement are the primary goals. Spatial location is seen as a critical factor for learning and specialization, and localization of the brain, in terms of modules, mental functions and regions, determine behaviour and thus self. In a vocabulary of discovery and action, the final frontier of the mind is mapped across neural geographies as techniques are developed that change, create and develop function. The mind itself can be known, and will, self and consciousness become a matter of metaphysics. Consciousness becomes 'a dialogue between the local and the global ... an emerging pattern ... something that must persist as a result of the input' (Interviewee A, from the International Neuroscience Conference, Wicklow, 2011). The idea of plasticity acknowledges the malleability of the human brain, but this plasticity is understood in terms of scientific interventions on neural development rather than dependent in lived experience.

In this understanding, self is simply a physiological process, 'a repeatedly reconstructed biological state' (Thornton, 2011: 47). Identity, self, learning and experience can be quantified and visualized in brain scans, which according to Thornton (2011), are themselves a very good example of how a neuroscientific discourse works, as though they carry the authoritative weight of science their meaning is not clear, they are mediated by the contexts in which they circulate and they can be used to support contesting claims.

Brain function occurs as along a process grid which 'lights up' in a similar way to a telecommunications network (another neuroscientific metaphor) when certain areas are activated. In sociocultural terms, this same process could be visualized in terms of scaffolding, where learning is built upon learning through sociocultural processes, such as socioculturalist Barbara Rogoff's planes of apprenticeship, guided participation and participatory appropriation (see Appendix C: Sociocultural Glossary). In neuroscientific terms, the brain is real estate; land to be rezoned. An area of the brain is agentive and can abandon its career laid out from birth and adopt new skills and tendencies; but in neuroscientific discourse, this occurs again without full consideration of the activity and world which make up the agent.

A neuroscientific understanding of mind as outlined here uses scientific terminology in an attempt to make everyday experience technical and measurable. Colloquialisms try to make the language of neuroscience accessible while the positivist medical language posits neuroscience as an alluring and active pursuit of health. Urgent but practical demands are made on the learner who is sucked in by the possibility of being able to simultaneously accept and deny responsibility for actions depending on context through the conflicting neuroscientific discourses. The central message seems to be that through knowledge we can create better selves, minds, communities and worlds. Mind becomes simply what the brain does, and life is calculable in terms of measurements and interventions (Thornton, 2011).

A sociocultural mind over matter

For I do not exist: there exists but the thousands of mirrors that reflect me. With every acquaintance I make, the population of phantoms resembling me increases. Somewhere they live, somewhere they multiply. I alone do not exist.

(Nabokov, 2013)

Sociocultural understandings of consciousness and mind see shared narrative as contributing to a person's selfhood in social and shared processes, not only neurological wiring. Sociocultural theory also has its own set of metaphors to explain brain creativity, one of which is the metaphor of an interacting landscape: 'The river only carves and the mountain only guides yet in their interaction the carving becomes the guiding and the guiding becomes the carving' (Wenger, 1998: 71).

Here, in the fluid movements of flowing brook and jagged rock, we see one become the other as learning and living, our minds and our selves, become one experience: our participation in the world. Etienne Wenger's important contribution to sociocultural theory through his understanding of the duality of participation and reification is explored in more depth in Chapter 5. Other competing metaphors of learning as a photographic camera from neuroscience and a full ship and crew from sociocultural theory again reveal the differences inherent in how both perspectives understand the mind.

> no single individual on the bridge acting alone—neither the captain nor the navigator nor the quartermaster chief supervising the navigation team—could have kept control of the ship and brought it safely to anchor. Many kinds of thinking were required to perform this task. Some of them were happening in parallel, some in co-ordination with others, some inside the heads of an individual, and some quite clearly both inside and outside the heads of the participants.
>
> (Hutchins, 1995: 5–6)

In the above quote, where Hutchins (1995) describes what happened when the steering gear of a ship, USS Palau, failed as it entered San Diego harbour, shows how it takes a full crew in interaction with each other with a range of experiences and a range of tools available to them to keep a ship afloat. This compares to the neuroscientific metaphor where a very simple mechanism inside a camera calculates and copies an experience to be stored as fact in internal memory. From a neuroscientific perspective, there is no interaction, no negotiation, and the end product is more important than the sociocultural process. This is a metaphor of acquisition rather than a metaphor of participation (Sfard, 1998).

Aligning with our exploration of culture in the following chapter, as socioculturalists we also understand mind as emergent, contingent, indeterminate, sedimented, performed and dynamic, not as something that can be pinned down and contained, and assumed to be stable across context, activities and people. A key means through which individuals organize learning and experience selfhood is through the 'stories of the self' that, just like Samantha, they develop, express or enact. We think of learning and selfhood as the very process of negotiating a world, and an identity within that world, and therefore our attention has to be directed to people's intentions as they express and enact them; that is, as they emerge in the discourses and scripts that inform the person's notions of a desired self.

In 1902, Charles Horton Cooley, an American sociologist, suggested that self is shaped by the reflected opinions of others as we become *looking glass selves*. Within this process Cooley explains we first imagine how we appear to others. We then imagine the judgement of that appearance, ultimately developing ourselves through the judgement of others (Yeung and Martin, 2003). This occurs through interactions where we also take on the role of the other, feeling empathy and seeing through someone else's eyes. In this way for Cooley 'the thing that moves us to pride or shame is not the mere mechanical reflection of ourselves, but an imputed sentiment, the imagined effect of this reflection upon another's mind' (Cooley, 1902: 184).

This sociocultural understanding of self and mind places the individual within a community, defining consciousness as relational, shared, emergent, mediated and distributed by the world in which we live and those we share it with. Within this world, the neuroscientific metaphor of the sleepwalker does not work as, simply put, someone would wake you up. In sociocultural terms, it is not possible to be unconscious, as in the act of living we are learning, and experience, living and learning are inextricably linked. Learning is not something you set out to do—measurable and defined within set boundaries—it is who you are, your development of self within the communities you participate in.

The language of neuroscience focuses almost entirely on the biological agent but reflecting these neuroscientific understandings of learning in a sociocultural discourse, we believe, returns this biological agent to the activity and world in which they are firmly embedded and which are also central to learning. In this analysis, we refer to Jean Lave's sociocultural concept of agent, activity and world (a definition of which can be found in Appendix C: Sociocultural glossary) and a concept that is explored in greater detail in Chapter 6. A sociocultural understanding of learning and self acknowledges changes in brain form and function, but rather than seeing the individual as acquiring learning, learning acquires us through the myriad of activities and social interactions we take part in within the different communities of practice—at home, school, work, etc.—of which we are a part.

Through social processes of participation (taking part in the world) and reification (developing artefacts and reifications of our practice to guide us in the future), we engage in meaningful experiences and we learn. From this perspective, our participation becomes a source of self. In this view, mind and cognition are distributed across and mediated by the various communities of practice or social networks of which we are a part. Learning is emergent and agency, or the strategic making and remaking of selves within structures of power (Lewis, Enciso and Moje, 2007: 4), is central to how we experience the world and negotiate selfhood. Learning is about performance rather than acquisition and the ability to 'become' a full member in our communities of practice.

Returning to an important point introduced in the previous chapter, using a brain scan to explain experience is also an example of the way neuroscientific discourses ignore the situated and constitutive nature of learning. A sociocultural understanding argues that agent, activity and the world *of which the agent and activity are a part* come together in a very unique and meaningful way when learning occurs, and this has to happen before any neurons can wire or fire. Going beyond learning, sociocultural theory also has something to say about the formation of consciousness and self, as in its exploration of the cultural and social construction of reality it makes visible what has previously been, and currently remains in neuroscientific discourse, invisible—how learning is situated in a world where we act, behave and think using tools and scripts we are not always conscious of. In its clinical separation of content from context, body from world and self from mind, neuroscientific discourse alone falls short of explaining the social and cultural nature of knowing and experience.

A fundamental concept of sociocultural theory is the idea that *mind* or *cognition* similar to culture is a culturally and socially mediated phenomenon. Mind and thought are understood as interdependent processes which undergo qualitative transformations or *mediations*. These mediations occur on cultural, social and historical planes through the employment of cultural tools and resources, language, social interaction and previous histories of participating in the world outside, rather than inside, individual heads. By contrast, understanding *mind* neuroscientifically, as previously discussed, allows a complete mapping of what is understood as simply neurological function.

From a sociocultural perspective, the cultural mediation of learning occurs through the use of cultural tools and artefacts such as language, symbols and shared representations. The social mediation of learning occurs through our interactions with others as we go about our day-to-day experiences. Thus, not only is our thinking mediated by culture and society, but also our actions become mediations based on cultural, social, historical and present experiences. Within this understanding, it becomes very difficult to do or think anything that has not been influenced by historical, cultural or social factors. Though this has always been the case, we can now understand this complex process in terms of our rich and varied cultural histories.

Sociocultural theory further develops our understanding of mind as mediated by explaining that cognition is also situated and distributed, locating learning between individuals within a group, rather than in individual heads and *minds*. In this view, mind becomes a truly social and cultural phenomenon as our social interactions and use of cultural tools become our experiences and learning in the everyday. Distributed cognition can be seen at a cultural and societal level in our developing of certain culturally acceptable traits and behaviours, or the following of certain cultural or historical traditions. Distributed cognition in everyday practice means that we change the date Christians celebrate Easter every year or that we normally wear clothes when we go outside.

Breaking the mirrors

Comparing sociocultural and neuroscientific discourses, it appears that woven together from threads of very different origins we have two very different vocabularies and theories for explaining some similar processes. For example, what neuroscience understands as localized in the brain, sociocultural theory, returning agent to world, sees as distributed across communities of practice. Where neuroscientific research talks about plasticity, sociocultural theory stresses experience as a part of the process. While not perhaps two halves of the same whole, elements of sociocultural theory can be compared and contrasted with elements of neuroscience to further our understanding of mind, self and learning.

Neuroscientific concepts, language and vocabulary challenge the sociocultural outlook on learning and human flourishing. The sudden and unrelenting tide of neuroscience and brain imaging is transforming our secular soul into a place for speculating about who we are in a 'molecularization' of life itself (Rose, 2007a: 15). The language of neuroscience offers 'a new grammar for understanding our minds' (Thornton, 2011: 17) where 'the cells that make up our nervous system describe sunsets, craft poetry, solve equations, remember birthdays, dream' (Niehoff, 2005, in Thornton, 2011: 56). Explaining learning through this new and extremely popular language make(s) up citizens in new ways (Rose, 2007a), fundamentally changing our understanding of concepts such as learning, self, mind and ultimately how we understand and live our lives. Language carries concepts.

At the heart of this chapter and this book is an understanding of the dynamic and mutually constitutive relationships between how we talk about our brains, cultural practices and our understanding of mind–the networks of selfhood. We view the brain as a discursive space where the language of neuroscience currently attempts to coordinate personal, social and biological dimensions of life and translate them into a common scientific language for living. Within this process, there is always the possibility of a neuroscientific takeover, hostile or otherwise, as its language fits with our current economic and wider social structures as 'neuroscience' has become the buzzword of the twenty-first century.

For example, as mentioned in Chapter 1, on 2 April 2013, American President Barack Obama announced the Brain Initiative (Brain Research through Advancing Innovative Neurotechnologies) making it very clear that the 'decade of the brain' has certainly not come to an end. Obama's goal is to map the human brain with initial funding of one hundred million American dollars. In his speech, he links benefits of this initiative for science, the economy and the entire human race:

> What if computers could respond to our thoughts or our language barriers could come tumbling down? Or if millions of Americans were suddenly finding new jobs in these fields–jobs we haven't even dreamt up yet–because we chose to invest in this project.... That's the future we're imagining. That's what we're hoping for. That's why the Brain Initiative is so absolutely important.... It's what America has been all about. We have been a nation of dreamers and risk-takers; people who see what nobody else sees sooner than anybody else sees it. We do innovation better than anybody else–and that makes our economy stronger.... The Apollo project that put a man on the moon eventually gave us CAT scans.
>
> (Obama, 2013: quoted online)

We wish to draw attention to this as we believe, as Thornton (2011) explains, that biological languages such as neuroscience do not make the brain or mind transparent to scientific knowledge; rather they 'reshuffle categories and fold the elusive qualities of choice, will and agency into the language of biology, attributing them to neurons or electrochemical processes' (Thornton, 2011: 57). We question whether or not the neuroscientific clinical and at times deterministic understanding of self provides a satisfying explanation of how the richness of lived experiences come to make up mind, and in this chapter begin to consider what a sociocultural discourse might have to add to the story. Table 3.1 summarizes the neuroscientific and sociocultural definitions of mind we have presented in this chapter.

Within this, it is important to remember here that language is never neutral but is deeply implicated in the production of our social and cultural worlds. The

Table 3.1 Two minds: the eternal reflection between two mirrors

A neuroscientific mind	A sociocultural mind
Chemical and neural processes	Social interaction
Neural networks	Communities of practice
Neural connections	Participation and reification
Plasticity	Experience
Spatialization	Mediation
Localization	Distribution
Specialization	Legitimate peripheral participation and full member status
Temporal	Meaningful and emergent
Action and discovery	Agency
A determined self	**A negotiation of identity**

metaphors for learning that align with particular perspectives offer us competing discourses through which we can engage with the world and develop an identity. The discourse an individual chooses goes a long way to making up our sense of self, as returning to our opening quote to this chapter reminds us.

> I like the strings. I always have. Because that's how it *feels*. But the strings make pain seem more fatal than it is, I think. We're not as frail as the strings would make us believe. And I like the grass, too. The grass got me to you, helped me to imagine you as an actual person. But we're not different sprouts from the same plant. I can't be you. You can't be me. You can imagine another well–but never quite perfectly, you know? ... Maybe it's more like you said before, all of us being cracked open. Like, each of us starts out as a watertight vessel. And these things happen–these people leave us, or don't love us, or don't get us, or we don't get them, and we lose and fail and hurt one another. And the vessel starts to crack open in places. And I mean, yeah, once the vessel cracks open, the end becomes inevitable. Once it starts to rain inside the Osprey, it will never be remodelled. But there is all this time between when the cracks start to open up and when we finally fall apart. And it's only in that time that we can see one another, because we see out of ourselves through our cracks and into others through theirs. When did we see each other face-to-face? Not until you saw into my cracks and I saw into yours. Before that, we were just looking at ideas of each other, like looking at your window shade but never seeing inside. But once the vessel cracks, the light can get in. The light can get out.
>
> (Green, 2008: 301–302)

Engaging with the debates inherent in mind/brain research, we believe that the brain, mind and more importantly the experiences we engage in through it are more complex than a simple neurological mapping can accommodate. The brain exists and functions alongside culture, experience and social interaction, where to remember an event is a complex process involving all senses as we *in our mind's eye* see, hear, feel, taste and touch the moment and those around us. We believe that neuroscientific language alone, as it powers learning theory and research, is not enough to fully articulate the complex nature of learning and living.

There is a danger that too much faith in form forgets about the importance of function and sociocultural as well as biological processes. When learning works, it works, but attempting to recreate the same experience elsewhere is not always successful. This is in fact due itself to the inherent social nature of learning. From a sociocultural perspective, the metaphorical neuroscientific loom becomes loaded with a host of new and multicoloured threads that can be woven together in new and meaningful ways. In this way, we present this text itself as a metaphorical loom where we attempt to knit together both biology *and* experience in a sense of self.

Understanding mind: putting the pieces back together again

> Most people are mirrors, reflecting the moods and emotions of the times. Some people are windows, bringing light to bear on the dark corners where troubles fester. The whole purpose of education is to turn mirrors into windows.
>
> (Harris, 2013: quoted online)

The central task of this chapter has been to break down into metaphoric or constitutive pieces sociocultural and neuroscientific understanding of selfhood and mind so that in the remaining chapters they may be pieced together again in a new understanding of learning. Taken apart, they expose and inter-rogate the assumptions of the other, but put back together in a very careful and specific way they offer points of connection and a new emerging under-standing of learning. Taking the superficial broken reflections and transforming them into windows to a new understanding is the task of the remaining chapters. We conclude with a few important points about learning in terms of the sociocultural understanding of mind outlined in this chapter.

Learning experiences radically alter human brain architecture. The ability of the brain to modify and reform throughout life as a result of learning and in response to environmental change confirms its unique plasticity. But under-standing selfhood and mind begins with the understanding that we do not exist in a vacuum. As social actors with personal and cultural histories and futures, when we act we shape and are shaped by the world at the same time. This process allows us to socially reproduce and transform the world in ways that are meaningful to us and that help us make sense of our experiences. This complex sociocultural process is often taken for granted and we do not see how our tacit beliefs and ways of being in the lived world influence who we are and who we can become—our identity, self and mind, as our present extends through our past.

Neuroscientific research into underlying mechanisms of learning and under-standing of mind is now painting a similar picture of how learning occurs over a lifespan, though in a very different language, explaining that our actions and self are dependent on the ebb and flow of brain operations and brain chemistry, on genetic inheritance, and on social/cultural systems that shape cognition, perception and emotion. According to this research, we live simultaneously in the present and the past, but from this position through brain plasticity we shape and reshape our brain by the degree and extent of connections between neurons in certain brain regions. In addition, we are shaped by our brain, trans-forming minds, selves and world. Through developments of and in meaning and physiology we learn. Cognitive processes and underlying neuroanatomy contribute to the sense of agency—the conscious experience controlling voluntary action, but this is only a part of the story.

On the one hand, one's unique genetic make-up mediates how the world environment affects brain, mind and body. On the other hand, genetic expression is malleable and is shaped by experience and the world environment. The task in question, as well as the other people, cultural tools and social and physical space in which the activity takes place, brings something unique to our participation and prioritizes the importance of developing specific selves. When we act, we act as a historically located individual, creating and created by personal and shared histories of participation and reification—our culture and our world are resources for identity development. Our performed, mediated and shared plastic identities influence the shared resources we can appropriate to participate. Engagement in activity requires mind, brain, gene and physical expression and interaction.

From a neuroscientific perspective, the brain needs a variety of learning strategies and experiences in order to orchestrate a complete learning experience, yet learning is still viewed as something to attain and possess, rather than something we do and become. Experience, emotion, environment and motivation stimulate and re-sculpt the physical brain throughout the life cycle. In a world where definitions and understandings of self can make all the difference between sane and insane, innocent and guilty, now more than ever it is important that we understand what it means to say we are ourselves or that we learn.

In an examination following his arrest, the perpetrator of the 2011 attacks on the Labour Party in Norway, Anders Behring Breivik, was diagnosed with paranoid schizophrenia and was declared criminally insane. In April 2012, he was declared to be sane. In January 2013, a lawsuit was filed against the University of Colorado, alleging that a school psychiatrist could have prevented the 2012 Aurora shootings during a midnight screening of the film *The Dark Knight Rises* by James Eagan Holmes, after he admitted he fantasized about killing a lot of people. Our point here is that, understood as a science, neuroscience holds extreme power over individuals, but as a science of behaviour with the influence to announce people as responsible or not for their actions, we too have a responsibility to interrogate its person-made tools and theories of self and mind. Mind exists not in individual heads, but in shared social practices and reifications of what is deemed of value to a particular community or society.

> As the brain becomes more sophisticated, it appears to exploit instinct less and less and instead uses increasingly the results of individual experience, of learning. Hence individuality, I would argue, becomes more evident.... It is in this personalisation of the brain, crafted over the long years of childhood and continuing to evolve throughout the life, that a unique pattern of connections between brain cells creates ... 'a mind'.
>
> (Greenfield, 2000: 13)

Conclusion

This chapter has revealed how sociocultural ideas such as participation, culture, meaning, relationships, agency and identity, though complex, are very helpful in understanding mind, selfhood and the ways people learn, how people extend their capabilities in different settings and through different experiences, and how they become expert participants in a valued activity. This line of inquiry into learning (in the broadest sense) offers very significant insights into how we foster (and constrain) human learning through our practices and our policies. It is a line of inquiry that merits much more attention than it currently gets by those interested in fostering learning, especially practitioners and policy makers. A key point is that learning and living are inseparable, yet practices in our institutions, such as schools and universities, sometimes deny this reality.

Sociocultural learning theory, often seen as the poor relation when it comes to understanding self, directs attention to such issues as: the learning opportunities available and denied in any given interaction; the resources–human and material–available in the environment; peer relationships; how people's ways of knowing are acknowledged/denied and built upon; how one is helped to grasp what counts as success in a given context; and how moment-by-moment interactions can be so pivotal for one's sense of self and therefore one's power to act and interact purposefully. Alongside neuro-scientific discourse, sociocultural theory deepens both our vocabulary and understanding of what it means when we say that we learn.

Chapter 4

The making of culture

Introduction

> Once upon a time, a little girl named Nell was assigned to prepare an oral report about her cultural background. Nell realised that she did not know very much about hers. What could she say that would give her report the flavor and color of 'culture'? Nell felt a wave of panic as she thought about what to show and tell. 'I'm not anything', she thought, 'I'm just an American'. Seeking to impress her teacher and classmates with at least some colorful details on her family's food, dress, and holidays, Nell asked her mother for help. But Nell was disappointed when, barely looking up from the vegetables she was preparing for dinner, her mother merely shrugged at the question, 'What are we?' She replied, 'I don't know. Some mix of Irish and English, I guess. It was a long time ago'. When pressed her mother could summon none of the colorful details Nell hoped to include in her report. Frustrated and desperate for a story, Nell tells us, 'I dreaded having to give that report'. So, she confesses, to make her cultural background interesting, 'I faked being from Poland'.
>
> (Florio-Ruane, 2001: xxiii)

This is a student teacher recalling what was for her a memorable multicultural festival she experienced as a child in her elementary school. We reproduce it here to highlight a take on culture as something exotic, as something to do with food and festival and as something only associated with people who come from the non-dominant group in society. Nell is seen as lacking in her knowledge of culture while her teacher and formal education could be read as trivializing it, associating it only with a static view—culture as equal to ethnicity. Is culture just a label for a group of people? As the researcher, Florio-Ruane says in her analysis of this vignette, the child's teacher and mother can be understood as indicative of an unreflective and taken-for-granted stance of the White middle-class on history, power and privilege where words like 'diversity', 'culture' and 'multicultural' pertain only to non-dominant, traditionally marginalized groups. We share Florio-Ruane's interpretation.

Another related conception of culture is that different groups of people live in different ways to other groups (usually the mainstream or majority) because they have different ways of making sense of the world. This culture as separatist or blanket view tends to position groups of people of particular heritages and loyalties in the same way and to ascribe stability to cultural ways of knowing. An example of this in practice, especially in post-primary schooling, is similar-ability grouping. Another example in Ireland (though not common), is grouping traveller children together for teaching. Yet another (far more common) example is single-sex schooling. The assumption underlying these practices is that there are two main cultural groups who have so much in difference and so much within-group consistency that they both benefit from separate teaching/ schooling. Cultural differences are seen here as individual traits. Beliefs in stable traits within individuals can manifest themselves in practices such as inflexible grouping which, in turn, is likely to influence teacher expectations and student achievement. The assumption of coherent and stable attributions of characteristics locates culture inside individuals' heads–the emphasis is very much on social categories and people as 'carriers of culture' (Gutierrez and Rogoff, 2003). This chapter examines the concept of culture in some depth.

It has been claimed that 'exciting' findings in 'cultural neuroscience' testify to the value of a marriage between neuroscience and sociocultural theory and, in particular, how cultural neuroscience has the potential to lead to improved education practices and mutual understanding across cultures (see Ames and Fiske, 2010). Our interest in researching this area more generally in this book, is to explore such a possibility or, more particularly, to discuss what might be gained in terms of our understanding of learning by such a marriage. What kind of a marriage is it or might it be, and what would it mean for our conceptualizing of learning? To our knowledge, this is the first comparative theorization of culture in neuroscience and sociocultural theory with reference to possible implications for learning.

In 1996, Michael Cole's sociocultural book introduced cultural psychology as a 'front and future discipline'. Borrowing this language, a special issue devoted to cultural neuroscience in the journal *SCAN*, cultural neuroscience is described as 'a once and future discipline' and as offering 'cutting-edge discoveries' (Chiao, 2010: 109). In this special issue, the neuroscientists Shinobu Kitayama and Jiyoung Park (2010: 126) proclaim that 'culture has become a frontier for neuroscience and, conversely, neuroscience has also become a frontier for cultural psychology'. A few years earlier (2007), the socioculturalists Wolff-Michael Roth and Kenneth Tobin made the point that sociocultural theorizing is on the rise and that culture is cutting-edge, frontier thinking. The concept of culture is central to sociocultural theory and now obviously central to cultural neuroscience as well. But, is the definition of culture shared in each case? How is it understood by neuroscientists–at least by those claiming to be cultural neuroscientists–and does it align with the view of socioculturalists? A fundamental theme in both perspectives, yet a word in common usage, it is important to tease out its meanings and their respective implications for how we might understand learning and the promotion of learning. This is the task we have set for ourselves in this explanatory chapter. While some analysts have sought to tease out the potential contribution of cultural neuroscience for the study of culture itself (e.g. Denkhaus and Bos, 2012), we are more interested in its potential for extending our understanding of human development and learning.

The next section introduces and analyses neuroscientific concepts of culture, primarily as reflected in the first generation of empirical studies. The chapter then goes on to consider culture from a sociocultural perspective, linking where relevant with neuroscience's desire to more seriously adopt a constitutive approach. Throughout, we draw out implications for learning and we identify potential overlaps and divergences. In the conclusion, we speculate as to the potential for a marriage, a living of separate lives, a merger or a takeover.

The importance of culture to neuroscientists

Cultural neuroscience stems from the expressed desire to recognize the mutually constitutive nature of culture, mind and brain, and throughout the literature there are several references to the work of various cultural theorists, very familiar to those who work within a sociocultural frame, such as Clifford Geertz, Michael Cole and James Wertsch, to name but a few. The logic used by neuroscientists in its embrace of culture stems from the claim that the brain requires culture; that experience, which is the basis of the neural plasticity in the brain, is organized by culture. The infrastructure of the brain is shaped by and shapes culture. There is a strong evolutionary, biological strand running through the rationale for neuroscience's interest in culture. It claims to advance a view of human mind as 'biologically prepared and yet supplemented, transformed and fully completed through active participation and engagement in the eco-symbolic environment called culture' (Kitayama and Park, 2010: 112). It is argued that those individuals who have the ability to acquire and practise the current culture's tools and tasks maximize their chances of obtaining fully-fledged status as cultural members, thereby enhancing their ability to attract a mate (e.g. Miller and Kinsbourne, 2012). Their fundamental interest is to understand brain mechanisms underlying processes such as perception, judgement and decision making, processes which they recognize are highly pertinent to acquiring competence in the valued culture.

The expectations that cultural neuroscientists have for their line of work are ambitious, and within them is an implied notion of culture. Among the issues highlighted in the literature as of research interest to them are the following:

- an understanding of the neural manifestations of socially shared meanings and practices;
- an understanding of the neural mechanisms facilitating cultural meanings and practices;

- the extent to which and how the genetically programmed maturation of cerebral hemispheres is fine-tuned by their interaction with the human environment, especially caretakers, and how this modulation of brain development is influenced by different cultural practices;
- the influence culture plays in subjective experience;
- whether adaptations by the brain to contrasting cultural environments become fixed or remain malleable in response to subsequent changes in the cultural environment;
- whether differences in how the brain approaches various environmental issues are simply pragmatic, or whether they reflect early learning that involves long-lasting adaptation by the brain as it develops and matures; and,
- the possibility of linking performance on cultural tasks to life stages, gender and other socio-demographic categories.

How culture is conceptualized

We examined how neuroscientists who describe themselves as cultural neuroscientists think about 'culture'. We paid attention to their definitions of culture and to how they operationalized it in their empirical studies.

Culture is defined as an amalgam of values, meanings, conventions and artefacts that constitute daily social realities. Three elements of culture are noted in the literature and are highlighted, in particular, in the lead article in the special issue noted above (Kitayama and Park, 2010). The first component of culture refers to 'explicit values' that are emphasized in a given group: for instance, independence is assumed to be highly valued in the West and interdependence highly valued in the East. The second component of culture, labelled 'cultural tasks', involves routines, shared scripts for action, and various conventions and appropriate behaviours designed to achieve the primary values, say, independence. Both these dimensions of culture emanate directly from the work of cognitive psychologists and anthropologists and are accepted by neuroscientists—this is part of the basis of the interdisciplinarity. The third component of culture is a mix of psychological and neurological tendencies. Differences in the neurological tendencies or brain pathways among groups for the same tasks are attributed to culture and, on the basis of the empirical studies we found, this constitutes a major line of cultural neuroscientific inquiry so far in the field.

Currently, the vast majority of studies aim to localize cognitive processes and rely, at least partially, on cognitive theory to interpret their results. To conduct these studies, the researcher typically operationalizes the construct of interest by designing a simple task to which participants respond. In some studies, participants look at a series of pictures and rate how strongly they feel about what they see. Such ratings are then typically correlated with measures of neural activity using brain-imaging technologies, i.e. Positron Emission Tomography (PET), Single Photon Emission Compute Tomography (SPECT),

Electroencephalography, Magnetoencephalography and Functional Magnetic Resonance Imaging (fMRI).

In their empirical studies, cultural neuroscientists tend to take for granted the claims of anthropologists, especially dominant in the second half of the twentieth century, about differences among groups of people in relation to a host of dimensions including the self, independence or individualism, interdependence or collectivism and, additionally, to take it that such evidence has implications for learning and development–anthropologists and cognitive psychologists having established such claims based on behavioural and belief measures obtained through inventories, questionnaires and psychometric tests. They are willing to accept, for instance, that people from a North American middle-class background and their Western European counterparts show more independence in placing a high value on a personal self, having personal goals, desires and needs, while people from an Eastern background (e.g. China, Korea, Japan and Taiwan) are more interdependent, placing more emphasis on social goals and concerns.

Emotions derived from independence, it is assumed at least in one series of studies, include pride, feelings of superiority and 'socially disengaging emotions' such as anger and frustration. Emotions assumed to be derived from interdependence include friendly feelings, respect, guilt and shame, the latter called 'socially engaging emotions' (Kitayama and Park, 2010: 118; Chiao et al., 2010). Assuming that socially engaging emotions are associated more with Asians and socially disengaging emotions are associated more with European Americans, they value and call for research that would explore cross-cultural variations on brain areas for these populations. Similarly, work by Zhu et al. (2007), Ng et al. (2010) and Ray et al. (2010) showing a neural basis of cultural influence on self-representation leads to the idea of a Western self and an East, Asian self. This line of inquiry shows that the medial prefrontal cortex is important for representations of oneself (as opposed to representations of related others) among Westerners, but not among Chinese participants.

The argument is that cultural tools and cultural practices have powerful influences on neurological pathways and that specific cultural tools and practices promote certain brain changes. There are several empirical studies, many still in press or only published in the past five to ten years, that justify their argument. In addition to those listed above, the neural correlates of a host of psychological mechanisms have been investigated: from empathy to language, from music to number representation, and from self-awareness to mental arithmetic. One such study shows that, for native English speakers, the left perisylvian cortices, areas usually associated with linguistic processing, are activated, while, for native Chinese speakers, a premotor area is activated. Other examples attest to different brain patterns for abacus experts in Japan and arithmetic processing in a sample of Chinese people. A study by Tang et al. (2006) recorded participants' brain activation as they carried out two types of mathematical task–an addition task and a comparison task. In each task, participants were presented with three numbers simultaneously. In the addition task, participants judged whether the third number was equal to the sum of the first two numbers, whereas in the comparison task, participants were asked to judge whether the third number was greater than both the first two numbers. In accuracy and response time, both Chinese and Westerners performed equally well but significant group differences emerged in regional brain activation, as indicated by fMRI. Western participants showed greater activation in the perisylvian regions, including in the Broca and Wernicke areas, in both tasks. Chinese participants, however, showed greater activation in the visuo-premotor association areas and this was especially evident during the comparison task. Furthermore, a connectivity analysis was carried out to investigate possible cultural differences in the functional neural networks involved in the comparison task. It emerged that different neural networks were activated in Western and Chinese participants. On the basis of these results, Tang and colleagues suggested that the culturally specific brain activation during numerical processing corresponded to the application of different cognitive tools that had been learned in the culture.

Yet some cognitive psychologists and some neuroscientists have been challenging the assumption of a linear relationship between perceptions and cultural context, especially country or ethnicity. The work of Richard Nisbett and Yuri Miyamoto (2005) exemplifies this in relation to the influence of culture on holistic versus analytic perception. Research had established that Westerners tend to engage in context-independent and analytic perceptual processes by focusing on a salient object independently of its context, whereas Asians were inclined to be more holistic by attending to the relationship between the object and the context in which the object is located. Their research explored mechanisms underlying such cultural differences and showed that participating in different social practices leads to shifts in perception. These findings point to a more complicated relationship between the cultural context and perceptual processes.

We would argue that there is somewhat of a disconnect between the claim to subscribe to a constitutive stance on culture, brain and mind, on the one hand, and the operationalization on that stance, on the other hand, in the empirical research studies conducted. The importance of values, beliefs, artefacts, cultural tasks and practices is acknowledged thus implying (a) the role of patterns and meaning, rather than mere group membership, (b) the idea that culture is not just in the head but is part of the environment, and (c) the recognition of context, all aligning with a sociocultural view. Yet, in the empirical studies culture is treated differently, as an independent variable with the neural dimension treated as the dependent variable.

An essentialist, bounded view of culture?

Cultural neuroscientists say that the new evidence from their empirical research studies is impressive. They conclude that the brain and its various neural processing pathways are influenced, sometimes significantly, by culture, and that as a consequence, when two or more vastly different cultures are compared, highly systematic differences in brain responses can be detected (Kitayama and Park, 2010). Culture's influence on the brain, they conjecture, arises from 'repeated participation and engagement in culture's conventions, routines, and socially shared scripts for action'. However, they go further than this. They also claim that because the brain reflects culture, brain activation patterns can provide important information about the very characteristics of the cultures themselves that are compared (124). So, from this claim it follows that the brain can tell something about culture.

Is the version of culture espoused in practice by cultural neuroscientists a separatist view, a bounded model, one that is not permeable? At the level of the empirical studies, it would appear so. While there are references to and studies of within-group variation in brain pattern and there are several overtures made to the work of socioculturalists, assumptions underlying the empirical studies would appear to be that:

- culture is an entity, stable and bounded;
- culture reflects itself in ideas that are internal to the person;
- culture is built into the person's brain as a result of experience;
- culture is something that is group- and geographically-based;
- culture can be established by the use of inventories such as questionnaires; and,
- culture can be measured and represented as brain images of activation.

Further assumptions include the following:

- people belong to just one culture, or at least belong primarily to just one culture;
- because people are assumed to belong to one culture, the assumption is that those people share not only the same values, but also have had the same experiences;
- because people can be categorized as belonging to a culture and because culture is viewed as a discrete entity, cultures can be compared and contrasted;
- people accept the dominant values of their community, country, ethnic group;
- variation with groups is ignored; and,
- geographical location is predictive of culture.

Culture and brain making each other up

There is plenty of critique of cultural neuroscientists' take on culture from within and without the neuroscience field (Mateo *et al.*, 2012; Denkhaus and Bos, 2012; Bao and Pöppel, 2012; Whiteley, 2012). We ourselves are less interested in whether their take on culture is 'right' or 'wrong' and more interested in its adequacy for a sophisticated understanding of learning.

While some of the assumptions above are challenged by a sociocultural view, there are important messages for learning and its promotion even at this stage. The emphasis on socially shared ideas and experiences moves attention for learning beyond the immediacy of the individual's brain and acknowledges the diversity and history of communities. To the extent that an activity is more or less prominent in a given culture, the expectation is that repeated participation in that activity would lead to cultural differences in functional connectivity and in the physical structure of the brain (Kitayama and Tompson, 2010). The various researchers noted above make this point repeatedly, whether the study is about number, music or language. Once people engage in the same activities or in 'scripted patterns of action' over a period of time their brains change accordingly. But interestingly, from a sociocultural viewpoint, that engagement may have to be 'active', i.e. conscious, wilful and voluntary. So it would seem that subjective commitment, personal goals, agency and internal satisfaction all matter. Neural activity increases when participation is meaningful to the person. Presumably, the converse is also relevant. People may resist and object to engagement in the mainstream culture of the group in question, they may engage in different pursuits, all with consequences for functional connectivity.

Another feature that is more implicit than explicit in the work of cultural neuroscientists is the role of social interaction and language, which we highlight in more detail below. But for now we note that the sharing of culture through social interaction and participation in joint activity signals the potential for cultural practices, values and beliefs to transcend geography, to travel and cross boundaries. Later, we discuss a take on culture where boundaries are not fixed, where the 'container leaks'.

Living culturally as opposed to living in a culture

While socioculturalists do not deny the importance of looking for patterns in how members of communities participate in everyday practices, they would guard against responding to people primarily on the basis of cultural or geographic background, sex, etc., preferring to build contexts for learners through shared experiences and interaction.

Socioculturalists think of cultures as practices that can be fixed/enduring, emergent and changing. Culture is not necessarily a stable phenomenon as empirical neuroscience research so far assumes. Regularities and stable characteristics are always in tension with the emergent goals and practices that people construct for themselves as they participate in activity. This conflict and tension contributes to the variation and change in an individual's and community's practice (Gutierrez and Correa-Chavez, 2006; Gutierrez, 2013). This view would suggest that we need to look not just at stability in culture, as neuroscientists seek to do, but also at the shifts and transformations and adaptive responses of individuals to the tasks at hand. Some cultural neuro-scientists are beginning to recognize a more dynamic version of culture (see Dominguez *et al.*, 2010, for example) but as we noted, its research applica-tion seems to be more problematic.

People draw on resources, practices, concepts that have proved helpful to them over generations. Over time, these practices, which might include, for example, ways of talking and belief systems including allegiances to particular values such as personal independence, can become associated with parti-cular groups. But to equate the use of these practices with race or ethnicity or geography (i.e. essentializing groups) is unhelpful. In sociocultural theory, the assumption that a particular group engages uniformly in the same set of cultural practices or does so in the same way is unacceptable (Rogoff, 2003). To do so may lead to overgeneralization and treating people as if they are independent of the contexts in which they find and create for themselves. Of greater interest than social categories or individual traits are the cultural practices people engage in, what people do as they move across everyday school, work and professional contexts that both shape and constitute their learning day by day. It is thus more helpful to think about people as living culturally rather than living in a culture.

The idea of culture as blanket or separatist, then, gives way to the metaphor of culture as fabric where culture and activity/context are inseparable at the level of individual, group and societal development (Nasir *et al.*, 2008). Culture as fabric is a richer and more fruitful way of thinking about culture if one is trying to promote learning. It focuses attention on resources available to support participation rather than on individual, family and community deficits. Differences are attributed not to group culture, but to learners having different histories as a result of their experiences in and responses to different communities of practice, traditions and institutions.

Although a given cultural group may share a historical, linguistic and geographical background, it doesn't follow that one would conceive of cultural groups as fixed, unchanging and homogeneous. Socioculturalists challenge the notion of culture as coherent and timeless and as something uniformly accepted and acceptable to a given cultural group. The socioculturalists, Gutierriez and Rogoff (2003: 22) sum up the position well:

> Examining cultural variation in terms of familiarity with different practices in dynamic communities organized in distinct manners is a very different approach than attributing a 'visual' style to Mexican children and a 'verbal' style to European-American middle-class children. We argue that is it more useful to consider differences in the children's, their families', and their communities' histories of engaging in particular endeavors organized in contrasting manners. This avoids the implication that the characteristic is 'built in' to the individual (or a group) in a stable manner that extend across time and situations, and it recognizes the circumstances relevant to an individual's likelihood of acting in certain ways.

Clearly, cultural neuroscientists are only beginning their foray into sociocultural psychology and therefore their conceptualizing and empirical work is at an early stage. In contrast, sociocultural perspectives on culture have an extended history and incorporate a complex, nuanced set of concepts that merit further elaboration here.

Boundaries are permeable

The Country of the Blind

A man called Nunez is standing on a peak in the Andes. He falls to the valley below but not to his death. He eventually discovers that the only people who live in the valley are people who have been blind since birth and they have been living here for some fourteen generations. Being an arch opportunist Nunez can see no threats or challenges ahead. As far as he's concerned, to be able to see 'in the Country of the Blind' is to have the cultural capital of a king. He proceeds to try to interfere, take over, and give orders at will. He predictably runs into trouble. The people of the valley successfully resist and eventually he becomes marginalized and excluded from many aspects of life there.

The people in the valley have ordered their world so they have no need to see. For instance, they have developed a network of paths and distinguishing notches and kerbing to enable themselves [to] navigate their way quite satisfactorily. Being blind, they have no need for language to describe anything that is seen, nor have they a word for 'see'. In due course one woman falls in love with Nunez. She seems to enjoy his illusions about being able to see and she also identifies with his now excluded status insofar as she too has been pushed aside for having the appearance of eye sockets.

One day the people of the valley decide to define Nunez' problem and find a solution for him. Their surgeon's diagnosis is serious: Nunez' eyes are diseased, it is concluded, he has eyelashes and eyelids which move as a result of which his brain is addled and he is in a constant state of frustration and destruction. There is only one solution to his desperate plight: his eyes have to be surgically removed from his head. In fear and trepidation Nunez immediately scarpers back up the mountain from which he fell.

Martha's Vineyard

Three centuries ago one person in every 155 who lived on a small island off the coast of Cape Cod, Massachusetts had a high rate of genetically inherited deafness. From historical accounts it would seem that deaf people on the island were thoroughly integrated into the community by the fact that all spoke sign language. For example, in a court case situation, a deaf and hearing person could be called upon to advise, adjudicate about another person, whether that person was hearing or deaf. Deafness was irrelevant for most things. By conventional social and economic success measures e.g. rates of marriage, mastery of a trade, deaf people were indistinguishable from their hearing counterparts. And historical records show that when older members were questioned about deaf neighbours, they frequently couldn't recall whether they were deaf or not, since everyone spoke sign language including even hearing people with other hearing people. So clearly it is possible to have a community where deafness does not exclude a person from participating fully in the life of the group. The deaf person can play an equal part in most aspects of life. Not being able to hear can be addressed by ensuring that everyone can speak sign.

On the other hand, the island was not insulated from the wider social landscape beyond it where deafness was viewed as a desperate affliction. And when the island was opened up to tourists, outsiders who of course couldn't sign, treated the insiders with pity and some called for remedies that included a eugenics programme for their erasure.

The first story above is a much shorter version of a short story by H. G. Wells. The second is a factual account. Both are paraphrased summaries of accounts offered in a seminal paper, entitled 'Culture as disability' by McDermott and Varenne (1995), professors who work at the Universities of Stanford and Columbia respectively. We produce them here to extend the notion of culture outlined above and to unpack a view of culture endorsed by socioculturalists.

In a veiled criticism of Wells' own take on culture, these authors question whether Nunez had to be so severely excluded from those who could not see. Was it all his fault, or was he called by others in the community to look bad, they ask. And they wonder how we are to respond to the blind woman who fell in love with him. McDermott and Varenne note that even in the 'Country of the Blind', a blind woman can be marginalized–her difference was not acceptable to the community. The point of the two stories is that culture potentially disables as well as enables. Culture is not necessarily benign.

Like the neuroscientific accounts above, the assumption in Wells' story is that there is a coherence and a boundedness about how the group lives, sees the world and constructs meaning. This is the view of culture as 'a container of coherence' (325) or blanket or separatist view. The trouble, as the second account particularly illustrates, is that the container leaks. First, no group is so completely isolated from other groups that some cultural influence isn't possible. And second, and importantly, coherence is not established by group members all being the same and knowing the same things and in the same way. And this is an important point that appears not to be taken into account by the cultural neuroscientists above when they compare Eastern and Western orientations on, say, interdependence and dependence.

Coherence is won by the 'mutually dependent knowledge' each person in the group contributes in the process of living and working together: 'Culture is not so much a product of sharing as a product of people hammering each other into shape with the well structured tools already available' (McDermott and Varenne, 1995: 325). This is a crucial point and perhaps distinguishes the cultural neuroscientist from the socioculturalist. The former assumes a shared culture while the latter does not, the latter realizes that culture has to be negotiated. The culturalist Clifford Geertz's famous quote is pertinent: 'man is an animal suspended in webs of significance he himself has spun' with culture being those webs and the analysis of culture 'not an experimental science in search of laws but an interpretive one in search of meaning' (Geertz, 1973: 5). We might replace 'hammering' or 'spinning' with 'negotiating'.

What meanings are being negotiated? While cultural neuroscientists appear to acknowledge such crucial aspects as values, artefacts, practices, and so on, they appear not to engage with meanings and interpretations. Rather, meaning is assumed to be given unproblematically. Etienne Wenger's research shows how meanings are not within people, but that they are made manifest in 'the dynamic relation of living in the world' (Wenger, 1998: 54). The problem with identifying people as belonging to a particular culture is the assumption that there is one way to be in a culture, that meaning is a given; i.e. that people live in a culture as opposed to living culturally. This, in turn, sets up norms and deviations from norms and ignores the diversity inside a group. Depending on how a difference or deviation from a norm is noticed, identified and made consequential in a given context, people can be either enabled or constrained. The key questions then become: when does a difference count and for what reasons? What does a community of practice pay attention to? What is meaningful in a given situation to a given group of people? That culture is not stable is an important message. That culture is not necessarily positive is another important message. Nunez' tellings to the people in the 'Country of the Blind' were irrelevant since no sightedness also meant no blindness. We pick up on some of these points later in the book when we consider notions of ability and talent.

Language as a tool of culture and culture as dynamic

Some cultural neuroscientists claim awareness of the dynamic and unfolding nature of culture, how it emerges in practice in the moment-by-moment engagement and participation of people in activity, and how meanings are constantly negotiated and renegotiated through interaction. In line with socioculturalists, they argue that culture involves shared structures of meaning in terms of which people understand each other's actions. So culture is distributed. Whilst such a conceptualization is evident in at least one academic paper co-authored by neuroscientists and cultural theorists (e.g. Dominguez *et al.*, 2010), the shift towards a programme of empirical research that would reflect this conceptualization has yet to be detailed, much less implemented. Socioculturalists, on the other hand, have been grappling with this more dynamic notion of culture for much longer, including applying it to the promotion of learning and to research on learning.

If culture involves the hammering of a world rather than merely a sharing of a set of values, negotiation is imperative. And language is the key vehicle for most humans for such negotiation. When we speak, we afford subject positions to one another. Language, including gaze and gesture, provides a lens on how people interact with one another and build, negotiate, reproduce and contest culture. Language both hides and reveals meaning: what is not said can be as revealing as what is said. Together, through the cultural scripts that are used and evoked in interaction, we can get insights into how culture is shaped and shaping: 'It is through and by language and discursive practices, that selfhoods are constructed, identities are forged, and social processes are enacted' (Gonzalez, 1999: 433). In interacting with others in classrooms or workplaces, people use language and other behaviours to try to represent themselves in ways they find desirable and in ways that their peers recognize as a desirable way to be.

The dynamic nature of social interaction–the fact that each utterance in a conversation can influence the next speaker's decision, turn and utterance– means that the identities that emerge and shift in the moment-by-moment exchanges between people in specific interactional situations can never be predicted to result in the desired effects being achieved. As Roth and Lee (2004: 282) observe: 'As any other conversation, the topic covered cannot be predicted in advance but emerge from the dialectical relation of individuals that constitute the conversation unit.' The effects emerge through negotiation and participation and involve social risk-taking, with the level of perceived risk potentially compromising learners' opportunities to participate fully in classroom lessons. Thus, some people may fail to benefit from what is available to be learned.

Conceptualizing culture as emergent and classroom interaction (all inter-action) as a means of doing identity work, and therefore learning, signals the merit of listening and noticing students' use of language to negotiate tasks and relationships. A focus on how people interact together, with its attendant emphasis on opportunity to perform a desirable self within the group, can help teachers understand how their learners develop and display competence.

Bakhtin's notion of language is especially helpful here and contributes to understanding of culture as emergent and language as a vehicle for negotiation and being. He talked about dialogicality, which extends language beyond mere face-to-face interaction. He attended to different social languages or cultural scripts by which he meant the language of different communities of practice or cultures. Bakhtin's idea is that when people speak, they speak in a social language at the same time. Although the speaker may not be aware of the influence of cultural scripts, these scripts shape what individual voices can say. Hence the idea of one voice speaking through another voice makes sense. Put another way, collective voices are in the self (Hermans, 2001). To an extent, cultural neuroscientists are persuaded by this when they talk about culture being constructed and constructing, but their empirical research has yet to reflect this.

In relation to the significance of language for culture, this means that the moment-by-moment interaction or micro-context of interaction and relationships, cannot be understood without some concept of the cultural scripts being drawn upon and evoked.

An example illustrates the case. In an interactional study designed to promote classroom learning in science, Stacy Olitsky (2007) argues that students will be more inclined to use science concepts and scientific terminology if by so doing they contribute to their social solidarity within the group. She focused her attention on how her learners used language to negotiate their relationships and their learning. Just because her students did not use the relevant science vocabulary (e.g. pressure, water vapour, vacuum, temperature, etc.) in making predictions, this did not lead her to conclude that they did not necessarily know these words or concepts or that they could not apply them. In other words, she did not interpret what they said in the class/lab interaction to necessarily reveal their lack of knowledge, suspecting (correctly) that in other social situations (e.g. small groups) this understanding was accessible to them. In addressing this issue, she says:

> I consider not only what a student appears to 'know' in his/her speech, but also other relevant issues such as how aspects of the student's identity (e.g. group affiliations, reputation, categories) may shape participation, how students have responded to each other's science-related statements over a variety of timescales (in previous years, that year, yesterday, and earlier in the class period), and whether a student would anticipate that making a particular statement would result in an [interaction] characterized by solidarity and high levels of emotional energy, or lack of solidarity and a loss of emotional energy.
>
> (Olitsky, 2007: 50)

This quote captures a sophisticated and dynamic notion of culture that is absent from the neuroscientific research on Western and Eastern populations on collectivism and individualism. From the perspective of trying to understand how people participate in a learning situation, Olitsky's study points to how viewing individuals as the unit of analysis and considering their stores of knowledge as if they exist somewhere in the head, is inadequate. Instead, how people relate and interact together becomes the unit of analysis.

The interactional situation sheds light on what might be salient for students, what they are drawn to, and, therefore, is an enormous resource for illustrating how learners negotiate meaning. It also sheds light on what might be salient for teachers—for example, the interactional patterns may be designed to support the authority of the teacher, rather than creatively supporting learners in completing a task, and this may be a factor in learners' competence and understanding not being rendered accessible. In such an interactional situation, 'teaching as display' may thwart the identity-performing opportunities or agency of students.

Olitsky's study showed how teacher uptake of pupil responses was very important (a) in demonstrating to other pupils that their bids for membership of their science community were legitimate, and (b) in influencing the quality of the contributions that pupils made. From the point of view of the argument here, her study reflects a view of culture as emergent, dynamic, unpredictable and facilitated hugely by language.

It also captures something of the notion that to understand learning requires attention to how people think as they engage in culturally shaped tasks, contexts and events. Learning occurs through participation and is essentially a transformation in one's participation. To understand it requires attention to people's roles and their understanding of their roles in those tasks and activities. Learning is not something isolated and separate from living–rather it is part of social and cultural life.

Conclusion

Despite some fundamental differences in the conceptualizing and operation-alizing of culture, cultural neuroscientists and sociocultural psychologists agree on a number of important points that we believe are helpful in promoting the idea of learning as a transformation in participation. The joint recognition of roles, activities, artefacts, interaction/language and context, as well as the learner or cultural participant as active agent, are all important philosophical points of agreement, even though, as we demonstrated, there is no evidence, as yet, that neuroscientists are applying this concept of culture in practice in their empiri-cal studies. In our view, and as we will develop further in future chapters, there are several take-home messages about culture that are highly pertinent to how we promote learning, regardless of where that learning might take place. We conclude this chapter by noting its key messages:

- treating social groups as fixed entities is problematic;
- group membership is never coherent and sealed off from the larger social landscape: boundaries are permeable;
- culture is a double-edged process that can both facilitate and constrain; and,
- describing what people do, as opposed to categorizing people into fixed groups, offers the potential to bridge cultures for learners.

Given the current state of conceptualizing and theorizing among cultural neuroscientists, there is little that would suggest a marriage of equals with socio-culturalists. Neuroscientists would need to revise their take on culture and, as we elaborate later, this revisioning may well be impossible for them, given how fixated they are on the brain as a physical organ. In the next chapter, we build on the analysis offered here and suggest a model of thinking about culture that challenges further the neuroscientific conceptualization portrayed in this chapter.

Chapter 5

A heuristic for avoiding a totalizing concept of culture

Introduction

In the previous chapter, we showed how culture as theorized by neuroscientists appeals to biology, geographical boundaries and discrete divisions between groups. They tend to adopt a totalizing view of culture as their starting point in their empirical studies, thus oversimplifying cultural differences. Arising from the narrowness of their definition of culture we believe it lacks the kind of vision and elaboration that would be helpful in an understanding and promotion of learning. Despite overtures to the work of socioculturalists, neuroscientists make the assumption that cognition takes place solely in individual heads; brains actually. Contexts are not elaborated in their view of culture. Culture, according to Jerome Bruner, is biology's last great evolutionary trick. If this is so, then educators and researchers need to adopt as rich a view of it as possible.

Thinking, acting, perceiving and meaning-making depend on features of the social situation, not just the mental structures and activities of brains. Understanding learning demands attention to how people participate in culturally and historically shaped events. A dynamic view of culture, adopted by socioculturalists, transforms how we think about learning: it includes a focus on how meanings are construed and communicated, how relationships are central to action, how available resources—ways of doing things and physical tools—are all implicated in what is possible and what is not possible to do in a given situation and therefore in opportunities to learn. Socioculturalists see culture as emerging in practice; it is not an entity. It is through enactment, practice, as people participate in activity that it becomes observable. Important though what we say about ourselves and what we think are, it is in what we do that identity emerges and that culture unfolds. We endow an identity with meaning through our engagement in practice.

In engaging in practice with others, in living culturally, we negotiate ways of being in that culture, we produce, reproduce and transform the culture as we engage in it. Practice makes practice. The formation of a community of practice involves, indeed requires, the negotiation of identities. Through this negotiation, which is a lifelong enterprise, culture is a constant becoming and not an essential essence or category and it is certainly not a trait, internal to the person. The opportunity to participate, the opportunity to learn, to negotiate meaning is fundamental to the creation of a community of practice. What counts as participation or what members of the community deem relevant and worth attending to is key and this varies according to the situation. Hence, there are two aspects: participation on the one hand, and what to pay attention to on the other.

What did our friend, Nunez, in the previous chapter, pay attention to? The salient identity of sightedness gave him a perspective on the world which resulted in him tending to interpret events and others' actions in this light, thus closing off other possible interpretations. He held to a social script of sightedness which of course was wholly irrelevant in the world the participants around him were figuring. Learning events and forms of participation are defined by their current affordances. What from all the potentially significant things actually become salient for an individual depends on one's reading of the situation. This inevitably depends on one's history of participation in other similar contexts and on the assumed expectations of significant others present (or indeed absent) in the group. McDermott and Varenne showed how Nunez did not understand the subtleties of the enterprise as the community of blind had defined it. In attending exclusively to being able to see, he lacked the perspectives the participants in the community used. His non-membership shaped his identities through his encounter with the familiar. Nunez manifested himself by what he recognized–he could only see that he could see and others could not. Although he could see, the 'Country of the Blind' was not transparent to him. He could not appropriate other things and so was marginalized and eventually alienated.

Some people are better equipped than others to control and shape their identities in a given situation, depending on their familiarity with it. For some people, the struggle to extend their competence in a given community, like a classroom, may be immense because the tools they bring to their learning, their identities and identifications, are not used, appear not to be relevant or meaningful. In a classroom, meeting or work situation, actors vary in the nature and level of their engagement. Some may view their role as integral to the smooth running of things while others may fade into the background. Lave and Wenger's notion of 'legitimate peripheral participation' explicates how learners may become thoroughly competent in, barely adopt, or even reject the roles and practices of the various communities they encounter. What is key is that the process of negotiation is vital to culture. The critical issue is negotiability, not authority. As we saw from the story of Nunez, the very process of identification constrains negotiability. We are at once limited and enabled by the scope of our identities.

This chapter pulls together various concepts highlighted in earlier chapters by elaborating on a model of culture that we think is extremely helpful for thinking about what's involved in becoming more competent in a practice. It entails two concepts from the socioculturalist Etienne Wenger (2008) that together provide an elegant heuristic that overcomes the problems of culture as applied by neuroscientists. These concepts are reification and participation.

Not simply sharing but negotiating

The one-dimensional view of culture evident in neuroscience treats only of the sharing of culture. Culture is taken as a given. The need for the negotiation of meaning is not in the equation even though it is part and parcel of living, part and parcel of everyday activity, even activities that are repeated and repeated and that have a routine quality to them, such as meeting the same friends for dinner, time and time again. Each time, as Wenger says, we negotiate anew, we give life to the histories of meanings of which that activity is a part. And each time that negotiation involves attention and adjustment as appropriate to the new, if ultra familiar, context of meeting friends for dinner. There is the historical dimension to this activity—the same people have met many times before, yet it requires fresh negotiation, ongoing interaction of give and take.

By participating in the world, we do not just invent meanings independently, and yet meanings are not entirely predictable or imposed on us. We participate, we act and at the same time we interpret, make decisions. Negotiating entails interpretation and action, processes which are not distinct but which are in a dynamic relation: new circumstances arise which require further negotiation and produce new relations with and in the world (Wenger, 2008: 33). Let's imagine a teacher in a classroom. As a member of a community of teachers in a school, an individual teacher contributes to that community, is a member of that community through her participation as a teacher. She negotiates her way in this community by doing and acting based on her own history in this practice and in other related practices. There is no other way of acting except through what she judges to be an appropriate way to act based on her history. However, various artefacts support her decisions and her actions, not least, for instance, the official, specified curriculum of the country in which she teaches. The specified curriculum, the syllabus, the textbook, captures something of the expected practice: it is a guide to action. As an indicator of what society values, the specified curriculum represents some ideal of participation. It is in enacting this curriculum that the teacher negotiates meaning.

Participation

In enacting the curriculum, the teacher engages in all of the following: doing, talking, thinking, feeling and belonging. We bring ourselves to the act of participating whatever that act is. It is an active process that involves bodies, minds, emotions and social relations. It is a social process but also a personal experience. As a member of the community of teachers in a school, an individual teacher represents the community in some way. She recognizes something of herself in others and they recognize something of themselves in her, which gives rise to an experience of mutuality. According to Wenger, it is this experience of mutuality that generates a sense of identity in the culture. He says we become part of each other. Yet he stresses that community is not necessarily harmonious. Akin to McDermott and Varenne's idea that culture has a lethal side, a community consists of all kinds of relations: competitive and cooperative, intimate and political, conflictual and harmonious (Wenger, 2008: 35).

Through participation, we shape our own experience and at the same time shape the practice of our communities. And the extent to which we feel empowered to participate is an important dimension of our experience. This sense of agency, the power to act, is an aspect that is ignored in the view of culture adopted by neuroscientists.

Reification

Like the example of the specified curriculum above, we project our meanings in a way that seeks to give them a reality. Wenger says that we project our meanings into the world and then we perceive them as having a reality of their own, independent of us. He points out that in the case of participation we recognize ourselves in each other, but in reification we don't necessarily recognize ourselves in those projections. Thus, he says that the contrast between mutuality and projection is an important difference between participation and reification.

Essentially, reification gives form to experience. He says reification produces objects that congeal experience into thingness. Such things then become a focus for the negotiation of meaning. Illustrative examples, in addition to the specified curriculum, include writing down a law, creating a procedure, producing a tool. In negotiation, having a law allows us to argue a point, having a procedure helps us to know what to do, while having a tool enables us to carry out an action. In essence, human experience is fixed into an object which then shapes our experience through usage. Reification is central to every practice and takes up much of our collective energy. It can take the form of the following: abstractions, tools, symbols, stories, books, computers, terms and concepts. Like physical tools, such as hammers, literacy and mathematics are also reifications; they are tools for thinking with and for negotiating in the world. Reification has a collective quality but it shapes our consciousness and ourselves.

Since meaning exists only in negotiation, the object, the reification is not the end of the process. To become meaningful it has to be appropriated locally into practice. A key difficulty with neurosciences' classification of people into broad categories, sometimes binaries like Easterners and Westerners, is that such categorizations give differences and similarities a concreteness that they do not actually possess. They do not capture the diversity and richness of lived experience.

Participation and reification forming a duality

Wenger explains how participation and reification are two dimensions that interact. They form a duality, they imply each other and they form a unity. They are not opposites. They are not mutually exclusive, since both are crucial to every practice. In their interplay they remain distinct but complementary. They can be thought of as opposite sides of the same coin. He poetically describes the duality thus: 'the river only carves and the mountain only guides, yet in their interaction, the carving becomes the guiding and the guiding becomes the carving' (45). To exemplify, the specified curriculum is just a representation, a form, it is not the curriculum. It is meaningless without participation. It has to be enacted. One can't stand for the other although they come about through each other and one can make up for the shortcomings in the other. For instance, limitations of specified curriculum can be compensated for through participation, through enactment. Also, the specified curriculum can, as a guide to action, amend a potential inadequacy in participation.

Reification is only relevant in the context of experience and participation. The specified curriculum, as our example, has a history and it assumes a history of participation for its interpretation. Participation entails reification as it requires things, artefacts, words, concepts, cultural scripts, in order to act. It therefore has a collective aspect. As they are not mutually exclusive, it is meaningless to think in opposites such as tacit versus explicit, process versus product, individual versus collective, formal versus informal, and so on. Wenger argues that both these dimensions can never morph into each other but the relation between them can change. So, tacit knowledge can be made explicit and vice versa. And such transformation changes the possibilities for the negotiation of meaning. In this sense, a given reification is not fixed: it doesn't just pin down existing meanings but is creating the condition for new meanings (Wenger, 2008: 43). As social and historical tools, artefacts and concepts, reifications get modified through usage. Think of language which is dynamic and living, changing to reflect the purposes and problems of its users. As such, tools extend what we can do, yet also constrain our doing.

This is what neuroscientists miss in their understanding of culture. The desire to classify, dichotomize and categorize pushes towards surface features and misses deeper dimensions. Wenger's framework of reification and participation, which can't be defined as independent of each other, extends how to think about culture and persuades us to consider how people act and what guides people's actions and, crucially, to do both at the same time. It overcomes the problems that remain for neuroscientists in their conceptualizing. It also provides a framework for the analysis of learning contexts as we show in the next chapter of the book.

Two examples differently productive of meaning

Two examples follow to exemplify the interaction between participation and reification in learning. The first example is one where the reification was intense and the participation constrained and unable to compensate for the inadequacy of the reification. Nearly a decade ago, the first author was involved in a study that examined inclusion and assessment practices in primary classrooms in England (Hall *et al.*, 2004). The example here is a vignette from that work.

One teacher in the study rigidly adhered to a script of assessment in such a way that it limited opportunities for many of her learners to participate meaningfully in the enacted curriculum. The specified assessment policy, and, more particularly, the aspect of the specified policy that dealt with assessment for accountability purposes, dominated her practice. She was teaching year six, the final year of primary school and the year in which results of the external, national testing of English, mathematics and science would be used to rank schools and to construct league tables of school results, which would be published in the press. The highly public and 'high stakes' nature of the testing had the consequence, at least at local school level, of making a teacher's 'success' or lack of it highly visible. The teacher in question was, unsurprisingly, deeply aware of the prospect of this publicity. For her, the script of success amounted to her learners achieving well in the standard assessment tests–pencil-and-paper tests that targeted specific, measureable and relatively narrow aspects of the curriculum (see also Hall and Ozerk, 2010). She was successful in her terms insofar as her pupils achieved at least in line with their nationally expected levels that year.

However, observation of her practice and interviews with her and with her learners indicated a heavy emphasis on procedure and an over-reliance on reification. Her practice showed how her overarching concern was getting her pupils aware of how to do the tests and demonstrate their knowledge in a strategic way, rather than participate deeply in meaningful educative activities. Lessons were devoted to test taking. There was a strong emphasis on surface features of language for instance (as opposed to, say, the originality of expressed ideas) in writing lessons along with a strong emphasis on linguistic terminology (e.g. metaphors, characterization, plot, suspense) without the opportunity afforded learners to come to appreciate these concepts through more authentic writing tasks. Concepts such as metaphors, suspense, remained mere reification for many learners because they seemed to lack the participation in writing that would provide a deep understanding of them. Dialogue was stilted, monologic and teacher-centred, with very limited opportunity for learners to debate, discuss or explore ideas in the contexts of their lives, their own writing or interesting writing of others. Such exploration was not deemed relevant since there was only one way of demonstrating one's success, and the rules of the game could be learned by all by listening to the teacher, answering questions in a whole class setting, and completing pre-set assessment tests and tests of previous years. Meaning-making was circumscribed and narrowed to how to pass the test. The result was that learners did not become more deeply involved in the practices of reading, writing, and so on. They did not participate as competent writers and readers, but as test takers. They did not transform their participation in genuine literacy activity by enhancing their competence in those areas in a deep way. Their transformation was in exam technique. Because reification dominated, participation suffered and learners couldn't experience themselves as moving more deeply into the practices (Lave, 2008) of reading and writing.

Moreover, the subjects that were part of the assessment regime were taught at the expense of those areas not externally assessed, thus denying opportunities to learn in those areas. The following is a quote from the same teacher, in which she is describing how the school goes about identifying the test levels at which different children are working:

> In year 6 science we've started [setting] this term . . . we gave the children a SATs paper before Christmas, did it as a SATs test and then we've gone through every question and tallied the responses and we have grouped the children into like 3a children which we need to push to a 4. Then these are our level 4s that we want to push to a 5. These are our just level 3c children or just not got a 3 and we want to get them to a good 3 . . . we are all [lists the teachers and support staff] going to target those children and give them what they need to meet the mark.

The quote is telling in relation to the duality of participation and reification, as implicit in it is the view, apparently shared with several in the school, that learners have to be pushed and that 'meeting the mark' is what matters. Authority, not negotiation, is what is privileged.

It would be both simplistic and wrong to blame the teacher entirely for her teaching approaches. She was but a partial, though important and agentic, player. Account has to be taken of the personal and consequential aspect of the assessment order as she perceived it, informed by the construal of the reification by the school staff and headteacher. The relation of reification and participation in this case (and indeed in many cases) produced a particular kind of meaning-making. One can imagine how a different configuration of the relationship would result in a different set of circumstances for learners' experience. The national policy with its strong emphasis on assessment for accountability set the conditions for the kinds of action the teacher took. The reification of success emanating from the policy on assessment influenced the potential for the negotiation of meaning in that classroom for an entire year, although it has to be added that the teacher's response was not inevitable or determined. Her consciousness was fundamentally shaped by a version of the national policy on assessment and her pedagogy was one where authority, and not negotiation with her learners, held sway.

As an aside, it is of note that at the same time that the research was carried out, there was a strong emphasis on formative assessment–the kind of assessment potentially and directly related to the promotion of learning. That kind of assessment involves feedback to learners, negotiation and sharing with learners as to what counts as success in an area, and access to learners' understandings and assumptions–aspects that can only be ascertained through dialogue, exemplification and discussion. However, the high-stakes nature of the assessment for system accountability and the personal stakes for individual teachers were such that it didn't feature, or featured marginally, in the practice in that classroom.

Wider policy imperatives, and their perceived relative status, generate cultural scripts that mediate, albeit in different ways, what people do. Some of this mediation can be so subtle as to be practically invisible. The issue is that in curriculum enactments cultural scripts or reifications are implicated–they become part of the lived world interactions during moment-by-moment processes of negotiation and engagement. The enactor, in this case the teacher, is the agent through which the reification gets negotiated and reproduced. In this sense, the teacher is never completely free to act because s/he is shaped by and is enmeshed in the external world. Put another way, the external is also in the person (Hermans, 2001). Rogoff (1995) cautions against seeing the social world as external to the individual, saying: a participant in an activity is a part of that activity, not separate from it. So, for example, in a sociocultural exploration of the pedagogy underlying an individual's practice, account would need to be taken, not just of that person's practice and expressed views, but would also seek to understand and make visible the constraining and facilitating influences of the social order on those practices and views. People do not construct interpretations and meanings unhindered by the external world, rather, meanings are coloured and shaped by the collectives to which they belong. Yet, individuals' responses cannot be predetermined or taken for granted: people may resist, accept or subvert the specified curriculum or policy, hence the need for studies that engage with the local and broader contexts of social action.

A second example, where the duality of participation and reification seemed to indicate a more productive relation of meaning, stems from a recently completed knowledge exchange initiative in our university and led by the first two authors. Entitled the Voice, Identity and Participation (VIP) project and funded by the Irish Research Council (IRC), it ran for eighteen months and involved a mix of twenty teachers from all sectors of the formal education system meeting monthly to participate in discussion, seminars, workshops and formal lectures on the theme of inclusion. The project provided a context for teachers to engage with new thinking emerging from research that had been conducted on inclusion and learning, much of it by members of the research team, and the main purpose was to draw out the pedagogical implications of that line of inquiry for the participants' own practice in their particular settings. There was an emphasis on participants' own histories of participation, views and issues and the strategies they might adopt in their classrooms and schools in the light of research on such aspects as racism, language/literacy, assessment, inclusion and mathematics.

The concepts–inclusion, voice, identity and participation–can be thought of as reifications. To the research team, they were redolent with meaning but had to be unpacked and elaborated and made meaningful by our participants who did not start off from a history of exploring such concepts and who largely adopted a layperson's understanding of these concepts. A fundamental theme permeating the monthly sessions was that of respect for learners' perspectives and everyday experiences, which the university team sought to model in their approach to the project. Along with the monthly meetings, public lectures and conferences were also organized, and these involved some group members as formal responders and rapporteurs. In the more informal meetings, participants were often asked to bring an artefact with them to the meetings to introduce their feelings towards a particular topic. These ranged from a twenty-six-year-old calculator, to Sesame Street characters, to an old Irish prayer to a song. One participant commented that 'the use of the artefacts allowed and encouraged deep consideration prior to each meeting'. He continues 'observing the artefacts of others and the stories that followed was for me quite eye-opening as the opinions, attitudes, struggles and feelings of fellow teachers began to emerge'.

Participants found the balance between both presentation styles, where they lead some sessions while other times attending lectures or panel discussions and conferences, conducive to learning and the development of their understandings. In the smaller sessions, identities developed as attitudes and stories from their settings opened up to the group. The public lectures allowed the coverage of material in a more direct way and participants found these evenings extremely informative and they were often discussed at the next meeting. Another participant commented:

> I often found myself compelled to action in my own classroom following the meetings. Listening to the experiences and reflections of others in the group brought aspects of my own practice into focus for me. The drive home after the group sessions felt like a fraction of the time it was in reality; my mind was still on overdrive thinking of things that had been discussed and how they related to me professionally.

Through critical reflection, the participants began to see themselves as inquirers who could take more and more responsibility in leading discussions and making presentations as the project moved forward. Seeing themselves as insiders in the academic world with something to teach as well as something to learn, participants actively began to apply key concepts (such as identity) to their own classroom work and even tried to share their insights with other colleagues in their schools.

Teachers and principals stated that they had become more aware of their own agency and power as teachers as a result of coming to an understanding of the significance of concepts such as participation, voice, meaning-making and the need for learners to make their own sense. In this regard, one participant mentioned how a mathematics pedagogy research from the University of London (Dr Jenny Houssart) had shifted her sense of herself and her practice as a maths teacher: 'the speaker . . . impacted on my classroom practice because I now look at the alternative creative answers–even the incorrect answers–that children give and I look for the hidden maths within these that might not necessarily be outlined in my aims or objectives'.

Alongside these specific examples, participants told us how their involvement in the VIP Group influenced their overall understanding and approach to their teaching practice. As the participant below clearly elucidates, the process of the VIP Project allowed professionals to think about experiences within a school or systems structure, and by implication across other schools. One participant stated:

> this project has undoubtedly opened my mind to the whole idea of knowledge sharing amongst colleagues. In bringing together the whole team from principals, senior-management to teachers this will enable better joined-up approaches to achieving educational goals. Knowledge grows not only from the reading of texts and data analysis but also through the exchanges among colleagues that occur during meetings of subject associations, in corridors, or over a cup of coffee so therefore unquestionably knowledge about teaching grows through informal and formal exchanges among teaching staff. Through interactions, teachers form bonds that result in an exchange of knowledge including the generation of new knowledge and this should be promoted in all schools.

We see this initiative as a case of a good fit of reification and participation. The projections of ideal practice encapsulated in concepts such as inclusion, participation, voice, etc., were made meaningful and proved to be genuine tools for action on the part of the participants (and indeed on the part of the university researchers involved in it who, of course, were also changed in the process). On the other hand, participation around the use of the reifications through dialogue, use of artefacts, use of formal presentations, research articles, annotations of research papers, and so on, was such that both processes–participation and reification–were complementary, though still distinct. The reifications were generative of meaning because participation was enabled and maximized.

Conclusion

The implications of Wenger's framework are profound. First of all, a focus on the supposedly solitary individual, separate from what makes sense in the collective, is inadequate. The notion that, say, thinking is spread across people and reifications is impossible to accommodate alongside a view that thinking is solely and entirely in the head. Reifications participate in the practices in which they are employed. In using language to get a job done, for example, making a list to remind ourselves of what we have to do today, we do not usually contemplate the nature of the words, the grammar, style or spelling–we take all that for granted–yet the words are part of the practice, humans have evolved them to enable our communication. Acknowledging this, points to the importance of including cultural tools in the analysis of thinking, cognition and learning (Rogoff, 2008a, 2008b). Sociocultural theory, as exemplified especially by Wenger, Lave, Wertsch and Rogoff, has indeed led the way to recognizing that thinking is collaborative and distributed across people. Accepting that human development is a process of changes in participation in activity, the assumption that thinking happens completely inside the skull is rejected and this challenges fundamentally the theory and methodology of neuroscientists. People's brains do not mirror their cultures. In order to understand mental activity one has to take into account the cultural historical setting and its available resources–all the things that shape mind, consciousness and identity.

A second, profound implication of Wenger's framework for education and the understanding of learning is that the negotiation of meaning is vital for learning, and that negotiation of meaning requires both participation and reification; action and interpretation. While people learn through their own participation, the negotiation of meaning has to be supported; it cannot simply be given or taken for granted.

A major difficulty with the neural geographic approach of cultural neuroscientists is that the categories of people they draw are not naturally occurring, but co-produced. On the basis of our argument, a key question becomes: what scripts or reifications are involved in the co-production of categories so people end up as 'kinds of people'? Additionally, what are the histories of those reifications? In answering this kind of question, we get at some understanding of how a person's characteristics get made significant. Who and what is involved in a person's 'report card'? Over time, a person's pathway is produced for them and with them. In the next several chapters of the book, we examine instances of such pathway production when we attend more directly to learning.

Chapter 6

Making connections
Learning and pedagogy

Introduction

This chapter explores connections between sociocultural theory and neuro-science. Our aim here is to acknowledge that sociocultural and neuroscientific understandings share some characteristics, or perhaps more specifically, connect, in terms of certain key concepts within both disciplines. Plasticity and experi-ence, brain circuitry and social experiences, language acquisition and culture, environment and agency, brain function and social meaning–all align in very particular ways to bring meaning to experience when explored socioculturally. Some pairings will be investigated further and problematized in later chapters of this book, but here the research presented is largely complementary and makes a case for a more open-minded and context- and social-based approach to learning.

This chapter also considers the concept of pedagogy and highlights the implications of a sociocultural understanding of learning. Connecting learning, culture and neuroscience, the research presented in this chapter confirms our belief that there is value in investigating sociocultural concepts such as culture, social interaction and meaning, and reveals that they can be gainfully employed in building learning theory.

Making connections

> The brain struggling to understand the brain is society trying to explain itself.
>
> (Blakemore,1976: *Mechanics of the Mind*, BBC Radio 4)

In previous chapters, we have explored sociocultural and neuroscientific dis-course and theory, making some claims about the nature of learning. Examining the connectivity and disconnect of sociocultural theory and neuroscience in the last number of chapters, our main aim was to explain our understanding of learning through theory building and a focus on developing our conceptual perspective on learning. Building on this, our main aim now is to exemplify and justify the claims we made in our earlier chapters, with reference to specific research, stories and practices. Trying to explain our selves, we employ both sociocultural and neuroscientific research to exemplify what it means when we say we learn.

This chapter looks closely at some of the connections emerging from neuroscientific and sociocultural discourse, before we move on to problematize the relationship between both perspectives in later chapters. Here, we acknowledge that sociocultural theory and neuroscience are saying some of the same things about learning but will argue that, when it comes to pedagogy, it is sociocultural theory that holds the explanatory power to apply claims about learning to actual learning contexts.

We begin by setting the context for this, explaining that, when it comes to learning, neuroscientific research alone cannot directly translate into educational pedagogy. We then offer a series of connections, as we understand them, between sociocultural theory and neuroscience, acknowledging where both theories may align and connect before we look deeper at the relationship between the two in later chapters. Prioritizing depth rather than breadth, we focus in this chapter largely on one connection as we see it: that between brain plasticity and the importance of experience. Other connections are also made between both perspectives but briefly, so as to allow scope for what is to follow in the remaining chapters. We conclude this chapter with our argument for a cultural learning science, to be further developed, and a connection of learning and pedagogy that, we believe, can only be fully achieved through sociocultural discourse. Reading a little deeper into why we say the things we do, Blakemore's quote raises the question throughout of what occurred or is occurring in society to take us to this place in our shared explanation of self.

In a nutshell: the problem with learning

Aligning with the language it uses to define brain function, a neuroscientific understanding of the brain and learning is deterministic, clinical, clean, ordered, simple—almost black and white. At the centre of learning is the computational brain, an inner sanctum that reproduces the world and can learn, rewire and even change its very structure if the environment is manipulated in specific and controlled ways. Learning is about management, hours on task that will develop more synapses.

Learning can be captured visually and is measurable and quantifiable in brain regions. Success and failure are located in the brain, a hardware system that gives everyone a get-out-of-jail-free card when it comes to explaining behaviour. But, of course, people must still feel like they have power themselves and can continue to improve their learning so brain-based strategies for learning and pedagogy, self-help books and courses flood the market in an attempt to assure the individual that they do have some sense of agency, albeit only within the structure of a neuroscientific understanding of the brain and learning. Speaking of psychology in 1899, William James famously said:

> You make a great mistake, if you think that psychology, being the science of the mind's laws, is something from which you can deduce definite programmes and schemes and methods of instruction for immediate schoolroom use. Psychology is a science, and teaching is an art; and sciences never generate arts directly out of themselves.
>
> (James, [1899] 2008: 13)

Just over one hundred years later, while still an important and respected field, the science of psychology has been ravaged by time and no longer holds the allure it once had as the next big thing. Moving with the times, our more sophisticated society finds new answers to old questions in neuroscientific definitions, placing the brain as God, while ignoring the defining role that culture, society and social interaction has had in the construction of this new 'truth'. The problem inherent in this process is that we, meaning teachers, policy makers and educational theorists, are still employing old models of learning to develop our understandings. These models, psychology and now neuroscience, are largely mechanical (in terms of brain function), but learning is not mechanical. We have split the atom and we have walked on the Moon. If learning was a mechanical process we would have devised the formula by now, or at the very least stumbled upon it.

The next big thing, neuroscience, now leads education and learning research, but just as William James claims of psychology, neuroscientific insights cannot simply be imported 'as is' into educational discourse and theory. Much groundwork needs to be done, as we begin to do here in this book, that moves neuroscientific discourse and research into the realm of our lived experiences of learning, so that what happens in the brain (developed through neuro-scientific discourses) is understood in terms of what happens in the world (developed through sociocultural discourses). The explanatory power of sociocultural theory fills in the blanks in neuroscientific terms to give us a new understanding of a science of culture and learning. Neuroscientific and socio-cultural discourses connect and disconnect to say some very interesting things about teaching and learning. Exploring these connections and disconnects within the wider social and cultural context, facilitates a dynamic and constitu-tive conceptualization of learning and construction of pedagogy. We now move to discuss some connections between neuroscience and sociocultural theory.

Connecting brain plasticity and experience

A brain system is made of many neuronal pathways, or neurons that are connected to one another and working together. If certain key pathways are blocked, then the brain uses older pathways to go around them. 'I look at it this way' says Bach-y-Rita. 'If you are driving from here to Milwaukee, and the main bridge goes out, first you are paralyzed. Then you take old secondary roads through the farmland. Then, as you use these roads more, you find shorter paths to use to get where you want to go, and you start to get there faster.' These 'secondary' neural pathways are 'unmasked', or exposed, and, with use, strengthened. This 'unmasking' is generally thought to be one of the main ways the plastic brain reorganizes itself.

(Doidge, 2007: 9)

The neuroscientific concept of brain plasticity connects sociocultural and neuroscientific processes in neural conversations about social networks. The fact that the brain is plastic, dependent and malleable based on different environments, experiences and social situations, confirms the importance of the environment and social interaction in brain function and learning. Neuroscientific research reveals that our brains are 'plastic', meaning our brain changes as we learn. Brain plasticity, or neuroplasticity, occurs in the brain at the beginning of life (when the immature brain organizes itself), when brain injury occurs (either to compensate for lost functions or maximize remaining functions) and throughout adulthood (when something new is learned). Brain plasticity is a physical process, as grey matter changes shape and neural connections are made and unmade. Gopnik *et al.* (1999) conceived of this process of the development of neural pathways as akin to growing telephone wires that communicate with each other.

Neuroscientific research reveals the extreme plasticity of the human brain. For example, Maguire, Woollett and Spiers (2006) studied London bus and taxi drivers and found that London taxi drivers have a larger hippocampus (in the posterior region) than London bus drivers. They explain that this is because of the specification of this particular brain region for acquiring and using complex spatial information in order to efficiently navigate through systems. Because bus drivers only follow a limited set of routes, and taxi drivers must negotiate all of London, this particular brain region is more developed in taxi drivers. Similarly, Mechelli *et al.* (2004) observed that learning a second language occurs through functional changes in the brain. Draganski *et al.*'s (2006) study of German medical students and non-medical students, three months leading up to a medical exam, revealed that the learning of abstract information caused changes in regions of the parietal cortex and posterior hippocampus.

In his book *The Brain That Changes Itself: Stories of Personal Triumph from the Frontiers of Brain Science*, Norman Doidge relates stories of many individuals who experienced illness or accident, losing function in their brain, only to later regain this functionality in a different brain region. This reorganization of brain function again reveals the extremely plastic nature of the brain as individuals paralyzed as a result of stroke regain their ability to use their non-functioning limbs. Doidge's description of the sea gypsies, a tribe of people who learn to swim before they learn to walk and are distinguished from other children in their ability to see clearly at great depths of water without goggles, exemplifies how cultural activities can change brain circuitry.

All these examples from neuroscientific research exemplify instances of brain plasticity from a neurological perspective but lack the ability to explain the learning process. To illustrate this point further, we quote here from www.positscience.com, a popular website about the human brain, with a tagline on their home page of 'Think faster, Focus better, Remember more':

> Changes in the physical brain manifest as changes in our abilities. For example, each time we learn a new dance step, it reflects a change in our physical brains: new 'wires' (neural pathways) that give instructions to our bodies on how to perform the step. Each time we forget someone's name, it also reflects brain change—'wires' that once connected to the memory have been degraded, or even severed. As these examples show, changes in the brain can result in improved skills (a new dance step) or a weakening of skills (a forgotten name).[1]

The idea here, that changes in the physical brain manifest as changes in our abilities, is typical of the closed and singular theorizing at the heart of these studies. Looking at one thing in one place at one time, the brain is supreme, and environment and experience secondary. Sociocultural theory calls this into question by asking if everything starts and ends with the brain, then what would have motivated us to ever learn these skills, such as dancing, in the first place? Neuroscientific theorizing falls short of the rich understanding sociocultural theory can bring to the idea of brain plasticity.

Brain plasticity reveals learning as a process of social cognition and shared consciousness. From a sociocultural perspective, understanding the brain and learning means first of all understanding the world around it, as all learning in the brain occurs through social interaction. To have meaning, our practices must be read within our own culture and our actions must be understood from a historical and situated perspective. In the words of Jean Lave, from a sociocultural perspective 'agent, activity and the world mutually constitute each other' (Lave and Wenger, 1991: 33).

The complexity of this sociocultural idea requires some further explanation. For Lave, learning occurs when agent, activity and world align in a very particular way. Lave uses the term 'agent' to stand for our performed, shared and mediated (plastic) identities, our socially constructed selves. These identities are fluid and emergent and may be different in different communities of practice. Who we are played out in the context of who we are allowed to be influences in every context the shared resources we can appropriate to participate in different practices. For example, taking a momentary interlude to present a single voice for the purpose of a story, in my role as a lecturer, I can only do my job and give a lecture if other people join me at the lecture theatre, sit down, take out their notes, listen and ask questions. As an agent, I can only be successful in my practice when the shared agency, mediated and distributed within the group, allows me to do so. As such, my individual actions have to be accepted as meaningful by the group. It is not just a matter of taking agency or control. Stepping into a boxing ring, we can imagine that in that arena I would be much less accepted to participate in that practice.

By activity, Lave refers to the particular task we are involved in, that which leads our engagement in communities of practice. Activities can be varied and many individuals can engage seemingly in the same activity while really their practice is motivated by subtle differences. For example, a group of workers in a tinning factory could all be understood as working together to complete orders, get their work done and keep their jobs. However, looking from one worker to the next could reveal many interesting differences.

Tinners work with heavy machinery and must ensure that their safety is prioritized at all times. Packers want to be seen as efficient and good workers but cannot work too quickly as they want as many hours on their time-sheet as possible. Movers want to get everything to delivery trucks as they are waiting but must ensure that their loads are not too heavy. Managers control all areas of this process but again have their own agendas as they go about their daily practice. This is to say nothing of the employee who turns up late and wants to ensure his boss does not find out, the employee trying to get away early to meet her boyfriend, the employee currently in a dispute with a number of other employees, or the employee who is seriously hung over and on a final warning. As each of these agents go about their daily work practice, the particular task in question brings something unique to our participation and prioritizes the importance of developing specific identities within that particular community of practice.

Finally, Lave uses the concept of world to signify how, when we act, we act as a historically located individual, creating and created by personal and shared histories of participation and reification. In this way, our culture and our world, alongside the agent and activity, are all resources for identity development and learning. For the tinners, this might mean that our hung-over employee, well-practised in activities that will allow him to hide his sickness, will work on the machine that stands on its own in the corner, sleep in the store room at lunch, compliment and schmooze the managers, and flirt with co-workers so that he can gain their help. For our employee in disagreement with others, it might mean alterations to his practice such as taking his lunch at a different time (knowing the time the others go to lunch) and the initiation of the company grievance procedures in a formal complaint against his colleagues.

Introducing the world once again to the agent and activity adds a richness and a complexity that captures more faithfully in sociocultural discourse the experience of learning and answers the question of how the brain achieves its extreme plasticity. While neuroscientific research posits the importance of environment in brain function, it does not exhibit in any way a sociocultural understanding of what this might mean in lived experience. The environment exists only as it is wanted to exist by those who manipulate it to enhance or diminish the growth of synapses in the brain. The brain is master, and everything else is almost irrelevant. Learning occurs in the brain. Experiences are represented in the brain with the goal to aid future learning.

In sociocultural terms, the brain is defined as a partner in the learning process. Jean Lave's concept of agent, activity and world working together to create a learning experience that occurs through social interaction, defines the brain as an agent, but emphasis is placed on social as well as neural networks as an individual's past histories, experiences and interactions come to bear on what is being learnt. The higher order mental functions that we experience as we wire and fire from a neuroscientific perspective are combined with Vygotsky's concept of intermental processes, where the cultural, social and relational aspects of learning become inescapable. From this perspective, learning and literacy, reading and writing are cognitive abilities, but these cognitive abilities depend greatly on human cultural evolution (Vygotsky, 1962).

This basic understanding of our practice, that it involves social processes dependent on cultural evolution, has only begun in very recent times to connect in sociocultural and neuroscientific perspectives, largely through the role brain plasticity, from a neuroscientific perspective, and experience, from a sociocultural perspective, plays in learning.

> What is the relationship between the brain and culture? The conventional answer has been that the human brain, from which all thought and action emanate, produces culture. Based on what we have learned about neuroplasticity, this answer is no longer adequate. Culture is not just produced by the brain; it is also by definition a series of activities that shape the mind. The Oxford English Dictionary gives one important definition of 'culture': 'the cultivating or development ... of the mind, faculties, manners etc. ... improvement or refinement by education and training ... the training, development and refinement of the mind, tastes and manners.' We become cultured through training in various activities, such as customs, arts, ways of interacting with people, and the use of technologies, and the learning of ideas, beliefs, shared philosophies, and religion.
>
> Neuroplastic research has shown us that every sustained activity ever mapped–including physical activities, sensory activities, learning, thinking, and imagining–changes the brain as well as the mind. Cultural ideas and activities are no exception. Our brains are modified by the cultural activities we do–be they reading, studying music, or learning new languages. We all have what might be called a culturally modified brain, and as cultures evolve, they continually lead to new changes in the brain. As Merzenich puts it 'Our brains are vastly different, in fine detail, from the brains of our ancestors. ... In each stage of cultural development ... the average human

had to learn complex new skills and abilities and all involve massive brain change ... Each one of us can actually learn an incredibly elaborate set of ancestrally developed skills and abilities in our lifetimes, in a sense generating a recreation of this history of cultural evolution via brain plasticity.'

(Doidge, 2007: 287–288)

Connecting brain circuitry and social interaction

Recent neuroscientific research using fMRI has begun to map the circuitry of the social brain and this, alongside the discovery of mirror neurons, confirms further the social nature of the brain and learning. Neuroscientific research has now identified specialized neural pathways and mechanisms evolved to process social information. Such specialized mechanisms include: the perception of social signs and symbols in the vomeronasal system, the formation of social memory through social recognition (in terms of gender, kin, status and individual), filial imprinting (by defining species and parental phenotypes), sexual imprinting (defining future potential sexual partners) and the broader identification of the neural consequences of social experience.

This research confirms main concepts of sociocultural theory, as now it is scientific fact that not only does the brain influence behaviour, but experience and social interaction influence brain development and learning. Sociocultural theory defines the brain as an entirely social organ and posits that this is because the meanings behind what we do as individuals are always social. We are, in fact, never alone when we are learning.

The example of an English college-student preparing a mid-term essay highlights this very well: as she enters the library she is accompanied in her mind by the college lecturer who will correct it, her old secondary school English teacher along with all the interactions she has had with her friends during and after her English classes. Inside the library doors she joins another community of practice, as every book she takes off the shelf opens up another idea, opinion and person to help her write her essay. In such an example, it is impossible to imagine an instance where learning could ever be the solo feat of perfection a neuroscientific understanding alone claims it to be. Is it possible to ever learn anything on our own?

This sociocultural understanding of learning is exemplified in Patricia Kuhl et al.'s (2003) neuroscientific study of nine-month-old babies exposed to the Mandarin Chinese language either through the medium of a television set or through interaction with real-life Mandarin speakers. Kuhl found that the babies who were exposed to Mandarin through the television set showed no more ability to discriminate Mandarin speech sounds than the control group. The other group of babies, however, who were introduced to Mandarin through social interaction, after twelve sessions displayed an enhanced ability to discriminate certain Mandarin sounds. More recently,

Christakis *et al.* (2009) conclude that the effect of conversations and social interaction on language competence is almost six times greater for children than just listening to adults talk. These neuroscientific studies evidence further that there is more to learning than just the arbitrary working of a computational brain.

The father of sociocultural theory, Lev Vygotsky, in his early writings supports this thesis and argues that individual mental processes have their origin in social interaction. He understood, as previously discussed, that cultural endeavours such as reading and writing are cognitive abilities that depend on human cultural evolution. His work champions social interaction, the mediation of language and the role of the accomplished other (and the zone of proximal development) in a social understanding of learning. Today, neuroscientific research supports this view of social cognition (albeit inadvertently) by revealing the massive interconnections that exist between different areas of the brain which suggests that learning can never be separate from emotions, meaning and experience (Fuster, 2003). In neural mapping, neuroscientists are finding immense connections between brain regions which are thought to localize emotion, language, social interaction. In this way, neuroscientific research is revealing how language development is tied to emotions, is tied to social interaction, is tied to experience in the world.

Connecting language acquisition and culture

A sociocultural understanding of the significance of culture in learning is supported by (if not understood fully in, as discussed in Chapter 4) neuroscientific research. Kenji Hakuta's (2008) neuroscientific study of language acquisition and bilingualism reveals the biological and societal characteristics inherent in the process of language learning. He highlights societal and cultural factors such as the social status of the language, the compartmentalization or representation of different aspects of different languages, the literacy history of the individual, participation in a bilingual speech community and historical circumstance as all playing a role in language learning. He concludes that, while language learning does have a biological basis, it is not something that we do in our heads, rather, it is an individual condition nested within a distribution of broader societal circumstances that cause language contact (Hakuta, 2008: 1).

His study of Canadian English-speaking and immigrant communities who begin learning French, reveals that bilingualism is usually attained by the English speakers because they want to gain access to the privileges of bilingualism. For the immigrants, on the other hand, because there is little or no societal value placed on their native languages, their native languages will have only a very limited range of use and are unlikely to survive in future generations as a result. In Hakuta's study, the differing social status of each language influenced the strength and stability of each individual's bilingualism.

Marshall *et al.*'s (2008) research with Romanian orphans revealed that the lack of high quality social interaction was instrumental in the children's failure to thrive.

Connecting environment and agency

Immordino-Yang and Fischer's (2000) acknowledgement that experience shapes brain networks confirms sociocultural research (Bussis *et al.*, 1985; McDermott, 1996) that endorses the importance of environment, of experience, of the opportunity to learn, of the chance to 'catch up', of the time to practise, and of access to the valued language and literacy practices in communities. Though coming from a different epistemological stable, neuroscience also confirms sociocultural perspectives on learning that challenge deficit models of learning and development (Curtin and Hall, 2013).

Rizzolatti and Craighero's (2004) neuroscientific study aligns with sociocultural theory (for example the research of Ray McDermott) in showing that children continuously and unconsciously learn from what is modelled by others in their experience–from what is available to them to be learned. In this way, neuroscientific research, if read alongside the world it so painstakingly tries to separate itself from, aligns with Lave's conception of learning as dependent on agent, activity and world and also with the neuroscientific concept of agency, previously discussed.

Connecting brain function and social meaning

In light of all the examples of research and stories presented in this chapter, it would seem that brain function and social experience are interdependent processes and both are necessary for learning to occur. In sociocultural terms, the meanings, participations, negotiations and intersubjectivities at the heart of social interaction provide the brain with rich experiences. Highlighting the importance of these experiences and their social and cultural dependence, as demonstrated in Chapter Three, reveals a fuller understanding of the learning process. Despite the plethora of 'brain porn'[2] that claims the opposite, the brain does not work in isolation. It cannot. As social beings, the meanings of what we do are always social. Culture, experience and opportunity to participate are essential to learning and the development of conscious and literate human beings. Experience is learning. Sociocultural research argues that it is through meaningful social experiences, and not committing information to memory in isolation, that we learn (Rogoff, 1995; Wenger, 1998). Mind and body, brain and social interaction are linked through neural, cultural and social networks and the uniqueness of each brain further evidences the importance of biology, experience and social interaction in learning and pedagogy. This new understanding is beginning to bleed into neuroscientific literature and research, but the links between neuroscience and sociocultural theory and the implications of these for learning are still to be made in any significant and meaningful way.

And now a disconnect: does size matter?

The neuroscientific and sociocultural research highlighted in this chapter speak very well to each other but only in a very specific way. Neuroscience provides in these studies a window to experience that sociocultural theory cannot–it shows us what happens in the brain when we learn. To say, however, that this explains learning is a very serious mistake. Given an artefact or subject of study, sociocultural theory becomes an analytical tool through which we can come to know our own experiences. Having explored some connections between neuroscience and sociocultural theory, we would now like to conclude this chapter by examining a disconnect, in recognition of the complex relationship between both competing discourses, which we will draw out in the remaining chapters.

Remarkable brains have long interested neuroscientists. Returning to the remarkable brain discussed in Chapter 3, when Albert Einstein died in 1955, for decades after his brain was carried around in 240 pieces in a jar by pathologist Thomas Harvey in an attempt to find out what was so special about the brain of a genius. While the brain was of average size, parts appeared to be bigger, and for a time it was wondered if Einstein was a genius because parts of his brain were enlarged. We revisit the stories surrounding Einstein's brain here to highlight our point that neuroscientific discourse alone is unable to explain what it studies because of its inside-out approach to understanding learning. Trying to explain experience in terms of brain is just not possible. Explaining brain in terms of experience provides richer understandings of experience.

Contemplating the same issue (the significance of brain size) but from the outside in, evolutionary psychologist Robin Dunbar, who we discuss in Chapter 3, has a very interesting explanation for why our brains are five to seven times larger than they would be expected to be for a mammal our size, and it is worth revisiting here. Dunbar claims that our brains are the size they are because of the extremely social nature of the world we live in. Drawing on further examples from research, he explains that birds of a species that flock together have comparatively larger brains than birds of those same species who are not a part of a flock. For Dunbar, our brains simply had to grow as they came in contact with increasing group sizes and we copy others in our attempt to learn about our self.

What is interesting about both of these explanations for brain size, neuroscientific and sociocultural, is that they both start at opposite ends of experience. Thomas Harvey attempted to find meaning for experience in the brain, while Dunbar attempts to understand the brain in terms of experience. The difference for Harvey and within neuroscientific discourse as a whole is that he simply had nowhere to go. A new brain science, as we outline it here, begins rather than ends with the brain, as we attempt to exemplify.

The heart of the problem

Other research completed by the authors also reveals that, within the world of neuroscience, shortfalls are beginning to be identified and possible solutions addressed. In an interview with the authors, one neuroscientist (Interviewee G, from the International Neuroscience Conference, Wicklow, 2011) suggests that neuroscientists need to find ways to capture individual variability if they really want to help their patients:

> What we are finding is that all the individuals with perinatal stroke, they all follow different pathways to recovery so the rule may be that there is no rule–that it's actually important to analyse people within an individual context so the driving force for much of what we do now is try to find tools, analytic tools, that take us away from doing mean level . . . and try and take into account as much individual variability and as many individual factors as possible.

He continues:

> The critical interaction between what an individual brings to the environment and therefore takes from it is going to be driven by the traits of the individual, the particular parts of the environment they will touch as a consequence of their traits and then their response to that interaction will be idiosyncratic. So when we analyse the world in a way where we try to squeeze out the variability and look at an average in the population we are doing disservice to the complexity of the actual interactions that are taking place . . . what's the best way to teach this child in this environment is going to require a deeper understanding of what that individual brings to bear and how best to capitalize on those traits.

While not using language that is particularly sociocultural, these extracts reveal the beginning of a sociocultural turn in the language of neuroscience. In his interview, the neuroscientist goes on to state that he finds it no great surprise that children of excellent athletes are often excellent athletes. Rather than explaining this solely in terms of genes and biology, Interviewee G suggests that also: 'We might argue that it's because they grow up in an environment that places a high value on it [athleticism].'

His no one-size-fits-all approach might be seen as creating difficulties in his work as a neuroscientist, but in practice the opposite is true. It is precisely because he is aware that no one-size-fits-all that he has had to look elsewhere, and to the discourse of sociocultural science, to explain his experiences.

Learning and pedagogy: a cultural learning science

> All human behavior and learning, including feeling, thinking, creating, remembering and deciding, originate in the brain. Rather than a hardwired biological system, the brain develops through an active, dynamic process in which a child's social, emotional and cognitive experiences organize his or her brain over time, in accordance with biological constraints and principles. . . . In the other direction, a child's particular neuropsychological strengths and weaknesses shape the way he or she perceives and interacts with the world. Like the weaving of an intricate and delicate web (Fischer and Bidell, 2006), physiological and cultural processes interact to produce learning and behavior in highly nuanced and complex patterns of human development.
>
> (Immordino-Yang and Fischer, 2009: 2)

Drawing on sociocultural and neuroscientific perspectives posits learning as culturally, socially and biologically dependent. Constitutive in nature, learning becomes the social ability to recognize signs, symbols and language shared by others in the culture, which we explore in more detail in a later chapter. This process is also dependent on the biological capacity of the individual to respond to these socially meaningful reifications of experience. In this understanding, learning is both a process and product—it is a process of participation in the world.

The implications of a sociocultural definition of brain and learning can be read alongside the neuroscientific research previously presented in Chapter 2, to enrich our understanding of learning. We use the headings, findings and implications here (see Table 6.1) to mirror Sousa's presentation, which we discussed in Chapter 2: 'Defining brain', so both can more easily be read together. The findings we present are the central concepts of sociocultural theory, while the implications illustrate what this theoretical belief might mean for our practice.

Connecting learning and pedagogy

A discussion of learning is incomplete without a consideration of pedagogy. While it is outside the scope of this book to develop specific applications of our understandings of learning for pedagogy in defined learning contexts, and as the following discussion will illuminate, we may not wish to do so, we include here a focus on pedagogy to make some brief but important points.

We begin with a sociocultural definition of pedagogy: our participation in practice as a result of our understanding of the nature of learning. Within this understanding, a discussion of pedagogy involves more than a discussion of teaching in schools. Whenever we engage in learning, we develop our

Table 6.1 A sociocultural understanding of learning: findings and implications

Finding	Implication
Learning is an activity central to, as opposed to separate from, day-to-day living.	There are times in our lives when the issue of learning becomes problematic and requires close attention, for example, in school or college; but there are also times when learning works, for example, when a baby speaks his or her first word. We can learn from these experiences.
Every situation is an opportunity for learning and identity development, however, individuals can only ever learn what is around them to be learnt.	The problem arises when an individual learns something in any given situation, other than what was initially expected as the learning outcome. Understanding this for educators means that learning cannot be designed. It can only be designed for.
Our understanding of learning is an integral part of our everyday lives. It is part of our participation in our communities and organizations.	Our perspective on learning is most important. What we think about learning influences where we recognize learning as well as what we do when improvements must be made.
We are social beings and this fact is a central aspect of learning.	Learning is a negotiation of meaning and identity formation in social practice. Meaning–our ability to experience the world and our engagement with it as meaningful–is ultimately what learning is to produce.
Knowledge is a matter of competence with respect to valued enterprises such as singing in tune, etc.	Knowing is a matter of participating in the pursuit of such enterprises, that is of active engagement in the world.
Mind is mediated by culture and distributed across communities of practice.	Meanings and our understandings of the world and ourselves are always mediated and develop in the social and historical processes of participation and reification.
What defines a community of practice is a matter of sustaining enough mutual engagement in pursuing an enterprise together to share some significant learning.	Therefore, communities of practice can be conceived of as shared histories of learning. If this is true, then learning becomes a fundamental characteristic of practice. As Wenger believes, learning is the engine of practice, and practice is the history of that learning.
Power and agency are central to learning (Lewis, Enciso and Moje, 2007) but this power and agency are not possessions, rather, they are distributed by and across communities of practice.	Learning and identity are not possessions. They involve the constant negotiation of social interaction and experience. In this understanding, it is the community, or more specifically its participants, that learn.

pedagogical practice and the practice of others, and an understanding of pedagogy encompasses:

> what is salient to people as they engage in activity and develop competence in the practice in question. It takes account of two phenomena and their dynamic relationship (a) the social order, as reflected in, for example, policy and its associated cultural beliefs and assumptions; and (b) the experienced world, as reflected in both the enactment and the beliefs mediating how it is experienced.
>
> (Hall, Murphy and Soler, 2008: ix)

School is one site where pedagogical practices are evident and the one that is traditionally linked to the word 'pedagogy'. The understanding of pedagogy implied in this context, however, as fixed and bounded is false. In their text *Pedagogy and Practice: Culture and Identities*, Hall, Murphy and Soler (2008) challenge this bounded notion of pedagogy by suggesting that in school contexts the focus should remain, rather, on the parallels in curriculum, introduced across three levels:

1   Curriculum as specified–to include social order and policies;
2   Curriculum as enacted–to include our own participation;
3   Curriculum as experienced–to include the experienced world.

An exploration of pedagogy in school contexts, then, would centre on the relationship between these three understandings of curriculum, on connections and disconnects, and does not constitute a definition of pedagogy itself.

From this reconceptualization of pedagogy it is clear that it is a shared, dynamic and relational process in either specific or broad contexts. In this text, our focus on pedagogy has remained broad, but that is not to say that this text does not include implications for learning in specific contexts such as the school or workplace. Though we do not develop our insights in these specific directions, the reader can take what is discussed throughout this text and apply it to any particular setting. It was this exact aim that necessitated our broad focus on pedagogical practices:

> This deeper and broader notion of pedagogy, which is not confined to a particular place, setting, age or stage, draws attention to the identities which are variously valued, reproduced and transformed as people participate in activity. Whether the practice is in relation to becoming a reader, a learner of mathematics in school, a teacher, an architect, a hairdresser and so on, how the cultural practice is mediated by one's lived experiences becomes significant for one's ability to demonstrate oneself as competent and be recognised by others as competent in a given practice. Pedagogy involves an appreciation of the

significance of experiences and mediational aspects as key to supporting learning.

(Hall, Murphy and Soler, 2008: ix)

Learning, culture and neuroscience

Consciousness has been described, in neurological terms, as the appearance of a world (Metzinger, 2010a), a:

> certain fluidity, flexibility, a context sensitivity. . . . We have the feeling of being present in the real world … You could describe it as a specific illusion, but it is a major neurocomputational achievement of the human brain–the sense of presence as a self in a conscious scene.
>
> (Metzinger, 2010b: 12–14)

In our neuroscientifically informed sociocultural understanding of learning, this 'context sensitivity' is biologically and culturally based. Everything we say and do as individuals, including the language and sign systems we use to express it, are cultural and social constructions. From this basic but powerful premise, all that follows must also be cultural and social in origin. Learning becomes a social construct and a social process.

Elsewhere (Curtin and Hall, 2013), the authors have suggested that from a sociocultural and neuroscientific perspective, learning is the appearance of a functioning, literate self, in a world the individual experiences as meaningful. This can only occur where activity, agent and world; experience, brain and environment align in a particular way and learning occurs through shared cultural tools in social interaction. This understanding is at the heart of this text. The brain scan is not the learning–it is a picture of a part of it. In this chapter, we have attempted to begin opening up what we see as new learning worlds, broadening understandings of what it really means to employ neuroscientific and sociocultural definitions of the word 'brain' to 'explain' learning. Charles Horton Cooley sums up very well our understanding of learning and experience in his phrase 'the looking glass self', introduced in Chapter 3, which he uses to describe the way that self is shaped by the reflected opinions of others around us. Seen differently by our families, our colleagues, our lovers, our friends, each hold up a looking glass to us in which we can see something of our self. As Cooley (1902: 152) states, 'I am not what I think I am and I am not what you think I am; I am what I think that you think I am.'

Conclusion

In investigating a number of connections emerging between sociocultural and neuroscientific concepts and theorizing (plasticity and experience; brain circuitry and social experiences; language acquisition and culture; environment and agency; brain function and social meaning), this chapter has explored what stories sociocultural and neuroscientific discourses are telling about learning. Emphasizing the similarities, this chapter has provided context for later chapters where sociocultural and neuroscientific pairings are not viewed as complementary or in such a straight-forward way. This chapter also introduced the concept of pedagogy to our discussion; suggesting a sociocultural working definition of the term allows for more meaning making and gainful developments to both theory and practice. We suggested how understandings in this text may be applied in any learning context, not just the narrow vision of learning as taking place in schools and colleges. Rather than explaining learning, neuroscientific research gives us another way to look at it. Applying sociocultural concepts will, we believe, allow us to further our understanding of learning.

Notes

1 http://www.positscience.com/brain-resources/brain-plasticity/what-is-brain-plasticity
2 Chabris, C. (2011) *The Invisible Gorilla: How our Intuitions Deceive Us.* New York: Three Rivers Press.

Chapter 7

Constructing success and failure

Introduction

One of the main arguments of this book is that human development is always positioned within social, emotional and cultural spheres and that these spheres need to be considered as part and parcel of how we think and act in the world. Another argument is that human development is also neurobiological development. People are inextricably cultural and biological. Building on the arguments about a sociocultural perspective on learning in the previous chapter, and in particular on the introduction to pedagogy towards the end of that chapter, this chapter focuses more specifically on pedagogy in schools. In doing so, it elaborates on the cultural dimension of learning (as opposed to the biological) with reference to common educational concepts such as ability, intelligence, giftedness, accomplishment, expertise, competence, knowledge, success, and so on. These are words that are redolent with meanings in educational contexts and in school contexts in particular. They are used liberally in educational and everyday discourse, not always in the same way, to be sure, as exemplified in the work of Michael Hand (2007) who, from a philosophical perspective, seeks to distinguish intelligence from other related concepts such as competence. While such work as Hand's is interesting, the linguistic and conceptual distinctions among and between these concepts are not what the focus is here. Rather, what is of interest is how these concepts are made meaningful, how they are performed, and how they are made manifest with consequences for people's living. They can be used, tacitly as well as intentionally and explicitly, to position, identify, control, empower, exclude, include, affirm, undermine, reward, punish, promote and demote—and this is not an exhaustive list. In other words, how they are deployed and understood in particular situations can have major consequences for who people are and what they can become.

Taking culture as an analytic concept (as described in Chapters 4 and 5) this chapter shows how notions such as ability, talent, creativity, are constructed and performed, rather than given and predetermined. Such notions are made real and meaningful through the process of negotiation where people have intentions, make assumptions and are variously constrained by the scripts and reifications–conscious and unconscious–available to them. We examine these scripts and make them visible through their enactment *in situ*.

Extending ideas highlighted in the previous chapters, then, we begin this chapter by examining enacted understandings of success, failure, expertise, ability, disability–regardless of what these terms mean at dictionary level.

Testing for success and failure

How do we understand and explain achievement, success, failure? How do we understand and explain ability? In education, and especially in matters of schooling, we refer to what an individual knows and is able to do in relevant situations. We assess achievement and so can describe success or failure and often this is done in relation to others. Ability is frequently talked about as if it is something an individual has, something possessed, an internal trait, a property that is inherent in the person. In much psychological literature, it is understood as a variable that is independent, timeless and static; a construct that is psychologically prior to other forms of expertise (Sternberg, 2008). Ability, on this understanding, is facilitated by culture and society, yet crucially separate from culture and society. It is thought of as something that is prior to learning. The work of the neuroscientists Haier and Jung (2008) represents such a position when they pose the question: why are some brains smarter than others? These researchers claim intelligence, indicated by scores on IQ tests, is located in the brain and that this presents 'a daunting challenge' for educators, who incidentally, they say, show a lamentable disdain for the neural basis of intelligence. For these, and likeminded thinkers, the hope is that educators can design unique educational interventions using 'brain data' to optimize individual potential.

A legacy of the fixed notion of ability has dominated schooling in a range of ways. One way is the practice of ability grouping (streaming), which is especially common in secondary schools. Despite its dominance and pervasiveness in educational discourse and practice, and indeed in policy and research, this way of thinking about ability is not as helpful as the richer, more nuanced perspective afforded by sociocultural science. The latter directs us to how ability, competence or expertise is extended to one, how it is claimed, and how it is jointly produced.

In a sociocultural view, as already elaborated in the previous chapter, attributes of ability include all of the following: history, culture and relationality, such that it emerges out of interactions with others. However, it is not something that simply emerges between individuals but also encompasses the wider sociocultural milieu in which the interactions take place. It is not separate from the sociocultural realm but is constituted by culture and society. At birth, we all enter a community whose extended intelligence we share, but throughout life, this intelligence or culture has to be negotiated and made meaningful in the different contexts of our lives.

Consider some of the mechanisms typically used in education to demonstrate the ownership of success or to show evidence of ability. The history of schooling is one where assessment is inescapable, and currently, schooling could be regarded as synonymous with testing, assessing and passing judgement, or, more specifically, having judgement passed on one. In his *Stories in an Almost Classical Mode* (1988), Harold Brodkey reflected on his schooling and childhood:

> but I did well in school and seemed to be peculiarly able to learn what the teacher said—I never mastered a subject, though—there was the idiotic testimony of those peculiar witnesses, IQ tests: those scores invented me. Those scores were a decisive piece of destiny in that they affected the way people treated you and regarded you; they determined your authority; and if you spoke oddly, they argued in favor of your sanity.
>
> (Brodkey, cited in Hanson, 1994)

Allan Hanson's book *Testing Testing: Social Consequences of the Examined Life* (1994), along with his other work (e.g. 2000), show how tests often produce the characteristics they claim to measure. They get to determine success and ability. As he says, 'the individual in contemporary society is not so much described by tests as constructed by them' (2000: 68), while others claim that tests legitimate the sorting of people into intelligent and not-so-intelligent categories (McDermott and Hall, 2007).

Tests are used to categorize and describe ability and disability, so we get the gifted, the talented, the genius, the slow learner, the disabled learner, and so on. Those so assigned are then recognized, act and come to think of themselves in these categories and also become living portrayals of what these words mean. Along with describing, even defining the person, such accounts then act to constitute the categories themselves. 'Intelligence', conceptualized by cognitive psychologists as indicated by an IQ score, is a case in point. In cognitive psychology, it is a unitary phenomenon; it is a quantitative, measureable thing and people have varying amounts of it; and, the amount of it one has is fixed for life by heredity. Taking it that one is hardwired for intelligence, it is not surprising to find that intelligence defines one. Hanson (2000: 67) cites a wonderful account of Victor Serbriakoff, who he shows was 'invented' by intelligence tests, describing him as follows:

> Told by a teacher at age 15 that he was a moron, he quit school and worked for years as an unskilled labourer. At age 32 he happened to take an intelligence test, which indicated that his IQ was a towering 161. His life changed totally. He tried his hand at inventing and received patents, he wrote books on his favourite topic (not surprisingly, intelligence), and he became chairman of the International Mensa Society, an organization with membership restricted to individuals with IQs over 140.

This is a classic case of how intelligence, ability to learn, acquires people. There is the temptation to equate 'intelligence' and achievement with self-worth, as

Hanson explains. There is a disproportionate sense of inadequacy on the part of those not scoring very well, while there is an exaggerated sense of exultation, and perhaps superiority, at the expense of others among those who excel. In this case, the IQ test is the representational device, the reification, for acquiring 'intelligent' people—it constructs them. But, and this is crucial, in the process, intelligence itself is constructed and made real. The intelligent person, the test, the IQ score are all constitutive. Challenging the conventional assumption that intelligence exists first as a thing and that IQ tests follow to measure it, Hanson's book argues that the concept of intelligence is a product of intelligence tests and that tests create what they are intended to measure. Focusing on disability, McDermott and Raley (2009) in similar vein show how tests are given and the results treated as real but always more real to the person tested insofar as the tests claim to get inside the child's head. They quip: 'the problem with global norming: our kids are getting toasted by tests' (p. 47).

Co-constructing success and failure

Here we show, with examples drawn from our own and others' research, what the material and social practices of ability are and how ability is hailed and recognized. We draw on studies from the literature where such formations become visible and, as such, are resources for readers who are seeking to understand and promote development and formation. These narratives draw attention to people's intentions as they are expressed and enacted, that is, as they emerge *in situ*. We have chosen accounts that highlight how failure is jointly constructed in school settings and yet where the people in question actually wanted to avoid failure. Thus, we are not focusing on people who resisted or did not care about school and learning. These are all accounts of people who wanted to succeed.

A case of not belonging to the community of 'successful' learners

We draw here on work funded by the British Academy and reported in more detail elsewhere (Hall, 2008). Daniel is in primary school. A range of popular cultural pursuits are personally meaningful to him and these pursuits—especially pop music, football, horror movies, computer games and the social networking site, Bebo—are all highly relevant to the desirable self he strives to enact. These are material and mediational means (Wertsch, Tulviste and Hagstrom, 1993) by which Daniel leaves childhood behind and moves into a version of teenhood and adolescence which for him include being cool and being popular. In the process, he positions himself and is positioned by others as 'not able' and 'not learned' and not successful in school. Ability and being learned, as defined by the school system in general and by his school in particular, is not a concept easily associated with the world Daniel is figuring.

He attends a rural primary school and has the same teacher for three years. Teaching is very much in a traditional, didactic style, involving much teacher talk, much time spent on individual writing assignments, answering questions posed by the teacher, completing worksheets and studying the textbook in the various subject areas. Classroom-based pencil-and-paper testing is routine and high marks and compliance with class procedures are public signs of achievement and success. Daniel dislikes school and his teacher. In his final year in his primary school, he is sitting apart from others in the classroom and is perceived by his teacher as a 'disruptive influence' because 'he talks so much'. His friends and classmates tell the researcher that he 'has a problem with talking'. Despite indications from many one-to-one conversations and focus group interviews with him that he desires to be successful in school, school is a place where he is literally silenced, where he certainly cannot author a learned self.

While the 'popular' and 'cool' identity that he projected could be expected to and did indeed affect the learning opportunities he would look for and take in school, his teacher and other pupils unwittingly colluded in producing him as different and deviant and as a powerless person in the classroom. He was marginalized and made to look a failure. The mechanisms by which this happened included all of the following: lack of opportunities to engage with peers; sitting in rows; his physical distance from all others in the room; low expectations on the part of the teacher for him; the way knowing could be demonstrated; how success was defined; and what constituted valid knowledge. Daniel himself didn't perceive what was available for him to learn in school had much to do with his life project. School seemed to contribute nothing to life in his family or his community, particularly the pop-cultural community to which he so identified. In this sense, he was agentic in his own construction as 'not learned' and 'not able'. The salient identity of coolness and popularity gave him a perspective on the world that resulted in him tending to interpret events and others' actions in particular ways thus closing off other possible interpretations. The particular perspective of being popular and cool was too rigidly held by him and constrained him from extending himself in other directions.

The considerable mismatch between Daniel's experience in primary school and his lived experiences outside of school meant that his capacities were underestimated. While the identity of learned boy was not seductive for him, neither was it extended to him in school. A key problem for him was his unproductive relationship with his teacher. Through her reactions to him, she extended to him a position of not belonging—she isolated him from the community of learned pupils. And over time, over many moments of sitting alone, separate from classmates, his 'not belonging' became accepted and taken for granted. Dorothy Holland et al. (1998) and Stanton Wortham (2006) describe how identities thicken over time and events. Daniel's long period of time with the same teacher and peers, in the same classroom, having more or less the same routines and practices, meant that his sense of himself and others' sense of him as not belonging to the community of successful learners were consolidated and made firm.

The process of doing so was largely invisible to all the actors. That Daniel was learning in school is unproblematic, but what was available to be learned was complexly problematic (Lave, 1996). He was shown and learned day by day that he was not able or talented. The point is that becoming learned, acquiring an identity of learned boy, is far from a lone activity: one cannot be learned, literate, numerate, educated alone. One has to be recognized and made such by the actions and interactions of others and the perspectives underlying those actions and interactions.

Grabbed by a label

The title of this chapter captures its main argument: that the performance or the social practice gives life to and makes real what ability/disability is. In effect, there is only the practice, or, as we noted earlier, practice makes practice. Also, meanings of ability, success, achievement, etc. imply their opposites so they have to be discussed in tandem, as dualities. An especially telling account of a child, Adam, by Ray McDermott (2001) is worth summarizing to develop this argument further.

Adam had been labelled as learning disabled by the school system based on his behaviour in school and on various tests which, it was assumed, specified his traits. However, following observations of Adam in different situations in school, the sociocultural research team noticed that what happened around him organized, displayed and represented him as a learning disabled person. In moment-by-moment happenings involving Adam, learning disability was on show, noticed, documented, remediated and explained.

As in Daniel's case, it transpired that many people were involved in Adam's depiction as learning disabled, an idea powerfully expressed as 'the acquisition of a child by a learning disability' (McDermott, 2001: 60). Adam had been observed in 'everyday life', in afternoon activity clubs, in one-to-one testing settings and in classroom lessons. It seems that the more formal, constrained and 'school-like' the setting, the greater the scope for displaying Adam as disabled. In everyday life situations, he appeared competent and did not 'stand out' from other children in any negative way. In Cooking Club activities, Adam was okay, especially if he could work with his friend who took responsibility for reading the recipe and working step by step to make the cake. If required to work with someone other than his friend, however, there were occasional arguments and taunting from others. This was also the case with classroom lessons, although here he was more frequently made noticeable by the adults in the room and by other children for having problems getting his work done. In the more formal, test-like situation involving answering questions in a whole-class setting, or doing individual written work, Adam was made most conspicuous. He became very obvious as an unsuccessful member of the class, not only by his poor performances in whole-class interaction and on the tests, but also by the outlandish guesses he gave as answers to questions. In these settings, he tried to divert attention away from what he could not do by acting out, crawling under tables, distracting peers. All this social work aimed at concealing his incompetence, of course, was exactly what fed into his visibility as disabled, and triggered various professional labels as to 'what was wrong with him'.

The more school-like, formal and constrained, the more Adam was marked as disabled–so being learning disabled became differently available to him depending on the context. McDermott's analysis shows how Adam's problems are not explicable with reference to the cognitive demand of the tasks set, even though it is obvious that everyday life is easier than a test situation. Rather, his problems could be linked to the arbitrariness (from his perspective) of the tasks set combined with the degradation he frequently experienced as a result of appearing a failure. Following careful observation of Adam over time, the researchers established that the entire class paid constant attention to his disability such that 'everyone knew how to look for, recognize, stimulate, make visible and, depending on circumstances, keep quiet about or expose Adam's problem' (66). American classrooms, McDermott claims, are organized so people can be caught not knowing things and can have labels ascribed to them such as 'learning disabled'. The various settings in which Adam found himself provided moments for his degradation–some in the cooking sessions, even more in classroom lessons, and many more in the testing situations.

We are arguing that in contemporary schooling, learning disability, and by inference ability, is everywhere–it is a position that will be occupied, taken up and made real by the interactions and behaviours of those in the setting. It is also made real by the wider society–the test designers, publishers, and the desire to rank individuals, schools, nations, according to achievement. Understanding someone as able, intelligent, talented, etc., by this analysis, is not accessible by looking inside people's heads, but by examining the relations between people. As in the account of Daniel, it takes many people, interactions, relations and conversations to produce someone as able or disabled. In line with the notion of culture put forward in Chapter 5, and as McDermott's work shows, the portrayal of one person's lack of intelligence and success is an opportunity for others to claim high intelligence and success.

Making sense: subjectivities

Two other noteworthy studies that extend our analysis, highlight the role of perceptions, or more precisely, subjectivities, in how success and failure are constructed in classrooms. Renee DePalma (2008) shows how success is less about learning and far more about gaining access to the definitions of success that count, and conforming to those definitions. Based on ethnographic research and close observations of one girl, Laura, in school, she describes the tools or reifications used, the ways of participating and assumptions made by Laura as she navigates her way through the various activities that made up her school day, and how inconsistencies among her mainstream and EAL teacher as well as her own interpretation of success militate against her construction as successful in school. He shows how the nine-year-old unintentionally participated in producing herself as unsuccessful. In the process, he challenges the idea that her failure could be attributed to any one individual–Laura herself or indeed just her teachers.

Though participating in an English as a Second Language (ESL) programme for over a year, Laura's teachers describe her as failing to learn English–the exclusive medium of instruction. She was in a classroom where the majority could cope with English as the medium of instruction. Both her mainstream and her ESL teacher were of the view that she could 'barely do anything' and was 'limited' in virtually all academic areas. She was described by her teachers as helpless, passive and silent, while, occasionally, classmates talked about Laura as if she was not present.

Yet Laura was a 'good' student conforming to the routines of the class: she completed her worksheet independently as requested, she did not have to be reminded to finish her work. In 'rug time' she was visibly attentive to the teacher, raising her hand to answer questions when requested to, and recognizing when it was okay to call out answers when the teacher did not insist on hands being raised before answering. Laura's diligence in completing worksheets and low-level colouring, cutting-and-pasting tasks often went unnoticed and unrewarded despite the fact that the teacher set the work. Most others were less conscientious and sloppy about their worksheets and moved on more quickly to their silent-reading tasks. Laura was definitely motivated to learn. But her mainstream teacher ultimately did not value her meticulously completed worksheets or her silence and reading-like behaviours during 'sustained silent reading'–turning the pages, looking at the pictures, checking the blurb. Her teacher knew she could not actually read or understand the words on the page. Laura's silence, reading behaviour, motivation–all went unnoticed.

DePalma recounts several incidents in which Laura's diligence, obedience and compliance are apparently inconsistent with success, and in fact prove to be the very features that add up to her failure as a learner in school. Only on one occasion (game day) did the teacher's and Laura's interpretation of success align and on this same occasion Laura was ecstatic. Just like Adam, Laura had absorbed the procedures and rules–explicit and implicit–of the different teachers' classrooms and she tried to appear as competent as she could in the face of different tasks and demands. She also knew the importance of decoding English text and reading for meaning but did not have the competence to do either. What emerges from the account is that while the various participants, teachers, students, are part of the community of practice called school, they experience it differently and do not share interpretations or definitions of success and failure.

In fact, conventional schooling discourages the sharing of subjective understandings of schooling practices. Curricular rigidity in Laura's case (for example the school/state-wide policy of not using learners' first language in school), combined with lack of communication among the various participants in the schooling enterprise, resulted in barriers being erected to Laura's success. From the point of view of the argument being developed here, an entire system comprising teachers, other pupils, Laura herself, the official curriculum and enacted curriculum (that only English could be used in school and the use of Spanish was deemed subversive) as well as the structure and organization of the school day, conspired to position and keep Laura as unsuccessful in school. It takes many people to construct the failing student.

Another example from the sociocultural research literature is worth noting here, not so much because it provides insights into notions of success and failure directly, but because it extends our understanding of where to look for explanations: in this case to the perspectives of other learners. Roberta Schnorr's ethnography (1990) involving seven months of classroom observation and interviews portrays a year-one, seven-year-old boy, Peter, who spends some of his day in a special education class and some in a mainstream class. Thus, he is part-time in each setting. The researcher sought to understand how other learners understood 'first grade', and understood themselves (and Peter) as class members. Posing questions such as: What is first grade? Where do you belong? What do you do? an image of Peter emerges. He is someone who does not belong, who is seen as an outsider, and not as a respected peer.

The title of the study 'Peter, he comes and goes . . .' sums up the message–he does not/could not share in the significant events of the mainstream class. Missing key events, assignments and experiences that constitute 'first grade', Peter is cast by his peers as not belonging to the group, to the class. He is excluded because he does different activities, not the ones that count as being in first grade. However, there are also other mechanisms that tacitly render him invisible in the class. For instance, his teacher frequently uses his table for class materials while he is out of the room so his space is not entirely his. Despite having a teacher who 'talked up' his strengths, his peers do not recognize or sanction him as a legitimate member. He simply does not belong.

Reification, collective voice, constrained choice

All these slices of classroom life point to what is typically invisible in classrooms; invisible because it is so taken for granted, everyday and unremarkable. Because of its social embeddedness, this entire process of performing ability and failure–or any other cultural phenomenon for that matter–is often as unconscious as it is invisible. Although people may well be participating in the same activity, they do not necessarily have access to each other's understandings and meanings. Understanding the process, as these examples show, involves both looking *at* and looking *beyond* the individual; beyond the skull and skin. To look beyond the individual is to think of the script, reification or the collected voice that informs notions of a desirable self.

It is also to recognize that there is a reification of ability/disability which circulates and is taken for granted within a system. Contemporary schooling, arguably, is built around documenting, diagnosing and discovering people with different abilities, and especially disabilities, and there are all sorts of reifications that guide our action in this regard, not least test instruments. The upshot is that people have to be found not knowing things: this is a cultural script that is taken so much for granted that it is not noticed by all those involved. There are positions, spaces for people to occupy, and the space of learning disability is a highly salient one which will find its occupant. One must display certain disabilities that are verifiable, but the system in the form of its teachers, assessments of what children cannot do and the range of institutional labels (e.g. ADHD, IQ, hyperactivity, English-language learner) is poised to discover, diagnose and verify learning dis/ability where dis/ability is assumed to be an embodied, psychological trait. Identifying and logging people's deficits are, in the words of McDermott and Raley (2009), 'the institutionally well-paid pre-occupations of consequence, the stuff of a child's school records, the stuff of the institutional biographies that record a child's problems in school files forever'. Equally, to inhabit the position of talented person, cool teenager, learned pupil, one must display certain abilities that are verifiable and recognizable to others who occupy, or aspire to occupy, that same position. The position of failing learner is necessary in order to recognize the successful one.

An important point in connection with the invisibility of the entire process of finding people intelligent and learning disabled, is that the actors involved do not generally contemplate or question the cultural script that guides their 'finding' actions. By its nature, a cultural script is a set of tacit assumptions about the way the world works. While teachers know the structures and procedures like tests and labels, they know these mechanisms by using them rather than by problematizing them. Understanding a cultural script or a reification requires making it problematic, challenging what is assumed to be natural and taken for granted–what we are attempting to do here with the above accounts from the field. Alan Hanson, interestingly, likens this work to pondering the grammar of one's language as one engages in conversation–people typically do not do such pondering. However, sociocultural theorizing involves just such problematizing and analyzing as exemplified by the above accounts where processes typically hidden are rendered explicit.

What we have argued in this chapter is that ability is not a construct residing in the head but is a feature that is inseparable from the surround, the environment. The person, of course, is part of the environment and the environment is in the person, so ability is constitutive: it is made up of the person and the environment. Both are enmeshed. The environment includes the cultural scripts that circulate about how to demonstrate success, how to be a learner, what knowledge and skills matter in a given situation, and so on. These cultural scripts or reifications are part of the social order, the social world; they are outside the head. Yet, they are also in heads, because people, inevitably can only use the cultural tools of the environment to negotiate their way in the social world–to act. As we elaborated in Chapter 5, reification is essential to participation–both are necessary for action and both form a duality. So, the tools themselves, whether ways of interacting, language used, scripts about ability, have a history of use albeit different applications and enactments depending on situation. What follows from this is that intelligence or ability is already located in the tools, artefacts and the scripts applied. Intelligence, therefore, is distributed across the people, tools, artefacts and scripts that are available as resources to accomplish things, hence the importance of focusing on the enactment of ability, the performance of success, and so on, as the above accounts seek to do.

A key pedagogical and research issue arising from the analysis in this chapter is: what are the opportunities for learning in a given situation and how is this learning valued? As a result of the constraining or liberating influence of a cultural script or collective voice, people do not construct meaning in a neutral space with equal opportunities to express themselves or act. How people come to end up inhabiting one position, then, and not others in a given situation, is more a matter of experience and differential treatment by other people than any kind of innate ability. This is further elaborated in the next chapter, where we discuss the enactment of talent.

Conclusion

A key point of our analysis in this chapter, in terms of what educators do, is to make what is ordinarily invisible, visible, and on that basis to consider ways forward pedagogically. We conclude this chapter, therefore, by referring to some of the possible pedagogical implications arising from just one of the telling cases above. There are also implications for researchers, but we address those later in the book.

We hold that to be found intelligent, successful and expert, or to perform as such, one must have the opportunity to learn and for some learners this may simply require more time and support. Opportunity to learn is a key concept in sociocultural understanding of development. As we could see from the above, the fact that all learners are apparently in the same classroom does not mean that all have access to the same practice and, thus, the same opportunity to learn. Revisiting the case of Daniel, we suggest that to extend his agency in school, to bridge the popular cultural and learned boy communities for him, his teacher might make elements of pop culture part of the enacted curriculum, thus drawing on his experience and ways of knowing outside of school. A curriculum that is permeable and able to build on his textual resources, particularly media resources, would recognize the cultural resources he already uses and values–in his case, for example, horror fiction, visual literacies or texting. The affordances of these media resources would allow him to bridge old and new situations. The potential transformation and recontextualization of horror fiction texts in new contexts would involve him as knower and expert, thus enhancing his status as learner in school and legitimating the genre as worthy of study.

But, in itself this is unlikely to be adequate as it may not sufficiently disrupt existing power relations and assumptions about who can learn. Daniel would also benefit from practices that involved him more centrally in learning tasks that would enhance his sense of belonging and engagement. As it transpired, in secondary school, Daniel was able to renegotiate the tension that had previously existed between doing cool teenager and successful school learner, beginning to attain at least a partial resolution in this tension. He was beginning to be able to create an alternative path in which affiliation with school practices could co-exist with affiliation with cool teenager practices. How was this achieved? His secondary school afforded him new opportunities—in the form of new sets of peers, teachers, curricula, activities and tasks—to disrupt and challenge existing conceptions of him as a person and as a learner, though this was no easy process. There were changes in his support networks that helped him do some resolving of the dissonance that had been there for him before. Teachers seemed to act as brokers of new possibilities for Daniel while new and different kinds of classroom activities (e.g. lab-based science, practical woodwork and cookery) afforded new kinds of participation opportunities. The reality is that people develop goals and agendas for themselves by evaluating what they have the potential to do within a given context. They negotiate the tools, relationships and roles that help realize those intentions about the desirable self one could produce in interactions with others. However, it could well have been otherwise, and his identity as not learned may well have calcified rather than disrupted. Such a transformation requires a new set of relations and participation patterns and a new set of practices—far from a straightforward or predictable process.

A sociocultural analysis, as indicated in this chapter, brings to the fore the surround and wider social milieu as well as the person. The focus is less inside the person's head and more on what is going on around the person. What are the opportunities to learn the valued knowledge or skill? This question becomes more highly pertinent. Opportunity to learn therefore is a vital concept that asks educators to reconsider time to learn. The unprecedented emphasis on comparing learners, on measuring progress and on diagnosing difficulty without sufficient reference to opportunity to learn, is challenged by a sociocultural perspective.

Chapter 8

Explaining talent

Opportunity to learn

Introduction

If one accepts the line of argument developed in the previous chapter, then from a research perspective, a bounded individual is not adequate as the unit of interest and analysis. Rather, attention must focus on the reifications and cultural scripts in operation around the individual, the interactions, the sets of relationships, the histories, the memories, the surround and the affordances of the environment. A key research question becomes: how is ability and talent performed collaboratively in a given setting? For cognitive neuroscientists, environment is conceptualized differently to how it is conceptualized for socioccultural scientists. It is seen merely as background and, as such, easily separated from the person who is the unit of analysis. Socioculturalists resist mentalistic and reductive analyses of human development where the individual and the environment are treated as distinct. Instead, as we developed in Chapter 3, a social view of mind is assumed.

In the introduction to this book, we referred to an incident in which a group of teachers who were participating in a knowledge-exchange initiative discussed their understanding of inclusive pedagogies. One participant, whose professional role involved teaching children defined as autistic, argued that such children are creative, talented and intelligent in ways other children, not so labelled, are not, and that the evidence for this stems from recent work on brain science. The controversial point being made was that these children see the world differently and that some are creative and talented by virtue of their neurological makeup and that their particular genius is innate (see http://www. ted.com/talks/temple_grandin_the_world_needs_all_kinds_of_minds.html). So, in this perspective, as in the TED talk just referenced, talent is an individual accomplishment but also is understood with reference to differences in brain structure.

How is talent explained? What are the social practices of talent? How is it shaped, recognized and promoted? In recent years, there has been a trend to identify and fast track those assumed to be 'gifted and talented' (G&T), with the rationale always framed in terms of making the most of human potential.

In England, for instance, the current educational policy is to identify some ten per cent of all school children as gifted or talented (i.e. gifted academically or talented in some aspect of sport or the arts). Those so identified are then supported in specialized, enriched learning environments, so that their special gifts and talents can be promoted and developed to the full (DCSF, 2009; Eyre, 2009). An Internet search of the phrase 'gifted and talented' yields all of the following: lists of 'gifted and talented' programmes; a welcome to the Irish Centre for Talented Youth; a report entitled 'Gifted and talented children in (and out) of the classroom' on the website of the National Council for Curriculum and Assessment (NCCA) in Ireland; and many more such references. The Irish Centre for Talented Youth at Dublin City University tells us why we should identify gifted and talented children. So, the assumption is that there is no doubt such people exist and the identification of talent is considered possible. At a recent conference in our University, the Provost of Trinity College Dublin proclaimed that his University's mission was to attract and cater for 'the brightest and the best' regardless of background. Companies search for 'top performers' and 'creative talent', and, increasingly, it seems competitive advantage depends on the contribution of a talented minority. Alan Eustace, a Google vice-president, claims that 'one top-notch engineer is worth 300 times or more than the average'. Presumably he means 300 times more profit. A close examination of the actual words and phrases used in various popular websites give clues into the thinking of the origin of talent or genius: that it is a genetic endowment, on the one hand, but that it can be developed, on the other hand, and the sooner the better. The way talent is talked about in such sites also aligns with our current preoccupation with education as a commodity and illustrates the cultural demands we place on intelligence, learning and achievement. Ray McDermott's words about genius are apposite: '[g]enius exists most obviously in institutions that celebrate the success of a few over the many: the normal over the disabled; the talented over the normal, and the genius over the talented' and 'because it is possible to be a genius it's possible to be a dunce' and 'because genius is rare stupidity is rampant' (2006: 287–288). These dualities speak to the arguments about culture and practice developed earlier, especially in Chapters 4 and 5.

Taking the theme of talent and creativity, areas of significance for education and particularly schooling, as a focus, we show in this chapter how sociocultural (cognitive) and neuroscientific research, despite their different theoretical orientations, coincide in recognizing the significance of experience, participation and opportunity to learn. We show how sociocultural theorizing offers understandings of talent and creativity that neuroscientific views ignore in practice (even if they do not reject them in theory). The purpose here is not to offer a review of studies on giftedness and talent, rather, we have selected studies to highlight what can be learned about talent, and ultimately learning, from an exploration of sociocultural and neuroscientific theory.

Access to the valued practice

A host of empirical studies conducted by psychologists on talent, giftedness and creativity in different spheres, attest to the essential role of opportunity to learn and to the role of others in the depiction of the talented person. Though few are framed in terms of sociocultural science, the studies are interesting as they confirm the ideas developed in the previous chapter in relation to the significance of 'the surround' and the networks of relations that are part of the person's lived world. These studies direct our attention to penetrative questions such as: what is available to be learned and to whom is it available? Who has access to the practice? What are the practices of talent and creativity, and how do people become part of those practices and communities?

The 'ten-year rule' is a common theme in discussions of high/elite performance in such areas as sport, music, chess and other pursuits. The rule states that one needs in the order of a decade of study or practice to perform at very high levels. To reach the highest standards of performance in a domain, what is needed, it seems, is deliberate practice defined as appropriately challenging tasks that are geared to improving the skill in question. For elite performance, supervised practice starts at a very young age and is maintained at high daily levels for a decade (Ericsson and Charness, 1994; Charness *et al.*, 2005). Learners must target improvements with the availability of appropriate feedback and repetitions. Appropriate feedback is the kind that enables the learner to bridge the gap between what they can do and what they need to be able to do so it is focused, timely and specific, and above all, understood by and used by the learner to improve performance (Hall and Burke, 2004). In school contexts, there is research to show that even in the same class not all learners are afforded the same opportunities or, more specifically, the opportunities they need to make progress (Ivinson and Murphy, 2007), though these are usually unintended consequences of particular pedagogic practices.

On the basis of their study of superior performance in sport and other domains, Ericsson and Charness also argue that extended training changes the cognitive and physiological processes to a greater degree than is generally assumed—a theme developed and confirmed in recent years by neuroscientists as they demonstrate the interconnection between brain and body (e.g. Greenfield, 2000). This evidence from neuroscience confirming the significance of experience aligns with well-established research from a sociocultural science showing the importance of having access to valued knowledge and skill and having the chance to participate in a community of practice.

Over thirty years ago, Benjamin Bloom (1982), a cognitive psychologist, provided evidence that confirms our sociocultural emphasis on opportunity to learn, though his focus, much like current studies from neuroscience, is on the individual with the surround treated as an independent variable. Focusing primarily on elite swimmers, musicians and mathematicians, he demonstrated the significance of a number of features in the explanation and promotion of talent, all of which align with the argument developed earlier about the broader social and institutional dimension and the inadequacy of focusing on the individual in isolation. Among the salient features are the following:

- involvement and meaningful participation in the area in question from an early age;
- at least one of the elite performer's parents having a personal interest in the area and giving the young person enormous encouragement and guidance;
- taking for granted that all members of the family would participate in the domain: such is the strength of interest at family level, and individual family members are not consulted about whether they wish to participate, rather it is simply assumed that they would;
- minor achievements and indications of capability are celebrated and rewarded;
- timely appropriate feedback is offered in a way that the learner can use to improve practice;
- public events provide encouragement to learning where the child's emerging capabilities are on show;
- talented children have opportunities to learn about the records and highlights of the talented in their field, to talk about them and their achievements with their peers who share their interests; and,
- in the adolescent years, between 15 and 25 hours per week are devoted to lessons, practice and other related activities in the field.

Interpreting Bloom's analysis from a sociocultural perspective, it is clear that these 'special' people participate in the wider community to which their activity belongs. The above features are, if you like, the social practices of talent. In Bloom's take on it, they lived and breathed their talent development—it determined their companions and the activities they would and would not engage in. There was, it seems, always the broader picture—concerts and competitions—which provide models for the individual.

We would argue that the individual has to invest in a particular identity: this investment goes beyond time and resources, it also includes imagination, identification with others more accomplished in the area than oneself, and the desire to be a certain kind of person, though all of this is facilitated through the existence of models and encouragement. The person is agentic and certainly not passive in their formation as a high performer. While Bloom's analysis leaves intact the idea of talent as an accomplishment of the individual, it is clear from the factors associated with its manifestation that talent is also a social accomplishment involving the recognition and identification on the part of society of the talented performance and performer, not to mention the social network and extended community that support, supervise and mentor her or him. Like ability and disability, like success and failure, talent is something that is as much part of the social as part of the individual—it is distributed across people and artefacts rather than possessed by the single individual and it is co-constructed through enactment. Once again, the social and the individual are entangled, it is not possible to separate out one from the other.

Talent as performed, situated and collaborative

In a recent sociocultural study about the phenomenon of talent as performed and emergent in settings, Sommerlund and Strandvad (2012) develop this distributed argument well, much along the lines of the studies on success and failure discussed in the previous chapter. What their study offers, in addition, is an invaluable and theorized insight into the enactment of talent in various art, film and design settings. We draw on it heavily here on two counts: first, because it says something interesting about the production of talent and, second, because it conceptualizes creativity from a sociocultural perspective.

The researchers demonstrate how talent is potentiality that is always in the making, ever emergent. Their focus is young Danish film directors and fashion designers. They show how a few talented people emerge from processes where most aspirants are turned down. As talent in a given area is displayed by the individual or by others, the talented person, they argue, is not simply described, but shaped. All the training, mentoring, assessments, evaluations and descriptions of the talent are performative, that is they function, not as neutral mechanisms, but as active ingredients in shaping what they depict, much like our argument earlier about tests constructing ability and achievement. Thus, the assessments and evaluations are not just reflections of talent but constitutive of it.

Three helpful concepts that framed their analysis will be borrowed here for our purposes in developing the idea of the performative turn in ability, talent and success, and in extending our argument that talent emerges through a range of mechanisms and artefacts that people deploy in a given social context. The first is the constitution of talent through identification and recognition by others; the second is what the researchers call the installation of talent in the individual through self-technology and work; and third is the materialization and expression of talent through the attachment of talent in networks.

The identification of talent or the recognition of potentiality is not simply a matter of being right or wrong but is a deeply performative act that influences who can be talented in the future and what counts as, say, a work of art. To exemplify this, one of us recently visited a family who had just bought a grand piano. Several other adult family members were also present. A girl in the family aged about fourteen demonstrated the new, much admired acquisition by playing, with due finesse, one of her examination pieces, following which one of the visitors complimented her by saying 'the piano becomes you Margaret and you become the piano'. This was a small though telling moment of talent shaping—a moment in the emergence, definition and public recognition of Margaret's potentiality as an accomplished pianist. Our reference to 'moments' is of note as it points to the emergent and dynamic nature of formation and shaping, how this shaping is always 'a work in progress' rather than simply predetermined. The grand piano, the performance, the applause, the compliments–all signal a promise, a tacit contract that has the capability to 'mobilise attention, guide efforts and legitimate actions' (Van Lente, 2000: 43) on Margaret's part and on the part of parents and teachers.

Over time, talent is enacted in a number of situations (competitions, practice sessions, lessons) involving the individual and various others (supervisors, teachers, mentors, judges, peers, competitors). Sommerlund and Strandvad (2012: 184) say that 'evaluators of talent are not simply right or wrong about the talent of the aspirants, but more or less powerful in colonializing a bit of the future by making their particular vision of talent come true'. In their fascinating work on the sociology of expectation, Nic Brown and Mike Michael (2003) talk about the future as 'an analytical object', a space that can be colonized and shaped as opposed to merely a neutral temporal phenomenon. The future is to be colonized in the present since the future (and the past, as our chapter on memory also shows) are constantly created and recreated in the present (Brown and Michael, 2003). This is partially achieved by directing attention, guiding efforts and legitimating actions in particular ways. While the events in the future are not predetermined–there is no guarantee, for instance, that Margaret will ever be an accomplished pianist–representations of the future act as potent resources in making up the present and the future and maximizing the chances that she will.

Based on several studies of creative talent drawing on interviews, artists' portfolios, artefacts and other documents, Sommerlund and Strandvad identified a number of complicated characteristics of talent in the sphere of film, fashion, art/design. One is the ability to challenge conventional rules of aesthetics without breaking them. Another is spontaneous expression linked with not being overly schooled or skilled which suggests to us a legacy of talent as inherent in the individual. Interestingly, the artistic product appears to be less significant than the talented personality. The self to be expressed or potentiality matters more than the artistic artefact. The self, it seems, can override the artefact produced, as revealed by interviews with evaluators who said that they sometimes change their judgements of the portfolio work having met the person. What is clear is that the self, the artistic product, and the interpretations and subjectivities of the evaluators are all enmeshed.

The empirical evidence and analysis offered by Sommerlund and Strandvad show how talent is conceptualized by the creative artists as a natural urge, an inner drive and something internal to the self such that the aspiring artist is compelled to be creative. To be creative is not a choice, it is who one is. The artist works extremely hard for little monetary reward but the work is essentially work on oneself to release the potential within. Hence, following Foucault, the authors call this a technology of the self. In the process of being creative, then, the artist 'creates not only art but also his or her own self' (187). The narrative of starting young was dominant in the interviews with aspiring artists. Because being artistic and creative was as much an expression and creation of the self as it was work, interviewees were willing to sacrifice freedom, material resources and family life to pursue their creativity. Thus, the would-be talented artists read the situation accurately—their views align exactly with those of the evaluators.

For talent to get expression, to be realized, there must be objects to manifest it. But for this manifestation other people are essential. Even for those who work in isolation, such as pictorial artists, galleries and magazines are needed to make the art available to the public. This means that various collaborators and other actors are necessary for the talent display and thus all become participants in the process of manifesting talents. As the researchers note 'The film director does not (usually) fund, photograph, edit, act in, or sell the film. The fashion designer does not make, sell, or market the clothes. Other participants are crucial and they come in many different forms, not only persons but also equipment and money' (191). Some of the talent, the researchers point out, is the ability to let others attach to you, to be attractive to others. The making of relevant connections and networks is pivotal to the display of talent—it is far from just a lone activity or just a technology of the self. And so, as in the case of ability/disability, it takes many people to create the creative genius.

An intriguing and paradoxical finding of this research on the process of talent is that the aspiring artist must not be seen to work too hard. Apparently a certain nonchalance is respected and rewarded. Once again, the aspiring artists as well as their evaluators share this view: working too hard can exclude one from the community of the talented artists. This contrasts with a mastery discourse or 'ten year rule' and the opportunity to learn noted earlier in this chapter and also with several of the indicators of high performance. It rather aligns with a mystery discourse with a perception on the part of the evaluators that somehow artistic talent is innate and natural.

The legacy of talent as innate has a strong hold on the part of the popular imagination. According to McDermott, an anthropologist and socioculturalist, the mark of 'a natural learner is to do well in school without trying . . . to look really bright one must learn a great deal, hide how it is developed, and then display it as instinctively known' (2006: 294). It would seem such thinking is not confined to the US. This is explicable, we would argue, with reference to dominant, individualistic theories of learning, which tend to locate learning 'in the head'. The assumption is that inside the skull lies the origin of one's development and the source of one's understanding. This in turn is dictated by one's inherent ability, which is assumed to be constant across settings and contexts and as such can be quite accurately measured, like in an IQ test. As such, other aspects (e.g. contexts, conditions of practice, opportunities, communities of practice, etc.) are denied relevance.

The study by Sommerlund and Strandvad was chosen as it illustrates the practices of talent in a given context and setting. Rather than assuming that talent conforms to a particular universal definition, it demonstrates what it is through exploration within a particular setting. Talent is situated and produced.

The 'surround', the environment, the actors, the artefacts and other features, like galleries, are all part and parcel of the enactment and, therefore, merit recognition. As they make clear, being recognized as talented in this domain is situated and collaborative, far from an individual accomplishment. What the researchers have not ignored is the range of people and processes it takes to produce and recognize talented artists.

Talent, like culture, as enabling and disabling

The above researchers adopt a situated view. This line of thinking forces one to contemplate the circumstances and cooperation and role of others that accompany wonderful accomplishments and achievements. Referring to the accomplishments and 'genius' of Louis Pasteur, McDermott (1996) observes: 'Pasteur did not do what he did because he was a genius, he was called a genius for what he did and how he convinced others of its importance' (294). A situated view, like McDermott holds, would acknowledge Pasteur's ingenuity in organizing others but would also reveal his struggles. However, the notion of the lone genius, the gifted person, is deeply attractive to societies 'anxious to celebrate one person at a time' (294). Addressing the alienating consequences of the attribution of genius, McDermott argues that 'the acquisition of individuals by genius' excludes some people while marginalizing others. He reminds readers how perspectives about Jewish intelligence offer 'a case study in how praise becomes blame' (Gilman, 1997: 30). Any theory of the person as a source of great achievement can be turned against the same person as revealed recently in a study by Jane O'Connor.

Recent research using discourse analysis explored representations of talent, creativity and giftedness in newspapers, and the results would seem to align with McDermott's cautionary note. Jane O'Connor's research entitled 'Is it good to be gifted? The social construction of the gifted child' (2012) as well as her book *The Cultural Significance of the Child Star* (2008) offers a sociocultural perspective on talent and giftedness. She shows how newspaper reports of sporting prodigies are characterized by admiration, those about musical prodigies are characterized by awe, while those about academic prodigies are characterized by pity. Her analysis focuses on three domains of giftedness: sport, music and academic giftedness. In contrast to those deemed gifted in sport and music, the academically gifted children were represented negatively in the popular press.

What could explain the fact that the exceptional in the more physical and artistic fields of sport and music were constructed differently from those labelled 'academically gifted'? She explains this with reference to broader societal constructions of childhood and its distinction from adulthood, and specifically expectations about childhood regarding vulnerability, dependency, lack of knowledge and expertise. The academically gifted child is seen as transgressing the boundaries between childhood and adulthood. The gifted child challenges the notion of childhood innocence and is viewed as (potentially) non-compliant and subversive. Other longitudinal research spanning some thirty years (Freeman, 2005), showed that those children labelled 'gifted' had more emotional problems than those 'identically able but unlabelled gifted' while there is also evidence that those labelled 'exceptional' academically feel under pressure to temper or hide their achievements due to negative responses and stereotyping from peers. Other researchers (Geake and Gross, 2008) have attributed this hostility to the perceived link between the elitist nature of academic giftedness and privileged backgrounds and prestigious futures. Reifications or cultural scripts about creativity, talent, giftedness, and so on, circulate. They can be recruited and applied in different situations and with different effects. Reifications of talent can be disrupted and challenged through practice–they are not fixed.

Neural correlates pointing to opportunity to learn

As indicated by a trawl through databases using the words 'talent' or 'genius', neuroscience is indeed beginning to show an interest in this topic. A tiny sample include the following: *The Creating Brain: The Neuroscience of Genius* by Nancy Andreasen (2005); 'Wetware: The biological basis of intellectual giftedness' (see www.hoagiesgifted.org/montage/v1n4p3.html); and, a Christmas Lecture given in Edinburgh University (2012) by Professor Seth Grant, entitled 'Madness, genius and the origin of the brain'. The educational press, too, is interested (e.g. Sousa (2006) *How the Gifted Brain Learns*). A recent article entitled 'What our nerves tell us about talent' (Dommett, 2012) appeared in the UK *Times Educational Supplement*, a publication aimed at teachers and educators. Its message was that talent is a function of heredity and environment–hardly new. Although little of substance was reported in the article, there is the claim that 'highly able adolescents seem to have increased brain maturity and neural efficiency in comparison with the average adolescent'. We are not told what counts as 'able', but one assumes it is based on some measures like IQ scores. The claim for a hereditary base to talent is on the grounds that certain skills (which are not specified in the article) can be mapped to brain regions such as the corpus callosum, which, it is claimed, is highly genetically influenced. More tellingly, the article goes on to point to neuroscientists' interest in 'the potential shortcut to talent and expertise' that is likely to be forthcoming in the form of cognitive-enhancing drugs, which of course already exist, though their impact is not fully understood.

Two decades ago, researchers drew attention to the role that early learning opportunities play in musical achievement and talent (Sloboda *et al.*, 1994). They are highly critical of the view that a definite set of underlying qualities distinguish the talented from the untalented. They argue that musical achieve-ment draws on different combinations of a large number of skills and is highly associated with early learning experiences and with the opportunity to practise, to refine one's skills over time. As noted already, focused training and deliberate practice is key for the highest levels of performance. Neuroscientists have recently provided evidence of the musical talent of some children from a very early age, identifying sensitive periods as at least partially instrumental for this accomplishment (Trehub, 2003). However, rather than being a sign of innate talent AP (pitch) seems to be a natural consequence of interacting with a musical instrument, such as a piano, at a very young age, thus highlighting the power of experience and opportunity to learn, albeit in the very early years of life.

In a literature review of the 'neural anatomy of talent', M. Layne Kalbfleisch (2004), a professor of cognitive neuroscience at George Mason University, challenges the thinking of Sloboda and others in tentatively suggesting that there is an underlying ability that could account for the exceptional performance in music and computation skill in mathematics, which she labels as 'an ability to understand intuitively formal rule structures' (Kalbfleisch, 2004: 21) although she is careful to point out that we don't yet understand the neural basis of a focal talent. Her epistemological assumptions as to how to examine the emergence of talent are entirely different to the sociocultural stance discussed above, based, as it is, on identifying the relationship between environmental input and cellular response as independent variables. Yet appropriate opportunity to learn is a constant in both perspectives.

Learning, she says, is a form of plasticity and is an interaction between the environment, relevant support and opportunity. It depends on multiple forms of memory and the functional connectivity of systems in the brain and, of course, it is the latter claim that distinguishes the neural orientation. With reference to talent she then says: 'when these factors interact in a way that allows an individual to perform at an extraordinary level, we observe talent' (29). While this appears to be a definition of talent it says nothing about its formation. In line with her emphasis on plasticity, changes in the brains of expert musicians (compared to non-expert musicians) attest to the impact of practice. She cites research by Munte et al. (2002) who note several functional differences in the brains of expert musicians compared with non-expert musicians, one of which is cortical representations of digits on the left-hand side being greater in musicians, especially those who started training at an early age. Another is the difference in the size and structure of the planum temporale, the anterior corpus callosum and the cerebellum. It seems that the size of the anterior midsagittal corpus callosum is larger in those whose musical training began before the age of seven. The size of the midsagittal corpus callosum is taken as a measure of the number of axons that cross the midline, indicating greater inter-hemispheric networking.

Based on the evidence available to her, Kalbfleisch concludes that talent, at least musical talent, is explained with reference to a mix of genetics and opportunity to learn. Since, on the one hand, changes in connectivity seem to involve the striatum—a structure that has considerable plastic capability and not influenced significantly by genetics–it follows that learning and practice are of major importance. Since, on the other hand, changes in connectivity seem to involve the temporal and frontal cortical areas, areas that are influenced significantly by genetics, it follows that musical talent is probably enhanced and constrained by both genetic endowment and opportunity to benefit from appropriate experiences. Four years later (2008), the same researcher concluded that despite some progress, giftedness and talent is a type of neural plasticity that, from a neurobiological standpoint, is not yet understood.

Other researchers from a neuro perspective are less cautious than Kalbfleisch, claiming a strong neurobiological basis to exceptional talent in mathematics, for instance (O'Boyle, 2008), while others are quick to capitalize on what are assumed to be the implications for educational practice (Sousa, 2006). The neuroimaging evidence for this claim stems from the following: enhanced development of the right hemisphere and an unusual dependence on its specialized visuospatial processing capacities, and a form of brain bilateralism involving heightened connectivity and integration of information between the two hemispheres. Michael O'Boyle (2008) compared morphological and functional characteristics of the brains of mathematically gifted adolescents and the brains of their average-ability peers. He defined maths giftedness with reference to scores at the 99th percentile on the Scholastic Aptitude Test (SAT) in the US, or the Numerical Reasoning test on the School College Abilities Test (Australia). His analysis led him to conclude that brain organization among superior achievers in mathematics is 'uniquely predisposed toward a high degree of inter-hemispheric interaction and is characterized by rapid and accurate information exchange between the hemispheres' (183). In a further study, also by O'Boyle, using fMRI, the amount of brain activity obtained was several times more than for the average-scoring students, and the overall pattern of activity was found to be distributed differently. In particular, he found bilateral activation of the right and left frontal areas, along with significant bilateral activation of the premotor, parietal and superior occipital regions and heightened activity of both the right and left anterior cingulate cortices in the maths–gifted learners compared to their more average peers. Their major claim is that the brains of mathematically talented adolescents are quantitatively and qualitatively different from those showing average mathematical competence.

Despite his claim that current understanding of the neurobiological basis of mathematics ability 'remains in its infancy' (O'Boyle, 2008: 185) it did not prevent O'Boyle from recommending how maths might be taught and assessed for those identified as gifted. Assuming that such gifted adolescents have 'specialized learning styles' and that they are not likely to use the same types of cognitive strategies as their more average peers, O'Boyle recommends several instructional techniques that would seem 'a natural fit' for them. These include tasks that are complex and multi-dimensional as opposed to tasks that are repetitive and perhaps dull, tasks and activities that require creative responses and problem solving, and tasks that invite synthesis and analysis. Such pedagogic guidance, arguably, is suitable for all learners in schools, not just those identified as especially gifted. The neuroscientific evidence fails to help us understand how people become talented, illuminating instead some of its correlates. However, from the point of view of our main argument here, opportunity to access the valued practice is pivotal in the claim to talent.

Some neuroscientists have sought to explain giftedness, creativity, intelligence and talent more generally. While the above examples pertain to specific domains, Shaw *et al.* (2006) examined the extent to which brain structures of gifted children differed from those of their not-so-gifted peers and, in fact, showed they were more like the brains of those older than their peers. Based on a six-year longitudinal study involving the use of fMRI with some 300 teenagers, their evidence showed that the nature of neural growth and change in the cerebral cortex was different for highly intelligent (as measured by IQ scores) and less highly rated peers. In the former, the cortices were thinner when the children were young but over time grow so quickly that by the time the more gifted children were in the teenage years, their cortices were thicker than average. John Geake, working at Oxford Brookes University, similarly reports that gifted young people show more brain interconnectivity and have more enhanced neural structures in the prefrontal cortices, areas that are responsible for cognitive control and memory. Once again, this evidence explains nothing about the nature of talent. Rather, it identifies neural correlates of IQ measures.

Where to look to enhance understanding of creativity

Before leaving this topic, it is worth highlighting the difference in the methodologies of the two perspectives for probing matters of talent and creativity. We have already described in some detail above a study on creativity from a sociocultural view. Since the premise is that creativity is always situated and always involves other people and structures, those other players and systems need to be considered as part of the process of understanding who acquires and who can acquire the label of 'creative' or 'artistic', and so on, and how they acquire it. The following abstract of a neuroscientific study on creativity shows up the difference in approach:

> In this article we provide a brief overview of contemporary methodologies used for the operationalization of creative thinking in a neuroscientific context. Empirical studies are reported which measured brain activity (by means of EEG, fMRI, NIRS or PET) during the performance of different experimental tasks. These tasks, along with creative idea generation tasks used in our laboratory, constitute useful tools in uncovering possible brain correlates of creative thinking.
>
> (Fink *et al.*, 2007)

What it clearly shows is that the understanding of creativity, talent, intelligence, and so on, is to be gleaned from measuring brain activity. The surround is not of interest and assessment tasks can be designed to allow subjects to demonstrate their creativity levels and assessment can take place in a laboratory. The focus could not be more different to the account of creativity described above. While socioculturalists point to the interactions, the networks of relationships, the contacts, the identities and the activities involved in the production of the creative artist, neuroscientists–following the kind of study described in the abstract–point to the importance of, for example, posterior brain regions along with more diffuse frontal activation (Haier and Jung, 2008). These particular authors speculate as to the possibility that neural factors may enhance the growth of regional grey or white matter in the brain and that if such factors exist, drugs could be developed to stimulate them. Yet, we note that regardless of perspective, attention to experience and the opportunity the person (or brain) gets is vital to their formation. As neuroscientist, Keith Sawyer (2011: 149) says in this regard: 'the importance of domain specific expertise is confirmed. Extensive training in a domain is associated with different patterns of brain activation' and also 'a broad range of creativity research shows the important role of domain-specific knowledge, acquired over time and represented in long term memory' (152).

Nearly all the neuroscientific studies that we found on creativity, giftedness and talent, mentioned the limited basis of the evidence and the need for more study. Yet the potential contribution that neuroscience could make to our understanding of such phenomena is stressed. In a systematic review of sixty-three neuroscientific studies on creativity, neuroscientists Dietrich and Kanso (2010) make a number of important points about the contribution of the research base. They surveyed the entire literature that relates creativity to brain activity and focused on divergent thinking, artistic creativity and insight. While these terms are defined in the various studies reviewed, we will not go into their definitions here except to say that they are applied consistently in the different studies. What is of note, however, are the findings of this thorough review of the field to date. It would appear that there is no evidence to support the notion that creativity is especially linked to either right or left brain and there is no evidence to support the ideas that any stages of divergent thinking show a laterality effect. It seems creativity, therefore, involves cooperation among different cerebral areas and involves both hemispheres. The reviewers conclude that no single brain area is 'necessary or sufficient' for creativity. In very strong terms, they report that no claims as to the possible neural mechanisms of creativity can be sustained on the basis of the evidence to date. They also conclude that the research area is fragmented and lacks a sense of an incremental building of the evidence.

Whatever the weakness of the research base itself, we suggest that the focus on correlates and brain activity generally means that we are a long way away from neuroscientific evidence that can explain the 'how' of becoming creative or talented. On this, studies like the one conducted by Sommerlund and Strandvad (2012) are important because they have implications for how we might support the development of talent.

Conclusion

The traditional idea of the gifted, the creative, the talented and the genius, relies on ranking people according to some measure of what it is assumed giftedness and talent is. The head of the gifted learns better than the rest! A sociocultural perspective challenges this view, focusing attention beyond the head of the one labelled 'gifted' and directing us to the contribution of others, context, relationship and opportunity to learn, as well as the actions of the individual. Talent and giftedness are jointly produced. It is a perspective that sheds more light on the formation of talent and the process of learning itself. Despite these differences in orientation, the themes of opportunity to learn, experience and participation remain undisputed features common to both perspectives.

Chapter 9

#Language

Introduction

This chapter links language, culture, plasticity and experience. We illustrate how our current understanding of what counts as language is undergoing massive transformation. Connecting closely with Chapter 4: 'The making of culture', we understand language as a fluid, dynamic, shared and relational process in which everyone does not participate in the same way. In our analysis of the relationship between language, culture, learning and the brain, we explore how our practices rather than our brains are affected by changes in participation and reification.

Viewing meaning as central, we ask why so many researchers pursue an understanding of how our changing practices affect our brain, but not our culture itself, or our participation moving forward. Our method here is to explore reading and writing from both sociocultural and neuroscientific perspectives, in an attempt to unfix language and problematize what we currently understand as meaningful practice. We conclude this chapter by putting forward what we feel is a more valuable way of understanding literacy practices, based on our discussion in this chapter. Defining literacy from a sociocultural perspective, we also discuss supporting neuroscientific and other research which suggests that if we want to understand such a complex area as language acquisition, multiple theoretical frameworks and perspectives may be necessary.

The problem with language

> I, myself, was always recognized ... as the 'slow one' in the family. It was quite true, and I knew it and accepted it. Writing and spelling were always terribly difficult for me. My letters were without originality. I was ... an extraordinarily bad speller and have remained so until this day.
>
> (Agatha Christie)

> Emotions, in my experience, aren't covered by single words. I don't believe in 'sadness,' 'joy,' or 'regret.'... I'd like to have at my disposal complicated

hybrid emotions, Germanic train–car constructions like, say, 'the happiness that attends disaster.' Or: 'the disappointment of sleeping with one's fantasy.' I'd like to show how 'intimations of mortality brought on by aging family members' connects with 'the hatred of mirrors that begins in middle age.' I'd like to have a word for 'the sadness inspired by failing restaurants' as well as for 'the excitement of getting a room with a minibar.' I've never had the right words to describe my life, and now that I've entered my story, I need them more than ever.

(Eugenides, 2003: 217)

Our relationship with language–oral and written–has always been a difficult and complex one. One of the reasons often posited for this in neuroscientific research is the fact that as human beings we were not born to read or write. We are simply not wired for it. Explaining this phenomenal feat in culture, genetic and neural engineering demands more than the neuroscientific nuts and bolts as the brain makes connections between existing structures in response to new demands and developments in our practice. It points to the plasticity of the human brain, and exemplifies the way in which the brain is shaped by experience. Aware of the extensive neuroscientific research available on language and reading development in the brain, this chapter employs sociocultural theory to make well known its explanatory power as a lens through which to examine experience. While neuroscientific research provides an image of what happens in the brain when we encounter a new word or read an old one, sociocultural theory puts meaning on practice and has some very important insights for our understandings of learning.

In this chapter, we build on our previous theorization of culture as unfixed, dynamic, distributed, simultaneously facilitative and constraining, where focusing on what people do rather than categorizing people into fixed groups is central. Developing the metaphor introduced in Chapter 4, of culture as the hammering of a world into shape, here we explore the ways in which, through negotiation, words give rise to worlds and vice versa. This chapter is about language: the big words, the little words and everything else in between.

We begin by presenting our understanding of the interplay between language, culture and brain and contrast this to the understandings emanating from neuroscientific and anthropological research. We explore the history of reading and writing from both neuroscientific and sociocultural perspectives, asking provocative questions about the future of language and learning. Understanding language as unfixed, just like the culture it helps to develop, mediate and enact, we question whether or not the meanings we now put on our words and practices will be understood by individuals in the future. We investigate the ways in which our language and our culture is changing in diverse and dramatic ways. We question why so many texts exist that explore the implications of these continual changes in language for our brain, yet absent are texts that look specifically at the implications of our changing language and culture for our participation. We conclude the chapter by developing this argument and teasing out some implications of this for our understanding of learning and language and our definition of literacy.

Language, culture and the brain

> From his beach bag the man took an old penknife with a red handle and began to etch the signs of the letters onto nice flat pebbles. At the same time, he spoke to Mondo about everything there was in the letters, about everything you could see in them when you looked and when you listened. He spoke about *A*, which is like a big fly with its wings pulled back; about *B*, which is funny, with its two tummies; or *C* and *D*, which are like the moon, a crescent moon or a half-full moon; and then there was *O*, which was the full moon in the black sky. *H* is high, a ladder to climb up trees or to reach the roofs of houses; *E* and *F* look like a rake and a shovel; and *G* is like a fat man sitting in an armchair. *I* dances on tiptoes, with a little head popping up each time it bounces, whereas *J* likes to swing. *K* is broken like an old man, *R* takes big strides like a soldier, and *Y* stands tall, its arms up in the air, and it shouts: help! *L* is a tree on the river's edge, *M* is a mountain, *N* is for names, and people waving their hands, *P* is asleep on one paw, and *Q* is sitting on its tail; *S* is always a snake, *Z* is always a bolt of lightning, *T* is beautiful, like the mast on a ship, *U* is like a vase, *V* and *W* are birds, birds in flight; and *X* is a cross to help you remember.
>
> (Le Clézio, 2010: online translation)

Language, culture and the brain are inextricably linked through the concept of meaning. To begin, consider the following sentence: Everyone was present so she decided that there was no time like the present to present the present. Reading silently or out loud we change in ever-so-slight ways our intonation and stresses in the word 'present' as we anticipate its meaning based on the context. This is just one small example, but read alongside our quote at the beginning of this section it makes very clear that the act of reading and writing is indeed no small feat and requires more than neurological processing. Attending to the meaning and the context as we read, we do what computers cannot and rather than just processing words we experience them, in this way they become meaningful.

Another example: 'To wound a friend is unforgivable' he thought as he wound the cloth around the wound. Here, though many of us would be less familiar with the word 'wound' than 'present' in any of its meanings and forms, we are still able to bring different meanings to bear on the exact same word by using context, the negotiation of meaning and past experience. Here, we recognize meaning because of our past histories of participation, our social pathways, rather than just the neural pathways of our brain. This is the understanding with which we begin this chapter.

In his (2012) anthropological text *Wired for Culture: Origins of the Human Social Mind*, evolutionary biologist Mark Pagel conceives of the interplay between brain and mind, language and culture in a way which is very illuminating to our own thesis. He begins with the claim that culture is roughly everything we do and monkeys do not. For Pagel, the development of culture marked the final shift in the balance of power between our genes and our minds. He tells us that the culture which we so readily take for granted today had to wait nearly the entire history of life on earth to come into being. Pagel explains that through our cultural inheritance, knowledge can accumulate, as good ideas are retained and improved upon, while others are discarded. He concludes that through this *process* we are the only species that acquires rules of daily life from the accumulated knowledge of our ancestors rather than from the genes they have passed on to us. Conceptualizing of cultural learning as something which is mediated and distributed in his own words:

> Our cultures and not our genes supply the solutions we use to survive and prosper in the society of our birth; they provide the instructions for what we eat, how we live, the gods we believe in, the tools we make and use, the language we speak, the people we cooperate with and marry, and whom we might fight or even kill in a war.
>
> (Pagel, 2012: 3)

He continues:

> A wolf brought up by sheep will remain a wolf and soon turn on its benefactors, but a newborn human must be ready to join any cultural group on earth, and without knowing which. It might find itself living on the arctic ice, the Russian steppes, or sailing across Polynesia; it might find itself in the Australian outback, the deserts of Arabia.... And so we have no choice but to evolve to allow our culture to occupy our minds, writing its language and story into our consciousness.
>
> (Pagel, 2012: 5)

Neuroscientific research has shown the many ways in which we are primed to learn language but it seems when it comes to the story of culture, for neuroscientists and anthropologists such as Pagel, it is one more akin to Locke's *tabula rasa* or blank slate, where the culture we become a part of becomes also a part of us in an almost arbitrary process. Neuroscientific research considers culture, as discussed in Chapter 4, in a very one-dimensional way–the brain needs culture and experience to build connections between neuron and synapse. There is nothing rich or illuminating, however, about the theorizing of culture in neuroscientific research, as the well-known neuroscientist Antonio Damasio revealed in his (2011) TED talk: 'The autobiographical self has prompted extended memory, reasoning, imagination, creativity and language. And out of that came the instruments of culture—religions, justice, trade, the arts, science, technology.'

Here, and in neuroscientific conceptions of culture, the brain holds supremacy over a culture, understood in terms of geography and ethnicity, as individual brains bend cultural experience to their own will and the unit of analysis remains the individual self and, in some cases, the individual brain. This is a part of the story we would like to develop in this chapter, building on Pagel's conception of human language as 'the voice of our genes' (Pagel, 2012: 275) by suggesting that though every newborn baby joins a culture not of its own choosing, becoming a part of this culture is far from an arbitrary process as through our *hammering*—our daily practice, our participation and reifications, our language—we shape and are shaped by the worlds we inhabit. Indeed, to quote Ralph Waldo Emerson (1876): 'Language is a city to the building of which every human being brought a stone.'

In sociocultural terms, the unit of analysis becomes the process of culture itself, the ebb and flow of meaningful participation in relation to the participation and reification of others. This constitutive understanding of culture, brain and mind, posits language as the single most important cultural tool we can employ to allow others to understand our actions and experiences, to understand the actions and experiences of others, and to negotiate a meaningful identity for ourselves in the different communities of practice we engage in every day. Culture exists in the environment and in interactions, not in individual heads or even set and bounded groups. Where we find ourselves and who we find ourselves with will have implications for the development of our culture, and therefore understanding how we use language to hammer our culture calls for a non-bounded, non-geographical understanding of culture.

Living culturally through our language and social interactions we follow and enact instructions for living, but what is easy to forget is that through our language and social interactions we have also created them. Understanding this simple but often overlooked fact explains the shared and relational nature of the 'hammering of culture' through language that is central to this chapter. Understanding culture as in a constant state of flux and understanding cultural differences not as static, individual, stable traits but dynamic and emergent enactments occurring in practice people use language as a cultural tool to hammer and shape the culture they practise and reify. People are not carriers of culture. Individuals develop a meaningful culture for themselves in their shared experiences through language—we are makers of culture as through the making we experience our identities as belonging or not belonging, aligning or misaligning with the hammering of others.

Talking heads

Americans eat oysters but not snails. The French eat snails but not locusts. The Zulus eat locusts but not fish. The Jews eat fish but not pork. The

Hindus eat pork but not beef. The Russians eat beef but not snakes. The Chinese eat snakes but not people. The Jali Of New Guinea find people delicious.

(Robertson, 1981: 63)

While Pagel understands language as genes talking, getting what they want, we wish to develop this perspective, exploring in more detail the interplay between brain and mind, language and culture he alludes to in his text. The closed and fixed neuroscientific understanding of culture, outlined in Chapter 4 of this book, would not see the eating habits of different nations as problematic, assuming a shared culture rather than a sociocultural negotiation of experience and meaning. For us explaining language, brain and learning the story is much more complex, involving an understanding of the mystery at the heart of what happens when we use language, a vehicle of culture, and even more specifically, when we read and write.

The invention of reading occurred a few thousand years ago and brought with it an intellectual and cultural revolution. Now able to record the practices of our societies through a mutually understood sign system or language our talking heads now had something to talk about–the development of culture. Groups of people were recording and passing on information through written and oral language from one generation to the next. Responding to this social and cultural phenomenon the human brain had to develop new connections between its existing structures to ensure the development and preservation of this culture, but the developments in neuron and synapse were secondary to the social processes that demanded them.

Understanding the development of reading and writing as it is outlined here as a cultural (social) phenomenon first, to which the brain had to adapt through building new connections between existent structures, calls into question current definitions we hold of words such as 'literacy', which will be explored later in the chapter. If the development of reading and writing was really a social process to which the brain had to adapt, why do some definitions of literacy remain as the ability to read or write? Within this definition, where is the understanding of the wider cultural and social function and forms of literacy?

Maryanne Wolf's book *Proust and the Squid: The Story and Science of the Reading Brain* explores from a cognitive and biological perspective the evolution of reading. Quoting cognitive scientist Steven Pinker, she relates how 'children are wired for sound, but print is an optional accessory that must be painstakingly bolted on' (Wolf, 2008: 19). Because we possess no genes specific to reading or print, we rearrange our brain when we learn to read, making connections between already existent visual and linguistic brain systems. However, what is most interesting to our argument is the neuroscientific finding that the extent to which we can accomplish this unlocking of words is largely dependent on the amount of language and reading we are exposed to as young children, with some studies revealing a gap of as much as thirty-two million words between average, young middle-class children and children from linguistically impoverished homes (Hart and Risley, 1995). This again confirms the social and relational element at the heart of language and literacy processes as reading becomes successful where children have had prior positive and meaningful experiences with words.

According to Wolf (2008: 27) and her exploration of ancient writing systems from tokens to dragon bones: 'With each of the new writing systems, with their different and increasingly sophisticated demands, the brain's circuitry rearranged itself, causing our repertoire of intellectual capacities to grow and change in great, wonderful leaps of thought.'

At the height of their success in around AD1500, the Incas developed khipus or talking knots, to record the history of their culture. In structure, a khipu is made up of a horizontal primary cord from which a number of pendant cords hang vertically. Each cord can have one or many knots. The colour of the cord, how they connect to each other, the types and numbers of knots and the spaces in between, are understood to signify numerical and perhaps even narrative histories of the Inca people according to Harvard anthropologist Gary Urton. Urton believes that unravelling the meaning behind these knots could reveal the information which tied together the entire Incan Empire.

This small story shows the ascendance of experience over physical grey matter. Though, for obvious reasons, we do not have any brain material belonging to Incan people, we can but wonder what a study of their brains would tell us about their culture and lives? The answer in this case, as in our understanding of meaning, culture and learning, is that culture and meaning exist alongside social interaction and experience through language without rather than within our heads.

Today, at the pinnacle of our own technological and scientific success, we are tying our own history and future together in a not dissimilar fashion. We replace the dyed and knotted Incan cords with the three-dimensional strands of double helix DNA twisting together in the shape of a spiral staircase, complete with steps and staircase sides. Travelling through nearly four thousand years of history, unlike Wolf we understand that it is culture and not our brains that have made this leap possible. Our development of more sophisticated cultural tools, moving from knots and dyed twine to microscopes and double helix, happened in the world first and in our brains second, as in social and cultural processes we made decisions about what was worthy of study and how this might be studied. By developing our words we were able to develop our worlds, or at the very least, our understanding of them in a social construction of knowledge. In Incan knots and DNA strands we record our selves. Having lost much of the history of Inca civilization, their knots now remain shrouded in mystery for interpretation today—analogously, we can but wonder what is in store for our own constructions?

#/Hashtag: 'A' is for Apple (iPad), 'B' is for blog

BN BHL8 BC BIB :(RUOK? <3 PLS CYE + IMM 2NTE. HV SM NWS 4 U. 121 LTR. OT NOOB N WRK – OMG! :X BT OH HM TRY ?^ WT TM GF. ROFL! GGOH! (>_<)
?4U. CLD U BY BDAY CRD 4 M TAM 10X. I 4GOT. GN. WTPA? CAC
TTYL BOOMS! LMS!

Bad news–I will be home late because the boss is back. I am sad! Are you ok? I love you! Please check your email and instant message me tonight. I have some news for you–Private chat later. Off topic–the new person in work–oh my God! I should keep my mouth shut but I overheard him try and hook up with Tom's girlfriend. I was rolling on the floor laughing! I have got to get out of here! Embarrassing!

I have a question for you. Could you buy a birthday card for me tomorrow am? Thanks. I forgot. I got nothing. Where is the party at? Can anyone come? Talk to you later. Bored out of my skull! Please like my status on Facebook!

Due to the popularity and power of neuroscience, there is an abundance of texts that aim to explore the implications of new technologies on brain function and processing; for example Nicholas Carr's (2010) *The Shallows: What the Internet is Doing to our Brains*. What are less plentiful in the literature, noticeable in their absence, are texts that explore the implications of new technologies for our practice, our participation and our culture in any direct way. Taking on this task, this chapter aims in its analysis and theory building to explore how our practices rather than our brains are affected by new technologies and cultural practices, and offers some tentative conclusions about the implications of this for how we live our lives and our understanding of concepts such as literacy, learning, language.

Understanding that culture itself, along with the language through which it is produced, is not stable and fixed is central to our thesis. Within this socio-cultural perspective, tensions always exist between different participation and practices as well as between participation and reification. In this way, it is just as important, or perhaps even more so, to look closely at the shifts and transformations of culture and not just what we take for granted as cultural practices as our emergent practices give meaning to future ones. We now move to employ socio-cultural theory as a lens to explore current linguistic and literacy emergent practices, which we believe mark a further shift and transformation in our words and our worlds. In this, we also exemplify the sociocultural understanding that within any given community of practice all individuals do not work uniformly together in the preservation of one shared and decided–upon timeless culture.

One cultural practice undergoing massive transformation today is language; in its broadest sense, how we communicate with one another to get things done. As we go about our day-to-day practices, the way we organize our participation through language, talk and text is shaping and constituting our learning in new and different ways. The quotes at the beginning of this section show very clearly that the coherence that we assume exists in culture does not occur simply when all members in a group act the same and know the same things in the same way. Instead, culture must be negotiated, as through meaningful engagement, language and agentic action, people hammer themselves, each other and the world, and culture emerges inherent to, rather than a product of, the process. Learning and living occurs simultaneously through language and social interaction. In this chapter, we pick up and illuminate an argument in Chapter 4, that it is through and by language and discursive practices, self-hoods are constructed, identities are forged and social practices are enacted. We also keep in mind Bakhtin's dialogicality, previously discussed, which extends language beyond face-to-face interactions. If who we are lies in what we do every day, then a discussion of current literacy and language *practices* is central to our understanding of learning.

Just like our ancestors, we also have something to talk about today, our story to tell and just like our ancestors, we have adapted and developed the tools at our disposal to reify this information and pass it on to the future generations. In the twenty-first century, however, the language and literacies we require to do this, aligning with the sociocultural understandings outlined in this chapter, are very different. They are multimodal–textual, visual, oral, digital, experiential. The vehicle has changed but the sociocultural aim remains the same. A twenty-first-century literacy and language requires much more than the ability to read and write and is driven by social meaning. Once more, we stand at an impasse and in the vast amount and diversity of ways of talking about and representing and recording our culture we are almost reinventing the wheel. Creating our own new alphabet in the twenty-first century, we can take and share a picture of ourselves with the world possibly faster than we can sign our name.

Breaking our collective voice with a necessary individual interlude, the following story details the experience of one of the authors. Attending a comedy night at our local opera house, I had a moment, akin to Eugenides' 'hatred of mirrors that begins in middle age'–I felt old. In the interval, as I looked around the auditorium I could see that many of the people who had stayed in their seats were now on their phones. I remembered receiving my first mobile phone when I was in secondary school and the revolutionary feeling that accompanied being able to text my family or friends–to send a line of text over the phone and have another one come back to you in response. And that was only twelve years ago. On that night in the concert phones were being used, but not to send out dated text messages but to post statuses and comments on Facebook, upload photos and videos of the event while there, and catch up on what their other friends were doing. All and any friends, open access, no number required. Individuals were 'plugged in' in a heretofore unimaginable scale to others. The implications of this for our participation in language, literacy and learning are immense.

Returning again to the quotes that open this section, it is clear that the way we are using language along with what counts as language has changed dramatically. The first quote in just under 160 characters (the length of one text message) conveys a meaning that using our twenty-six-letter alphabet requires 525 characters to convey. Speed and cost effectiveness play a role in this new development of our language, but that is only the tip of the iceberg. As we engage more and more with digital practices and literacies (Twitter and Facebook, for example) where we communicate using a variety of modes—written, visual, musical, photographic, video—we are through our participation changing our understanding of what counts as language.

The mobile app, Instagram, allows people to almost exclusively take and share images and photos in a visual representation of their lives and their selves. There is an option to add text but people predominantly use this app to share photos solely, exemplifying the sociocultural turn we believe currently exists as people are developing new ways to develop culture through their language and participation, changing the shapes of themselves and their worlds and also the very shape of the hammers which they employ to achieve this process.

An even more novel idea, Snapchat is an app that allows people to send their friends a photo or video, which, once it is opened on the recipient's device, can only be looked at on screen for a few seconds before the video or image is deleted from the recipient's device. While the image is on screen, the viewer must make contact with the touch screen which inhibits them from taking a screen shot of the image. Introduced in 2011, it wasn't until 2013 that it was announced that these images are never deleted. The point here is the alarming rate with which technology is moving forward without any exploration of what this means for practice.

The two texts presented at the beginning of this section share the same message but project different social worlds and prioritize different ways of making meaning. These differences in what these texts do and the way they do it point to the fact that the work of reading lies not in the words but in our interaction with the text in whatever form it is as we try to put meaning on symbols. If negotiating a reading path is understood as a cultural decision (Kress, 2003) then living culturally we fragment, shift and change our social positions in relation to what we understand as meaningful practice.

As our participation extends and diversifies in many different directions and occurs through different media and platforms, we are simultaneously changing the way we communicate—our language is becoming more fluid and diverse along with the culture it supports. For example, in Australia, a government initiative has set up an 'RUOK? Day' to promote awareness of suicide prevention on social-networking sites. The Oxford English Dictionary now includes 'initialisms', terms such as 'OMG', 'LOL', 'TMI', 'FYI', 'BFF' along with words such as 'totes' (totally), 'whatevs', 'onesie', 'guyliner' and 'droolworthy'. Recognizing the history of participation that these words now have, they are included in the Oxford English Dictionary and the implication of this for our language and culture as well as our brain must be interrogated. There are sites online where 'savvy' parents can blog and ask what certain acronyms that their children use mean, including POS (parent over shoulder) and PIR (parent in room).

While our new social-media alphabet still centres on meaning and social interaction, what counts as meaningful has now drastically changed as we use Twitter, Facebook, Instagram, Four Square, LinkedIn, Pinterest, YouTube–the list goes on and on–to portray our identities in text, photo, video, bulletin boards, news feeds. Nothing is simple or neutral and words can be used to disguise as well as illuminate as we literally talk in code. Punctuation is an accessory rather than a necessity and meaning exists in the world and how we use them rather than in the words themselves. As people communicate in abbreviations rather than words, layout and capital letters create a sense of urgency and primacy around what is being communicated. This is a far cry from the traditional literacy practices we are familiar with and assume as a part of our culture but that we no longer employ as we live culturally in a negotiation of meaning.

Where previously we have used our traditional alphabet to bridge written and spoken text, today, as the quotes discussed exemplify, this bridging is becoming more and more difficult in light of new linguistic and cultural practices emerging as a result of our social interactions. Now more than ever, understanding text in terms of practice, what it does as opposed to what it is, is essential to our understanding of language. Who is saying what, about what, in what contexts and to whom? This understanding posits social processes and interactions as central to meaning and learning. It is precisely because our social interactions, our hammering of culture are not fixed or stable that the tools we use to promote them also remain in this constant state of flux. With an unprecedented number of ways to express ourselves and our culture, this understanding is so important today, as neither the language we use nor the culture developed in it is stable and we cannot expect them to be so.

In his (2010) book *Language, Learning, Context*, Wolff-Michael Roth explains that talking a language is learning a language. His text supports our argument and necessitates a sociocultural process approach to understanding language learning, rather than neuroscience's overly simplistic acquisition approach. For Roth, there is no real difference between knowing a language and knowing one's way around the world. Looking at an excerpt of classroom life (recorded Fragment 1.1c in his text), he stresses the importance of bringing ideas such as society and culture to bear on an analysis of learning and language:

> To begin such an analysis, consider this: the participants to the situation in Fragment 1.1c do not just talk for the sake of talking. They talk in a

particular institutional setting that their talk simultaneously produces and reproduces. Connor, his teacher, Cheyenne and Jan do not merely talk cubes and squares, they actually produce a lesson. This lesson is part of a societal activity called schooling. In schooling, society has a mechanism to reproduce its culturally embodied forms of knowing.

(Roth, 2010: 19)

In this quote, context, meaning and practice are all made in social interaction as learning becomes shared, relational, distributed and mediated through cultural tools such as language and sign systems. The embeddedness of learning in the world that produces it in this excerpt highlights very clearly the need for a study of language to incorporate a study of life, practice, experience and culture. Taking this idea even further, Roth suggests that in broader terms information, ideas and concepts are also never presented in exactly the same way and instead emerge as 'situated performances, making use of the resources at hand, conti-nuously transforming the self–transforming participative thought that goes with the activity' (Roth, 2010: 72). For Roth, this amounts to a level of passivity rather than agency whenever an individual engages in a language which is not their own, as it is the language that speaks and not the individual.

The roadmap of culture

Language is the roadmap of a culture. It tells you where its people came from and where they are going.

(Rita Mae Brown, quoted in Samovar *et al.*, 2009: 221)

Not having the right words to describe our worlds, as referred to by poor Jeffrey Eugenides in one of the opening quotes of this chapter, exemplifies very well the concept of passivity Roth develops in his text. It is not that we do not have the right words. There is in fact no great mystery at the heart of the reading process and for what it means to be literate. Reading and writing are socially developed 'roadmaps of culture' in which, regardless of where the extract comes from (be it *Heat* magazine's gossip column, or the *Encyclopaedia Britannica*), it is meaningful because it creates, enacts and perpetuates meaning about who we are as a people, what we believe in and what we may do next. We love or we loathe, identify with or completely unrelate to what is written, but at the heart of the process is our experience in relation to the experience of others. It is not that we do not have the right words. Today, we have an almost infinite means of expressing ourselves in social interaction with others but these modes of expression–language, text, image, screen–are also dependent on context and social relations. The tool does not always fit the purpose and must, can and will be adapted by individuals and communities as they come to 'talking the talk' in their own particular worlds.

Having established language as a tool for dynamic culture *processes*, we would now like to conclude this chapter by exploring how we might reconceptualize our understanding of contemporary language and, more specifically, literacy in this light by asking what implications our current linguistic and literacy practices, previously highlighted, have for our future participation and learning. Today, demographic trends reveal time after time that people spend more time engaged in social, emotional and non-traditional textually driven literacy practices than in reading and writing as they are conventionally understood. For example, a Time Use Survey published in Ireland in November 2005, revealed that the three main activities undertaken by Irish people are sleeping, working and watching television. Eighty-two per cent of Irish people spend over two hours every day watching television, compared with only thirty-eight per cent spending a maximum of thirty-seven minutes per day reading or listening to the radio. Further, forty-nine per cent of Irish people spend an hour and a half every day chatting with family and friends or texting and talking on the phone. Such trends do not support the very narrow and traditional view of literacy as reading and writing we currently hold and are in fact strengthening in educational reforms and cultural processes which focus on literacy and numeracy in their most constricted form. This is also an example of the ways in which culture can constrict as well as facilitate.

Educators, politicians and government leaders want and need their students to be 'literate' when they leave school and in Ireland a current strategy of more time on task (supported by neuroscientific research) is being employed to raise literacy and numeracy levels. However, sociocultural theory offers an alternative way of understanding the problem. As early as 1982, Shirley Brice Heath's sociocultural research with working-class children revealed that despite their ability to perform comparably with middle-class children in school in entry-level grades on literacy tasks, these working-class children fell progressively behind in later years. She argues that this is because in the later grades, being literate was assessed as the ability to draw on particular ways of talking, believing, valuing and acting that go beyond literacy bits and are differentially available within the social practices of different social groups (Heath, 1982). Here again, literacy is a social process of negotiation. It is more than something we have and do in our heads.

A sociocultural understanding of literacy begins with the acknowledgement that becoming literate involves process as well as product. Structural changes occur in our brain as we develop in a variety of literate practices, but this process is secondary to the social engagement and experience of negotiating meaning for ourselves through our practice for everything we do. Paolo Freire, in his (2007) *Pedagogy of the Oppressed*, was one of the first theorists to conceive of literacy as inextricably tied to social practice. For Freire, the word and the world are dialectically linked and thus it is impossible for literacy to exist outside of social practices. New social practices call for new ways to express ourselves. Through social practice and hours spent texting and on sites such as Facebook and Bebo, we have given meaning to 'words' such as 'LOL', 'TTYL', and so on. Participating in the world in new ways, we needed to update our language to successfully and meaningfully continue to preserve our culture, and this process, occurring though language and social interaction, in turn becomes a part of our future participation.

Colin Lankshear advocates this belief in his (1999) paper 'Literacy studies in education: Disciplined developments in a post-disciplinary age', arguing that traditional conceptions of literacy are over simplistic, as reading and writing can only be understood in the context of the social, cultural, political, economic and historical practices to which they are integral. As he states:

> There is no practice without meaning, just as there is no meaning outside of practice. Within contexts of human practice, language (words, literacy, texts) gives meaning to contexts and, dialectically, contexts give meaning to language. Hence, there is no reading or writing in any meaningful sense of the terms outside of social practices, or discourses.
>
> (Lankshear, 1999)

Without social context and shared experiences and practices, Lankshear argues that we simply cannot make sense of our literacy experiences. His example of the different experiences of a Christian fundamentalist and a liberation theology priest reading an extract from the Bible clearly elucidates how past experiences and social practice come to bear on literacy practice. Traditional literacy theories, including conclusions drawn from neuroscientific research, decontextualize literacy bits from the social practices in which they are produced and embedded while failing to acknowledge that without these social practices and experiences, literacy becomes meaningless and incoherent. While neuroscientific studies interpret spatially, temporally and contextually isolated fMRI scans in practice literacy learning cannot be decontextualized from the circumstance in which it occurs, as this is what gives it meaning.

James Paul Gee's sociocultural work on situated meanings and 'Discourses' provides a very clear picture of *how* this new understanding of literacy might occur in practice. In his (2000) article entitled 'Discourse and sociocultural studies in reading', Gee explains that language is given its meaning in use through its association with the situated meanings, cultural models and the sociocultural groups that socialize learners in communities of practice and literacy practices. Different individuals employ different cultural models of what it is to read and write different texts based on their alignment within specific communities of practice. He argues that texts are always connected in many different ways to many different worlds, and to be able to read and write such worlds individuals need to understand and buy into the practices and communities embedded in the text.

This understanding of literacy, as a complex social practice of recognizing patterns of world building, and coordinating shared experiences into a socioculturally meaningful dance (Latour, 1991), is achieved in practice through what Gee terms 'Discourse'. Our earlier discussion of different textual practices where very different-appearing texts can convey on the surface the same meanings, exemplifies Gee's conception of 'Discourse', highlighting how language is endowed meaning from the cultural and sociocultural models adopted by different communities of practice as they go about their day-to-day practices, and an understanding of those worlds is a prerequisite to engaging culturally and literately in their practices.

For Gee, once literacy is understood as a complex social practice, literacy instruction is viewed as apprenticing students into the discourses and social practices of literate communities. It requires skills of reflection, abstraction, analysis, interpretation, social and cultural literacy, problem solving, dialogic communication and collaboration. Discourses are socially recognized ways of using language (reading, writing, speaking, listening), gestures and other semiotics (images, sounds, graphics, signs, codes), as well as ways of thinking, believing, feeling, valuing, acting/doing and interacting in relation to people and things, such that we can be identified and recognized as being a member of a socially meaningful group, or as playing a socially meaningful role (Gee, 1996).

In his (2003) text *Literacy in the New Media Age*, Gunther Kress charts this move in literacy practices by understanding it as occurring predominantly as a move from writing to image, and aligns this with a move from book to screen. In terms of present and future practices, he makes the very important point that in this sociocultural turn in an extension of what is meaningful and counts as language, the world told is a very different world to the world shown. He explores how text is logically temporally arranged, while when it comes to image, the logic of space is all important.

In his example of teaching a biology class about the structure of cells he compares the use of language saying 'Every cell has a nucleus' versus asking the students to draw a cell. Through language, and saying that every cell *has* a nucleus, Kress claims that this signifies a relation between two things. He goes on to suggest that any sentence we use in the English language requires a verb and so conveys a meaning that is relational. Drawing the cell, in contrast, does not require this commitment to relations but a commitment to a location in space.

A fundamental difference between these two modes is that when we use words, we use our imagination and past experiences to fill these words with a meaning that makes sense for us and our participation. Kress's example of someone telling us that they have a new car reveals that the words themselves hold very little meaning—we do not learn anything specific about the car. Organized temporally, Kress argues that within language there exists a reading path we must follow. When it comes to images, this reading path is drastically different as we attempt to put meaning on images but they themselves are already full of meaning in their specificity and having been chosen by the creator of the image. This process is very clear when we consider how disappointed we can feel when, having read an excellent book, the film version just does not live up to our expectations. He concludes:

> It is now impossible to discuss alphabetic writing with any seriousness without full recognition of this changed frame.... The pressing use of image is forcing a reassessment of what writing is, what it does and does not do, and what it can and cannot do, it forces an insistence on its very materiality–the physicality, the materiality of the stuff that is involved.
>
> (Kress, 2003: 10)

Aligning with our understandings of language development and learning from this stance, Kress argues that the real problem occurs here when we try to confront this changing world with theories (such as neuroscientific discourses), which assume and were shaped to talk about a world that is stable, fixed and united. Kress is interested in his text in 'the materiality of the resources, and in how humans work with them in the demands of their lives' (Kress, 2003: 13). Moving the story forward, we take into account Kress's own assessment and move the focus to participation and practice in our search for meaning.

> I am aware that this partial focus needs to be complemented–matched– with the interests and the work of those who look much more and in great detail at practices ... And the stuff [materials involved in the practices] is culturally remade precisely in those practices. Theories are designed–like all tools–to do specific things. Extending one theory too far, into a domain for which it was never meant, does no one a service.
>
> (Kress, 2003: 13)

Dear sociocultural theory, we need to talk .Neuroscience.

> I think that because neuroscience throws light on underlying mechanisms, it will enable critical analysis of current theories of education which do not necessarily agree with each other. For example, a psychologist who has had a large impact in education is Vygotsky. Vygotsky foregrounded the importance of cultural tools like language for the process of learning. Work in basic neuroscience is showing that we all have social brains. We have relatively complex brains as humans because we live in complex social groups, and we have a complex signalling system called language for organizing these social groups. This recognition of the key role of social interaction for learning and shaping our brains, tied fundamentally to language, ties in very well with some of Vygotsky's theoretical claims about the importance of language and social/cultural systems for learning. For example, it offers a new way of thinking about talking, and why talking is a very important part of education. Communicating about ideas and

reflecting on ideas is one way in which the brain can change itself. Arguably, neuroscience is thus supporting the theory of someone like Vygotsky over other pedagogical beliefs that children work best when talk in the classroom is minimal.

(Goswami, 2011: personal correspondence)

To conclude, from a sociocultural perspective, literacy is understood in terms of socioculturally situated practices. Meaning, central to any significant human undertaking, is made not in the decoding of characters but from experiences, shared between learners and guided by teachers. Where these practices 'match' an individual's previous histories of participation they can employ and develop literacies in practice. Thus, to become literate is to be apprenticed in certain *social* practices. Broadening our understanding of literacy even further in this way, sociocultural theory argues that we are literate to varying degrees in everything we do. When we participate in any activity or within any community of practice, we need to know the rules of the game, so to speak, and so recognize literacy in all aspects of participation.

Central to our successful participation in processes in which we are in varying degrees literate, is meaning. Neuroscience's heavy reliance on biological inputs and underlying mechanisms, on the other hand, while providing a way of looking at learning and language development, are but one side of the story. Usha Goswami, director of the Centre for Neuroscience in Education at the University of Cambridge, summarizes this neuroscientific perspective very well:

> I think that neuroscience offers us new methods for analysing the processes that underpin effective learning, for example processes like language and attention. . . . It is becoming increasingly clear that biological inputs like the way that people move and the sounds that people make are effectively rhythmic stimulus streams that are analysed by the brain in rhythmic units. For speech, this means that syllables, and the way that the jaws open and close as syllables are shaped by our motor apparatus, are fundamental to language acquisition. For example, this would suggest that time in nursery is well spent in rhythmic activity such as dancing and singing, such as moving in time with a beat, and matching language and motor rhythms. This is an example of how neuroscience, by understanding underlying mechanisms, can offer support for some aspects of educational knowledge (such as the importance of nursery rhymes and music with young children) and question the central importance of others (for example, synthetic phonics).

(Goswami, 2011: personal correspondence)

Sociocultural theory takes a much broader focus, understanding that everything we do, from learning our ABCs, to updating our statuses on Facebook, remains meaningful to us in our negotiation of identity, but in the twenty-first century where and in what we find meaning for our practice has changed drastically.

A new social-media alphabet, which goes above and beyond our traditional twenty-six letters, forces us to find meaning in new and diverse linguistic and social practices. While we do not need a word to describe 'the sadness inspired by failing restaurants', we have moved beyond twenty-six letters in our representations of our selves. We now need words like 'hash tag' and the tool it names so that in an online labyrinthine void, our voices can be heard.

Telling a story in the twenty-first century requires reaching an audience that spans many different words and worlds, far more than we can make out of twenty-six letters alone. This chapter has attempted to chart how, through our language and our participation, we have come to stand today at an impasse, where what we count as language demands a recount and needs to be interrogated in terms of its implications for our practices and not just our brain. Alongside this, we would like to suggest that in a world with a population of seven billion, we have possibly as many languages, as activity, agent and world align together in a very unique way for each individual as they go about their negotiation of meaning in daily practice. Hammered and hammering the chances of finding someone else who speaks exactly the same language as us (in broad terms) is possibly seven billion to one. As our use of language shifts and changes, so too we need to move forward in our conceptualization and theorizing around the social processes inherent in our practices–our language.

> The major task is to imagine the characteristics of a theory which can account for the processes of making meaning in the environments of multimodal representation in multimediated communication, of cultural plurality and of social and economic instability. Such a theory will represent a decisive move away from the assumptions of mainstream theories of the last century about meaning, language and learning. The major shifts concern a whole range of hitherto taken for granted understandings, for instance about stable systems of representation, about the stability (guaranteed by the force of convention) of rule systems, about the arbitrariness of the constitution of signs. In all these, a major feature was the assumed centrality of language and, deriving from that, the assumed foundation of 'rationality' in language. In these theories, language 'users' were marginal to the system of the language in the sense that their actions had no significant effect on the system; users used the resources of the system, they did not change it. A fully requisite theory will rest on the understanding that the resources of representation are always in a process of change. While there is–necessarily–convention, the stability of the resources for representation is always contingent. The assumption that there are rule systems will be replaced by an understanding that systematicness is socially produced, and is a sometimes more and a sometimes less useful fiction. The signs of all representational resources are recognized as 'motivated' conjunctions of form and meaning, produced out of the interest of the sign maker, whose 'use' of representational resources is agentic and

transformative. Sign makers act out of their interest but with an awareness, more or less explicitly held, of the history of the resources, expressed as the force of convention.

(Kress, 2003: 168)

Conclusion

In this chapter, we discussed language, culture, plasticity and experience. We began by outlining the problem with language as we understand it. Wired for language acquisition but completely biologically unprepared for reading and writing, we suggest the extreme plasticity of the human brain in this regard, as it literally rewires itself, making new connections along existing structures, reveals the centrality of experience and meaning in learning. In our analysis, learning to read and write happens first in the world and then in the brain.

Understanding language, culture and the brain as inextricably linked through the concept of meaning, we then moved to discuss anthropological and neuro-scientific perspectives on culture, revealing their shortcomings and direct inability to meaningfully explain practice, when compared with a sociocultural analysis of the term. Understanding the constitutive nature of the relationship between mind, culture and brain imbues language with real significance and meaning as language is the most significant cultural tool we employ to share experiences with others. The process of culture itself is not the tabula rasa effort some neuroscientific research assumes as we grow up in our own culture we individually and collectively develop and adapt it on a daily basis. We discussed current changes in language, such as text messaging, to illustrate this point further.

Changes in language are not arbitrary, nor are they shared and understood by all members of a particular culture (under a neuroscientific definition of the term). What becomes central for us in this process is that social processes and interactions are literally making new meanings for what counts as language. Understanding language as the roadmap of culture, we suggested that changes in practice need to be investigated in terms of their meaning for future participation. In the instance of language, we argued that current changes call for a more sociocultural understanding of literacy and concluded our chapter by outlining what this might mean for our understanding of literacy and learning. In doing this, we drew on neuroscientific and other research which also points towards the need for the opening up of neuroscience to a more interdisciplinary approach, if it is to be applied to our understanding, our language and our culture in any meaningful way.

Chapter 10

Emotion

My many coloured days

Introduction

In this chapter, we explore sociocultural and neuroscientific perspectives on emotion, considering learning and experience from the perspective of the whole self. This is despite the fact that there are difficulties about the way the affective is conceptualized in the literature generally. The now well-known work of Gardner (1983) and Goleman (1995) and the notion of 'emotional intelligence', have undoubtedly spotlighted the importance of emotion in all aspects of life, including learning. However, from our point of view, their notion of emotion is problematic as it leaves intact the idea that emotion is something one possesses—a quotient. This view aligns more with the neurological than the sociocultural. In education research on learning, there has been a significant interest in the theme of engagement (Ellis and Coddington, 2013) but little theorization of emotion as part of the engagement pedagogies advocated in such studies. This chapter makes a first attempt at further theorization of emotion as a part of participation. The accounts and discussion here foreground affect and illustrate the enmeshed nature of the affective, the bodily and the sociality in learning.

The colour of emotion, learning and experience

> Life is like a train of moods, like a string of beads, and, as we pass through them, they prove to be many colored lenses which paint the world their own hue.
>
> (Emerson, 1993: 85)

As we argue in Chapters 6, 7 and 8, learning involves becoming a different kind of person in line with a transformation in identity in a social context. We can say that the self is constructed through participation in practical activity where recognition by others and one's own desires for recognition are central. Identity, relationships and power are all pivotal to participation, and emotion is an inescapable feature of participation and learning. Becoming a more fully participative member of a community of practice inevitably entails struggle, transformation, personal change, and accompanying feelings of success and failure, feelings of pride and shame, and so on. As such, emotion is produced in social relations. While personally felt, it is relational–affect is socially and biologically produced but has bodily effects.

The desire to be recognized as a particular kind of person highlights the way emotion is complicit in but inseparable from learning in a sociocultural perspective. People respond to the affordances and constraints of the situation as they perceive them, and learning involves becoming increasingly aligned with those affordances and constraints so one experiences oneself as a player, a member of a community, though such membership is never a once and for all thing. It has to be more or less constantly struggled over and fought for as the community itself changes and new affordances and constraints may apply and as the person changes over time. Indeed, membership may only be the start of the process (Packer and Goicoechea, 2000) since identity is a constant becoming which has to be struggled over.

In the context of learning, then, knowing or being able etc. is not necessarily the end but the means to recognition by others. There are both benefits and costs to membership as we saw in Daniel's case, for instance, in Chapter Seven–being a cool teenager seemed to win out over being a learned boy. He seemed unable to resolve the tension that was there for him in those two salient identities while he was at primary school. Thus, communities of practice are not necessarily harmonious and benign; conflict, tension, struggle are inevitable. Culture can indeed have a lethal side. Of course, harmony, joy, satisfaction, and so on, are also part and parcel of participation in communities. All to say that emotions in such a perspective are key. How people feel about their participation is central to their participation and therefore their learning.

Seeing red: neuroscience and emotions

On the final day of the Masters, Augusta 2011 Rory McIlroy's golf game unravelled. He held a one-shot lead when he walked off the ninth hole. After a triple-bogey seven at the tenth, another shot went at the eleventh and two more at the twelfth. He smashed his drive into Rae's Creek at the thirteenth. McIlroy dropped his head on his right forearm, his body slumped in confusion and embarrassment. He bogeyed number fifteen. By the time he staggered pitilessly off the final green for a back-nine forty three, his shirttail was hanging out of his trousers. As he left the course, Masters Patrons rewarded him with a standing ovation and cheers. A distraught McIlroy later recalls what happened during his performance 'for 63 holes in this golf tournament, I was leading and just a couple of bad holes on the back nine just sort of derailed me'. He continued, 'I don't know if people were just feeling sorry for me or what' but 'I'm incredibly grateful for it. I really appreciate it. It was a very tough day for me out there'.

(Mihoces, 2011)

Describing the experience of Rory McIlroy at Augusta in 2011, one neuroscientist interviewee tells us:

he needs to myelinate more—yes he fell apart ... he completely imploded, he fell apart. He started golfing like an amateur. Emotion trumped cognition. Absolutely, he lost focus. Golf is such a mental game—you have to be good but you need to focus, filter out, at that level all the attention, expectations, and emotions. You need to focus.

(Neuroscientist I, from the International Neuroscience Conference, Wicklow, 2011)

In this description, biological and neurological factors are understood to contribute to the physiological response, which results in the production of emotion. The 'affective network' of the brain as defined by neuroscience, comprises a set of structures in the centre of the brain collectively known as the limbic system or the 'seat of emotion'. According to neuroscientists, the limbic system houses the brain regions that play a key role in emotional processing, including the amygdala and hippocampus. The limbic system is intricately connected with cortical areas involved in cognitive processing, and neuroscience claims strong connections between the emotional system and other systems in the brain.

In our sporting vignette and the following neuroscientific explanation, the body of Rory McIlroy is overtaken by reactions that he had not consciously initiated, and which he in that moment cannot control. Myelination and focus would help Rory but in this instance, from a neuroscientific perspective, he can absolve himself from blame for the loss of the competition. In an unfortunate turn of events from this biological perspective Rory is the victim of an emotional hijacking where:

a center of the limbic brain proclaims an emergency, recruiting the rest of the brain to its urgent agenda. The hijacking occurs an instance before the neocortex, the thinking brain, has had a chance to fully glimpse what is happening ... this happens to us fairly frequently.

(Goleman, 1995: 14)

Discussing his understanding of neural takeovers, psychologist and science journalist Daniel Goleman portrays succinctly a neuroscientific explanation of emotion. Though not a neuroscientist, his work links the brain and emotions—see, for example, his (2011) text *The Brain and Emotional Intelligence: New Insights*. Swept over by a wave of emotion, the individual is rendered momentarily powerless against it. Emotion is understood as neurological affect and physiological response, and the wider social and relational context is ignored. The metaphor of emotion as hijacker may in this context make us smile sympathetically, but, connecting with one of our central concerns in this text, probing further what this might mean if we were to apply it to our practice could be quite disturbing and chilling, as Goleman's own vignette of a burglary gone wrong reveals:

> As Robles tells the tale years later, while he was tying up Hoffert, Janise Wylie warned him he would not get away with this crime. She would remember his face and help the police track him down. Robles.... panicked at that, completely losing control. In a frenzy, he grabbed a soda bottle and clubbed the women until they were unconscious, then awash with rage and fear, he slashed and stabbed them over and over with a kitchen knife.... Robles lamented 'I just went bananas. My head just exploded'.
>
> (Goleman, 1995: 14–15)

Imploding and exploding heads serve as a very apt metaphor for a neuro-scientific definition of emotion. Lacking the explanatory power to theorize upon and develop what is produced on brain scans investigating emotion precisely because neuroscientific research refuses to look beyond the brain scan, neuroscience falls short when it comes to adding to our understanding of emotion in learning.

The Rory McIlroy vignette illustrates a range of emotions–derailment, upset, confusion, embarrassment, gratitude–but what a neuroscientific analysis does not acknowledge is that all of these emotions occur in the social context of the golf Masters, amid the performance of identity. The feelings and behaviours are not random neurological phenomena but, rather, are constituted amongst others (team players, caddies, patrons and media).

As far as we can establish the findings from research on emotion in neuro-science that could be linked to learning are more confirmatory of what we know already than ground breaking in development of our understanding. In a paper with the promising title 'We feel, therefore we learn: The relevance of affective and social neuroscience to education', Immordino-Yang and Damasio (2007: 3) claim that advances in their field are highlighting connections between emotion, social functioning and decision making and they make the point that attention, memory and learning are 'subsumed within the processes of emotion'. Yet, they appear not to be in a position to say what the nature of the connec-tions are and how they may impact learning or education more generally. They conclude that the research has 'the *potential* to revolutionize our understanding of the role of affect in education' (our emphasis) and that in due course a better understanding of the neurobiology of emotion will provide 'a new basis for innovation in the design of learning environments' (3) and 'for the science of learning and the practice of teaching' (9). Thus, it would seem that right now understanding of emotion in learning does not uniquely implicate neuroscience and that, at best, evidence is patchy and inconclusive. Aspirations are high but the claims appear weak evidentially.

Feeling blue: experience and sociocultural theory

> Patricia, a high school student, struggles with mathematics. The last few times she answered a mathematics question she got it wrong and felt terribly embarrassed, which formed an association with mathematics and negative emotions. Her teacher had just asked her to come to the blackboard to solve a problem. This caused an immediate transfer of this emotionally-charged association to the amygdala, which elicits fear. Meanwhile, a slower, cortically-driven cognitive appraisal of the situation is occurring: she remembers her difficulty completing her mathematics homework last night, notices the problem on the board contains complicated graphs, and realises that the boy she has a crush on is watching her from a front-row seat. These various thoughts converge to a cognitive confirmation that this is a threatening situation, which reinforces her progressing fear response and disrupts her ability to concentrate on solving the mathematics problem.
>
> (Hinton *et al.*, 2008: 91)

We present this second vignette from Hinton *et al.*, exploring emotion in practice, to compare and elucidate exactly what a sociocultural analysis can add to a theorization of emotion. While still including a description of brain processes, Patricia's story embeds neurological effects in sociocultural practice and highlights the importance Patricia's understanding of her own identity plays in the process. Sociocultural theory understands emotions as shaped, experienced and interpreted via social and cultural processes in a negotiation of meaning and identity. Emotion is more than an inner state; it is relational and part of a history of shared experiences. Emotional states interweave nature and culture and emotionality itself 'lies at the intersection of the person and society, for all persons are joined to their societies through the self feelings and emotions they feel and experience on a daily basis' (Denzin, 1984).

Emotions, as understood socioculturally, play a central role in contributing to a sense of self, of being-in-learning, to the construction of an identity. In the mathematics vignette, Patricia becomes frightened in response to a perceived stress-provoking situation. Her emotional experience disrupts her thinking and working memory but the extent to which it is acted upon is mediated by context and previous experience.

Patricia experiences powerful emotions in the social and cultural context of the mathematics classroom. Emotions change readiness for action—and for Patricia's identity this means a disengagement with mathematics. Stress and fear become features of the practice for Patricia. How Patricia processes, expresses, communicates and regulates her emotions relates also to the social situation and social interactions. Patricia's identity is constrained within a social space that does not enable, honour or encourage her to articulate her knowledge without fear; to participate on her own terms. Understanding learning as a process of becoming within social interaction, Patricia's becoming, just like the experiences of Daniel and others illustrated in previous chapters, as a result of the emotions experienced during practice, may involve feelings of disappointment and marginalization that have a negative impact on her learning process.

Patricia recalls 'the last few times she answered a mathematics question she got it wrong and felt terribly embarrassed', 'remembers her difficulty completing her mathematics homework last night, and notices the problem on the board contains complicated graphs' (Hinton *et al.*, 2008: 91). Patricia's positional identity is constrained in relation to others. It is bound by the space and her history of participation in mathematics. What is clear throughout the exploration of this second vignette, is that Patricia's emotions are a part of her experience of defining, negotiating and acting of self in the social space and order of the classroom. Her emotions are experienced in the context of interpersonal relationships with others. Through Patricia's vignette, we see emotions as anchored in the bodily self and embedded in the sociocultural space and learning and identity practices.

In this chapter, we have begun to develop the very complex area of emotion and its importance to a sociocultural understanding of learning. Due to the elusive nature of emotion which sweeps over us or just as quickly slips away we conclude this chapter with a story from the world of neuroscience, which aims to illustrate in some way the sociocultural processes of emotion.

Colouring emotion

> Monday is yellow; Tuesday is quite a deep red; Wednesday is sort of a grass green; Thursday is a much darker green but still quite bright; Friday has always confused me, it's either a very dark purple, blue or gray; Saturday is white; and Sunday is sort of a light peach colour. For anyone who doesn't understand what's happening here, I have a neurological condition called synesthesia which means that I 'see' words in colours.
>
> (Stephanie Carswell, quote from http://en.wikipedia.
> org/wiki/List_of_people_with_synesthesia)

Synesthesia is a neurological condition in which stimulation in one sense leads to an automatic and involuntary stimulation of another sense. In the above quote, Stephanie sees words in colours. The title of this chapter on emotion 'My Many Coloured Days' is borrowed from the popular Dr Seuss children's book, which tells the story of a young child who appears in one particular version first in yellow, then blue and then purple, before metamorphosing into many animals, all a different colour and each portraying a different energy.

For us, the neurological condition of synesthesia, on which this text is also based, provides a very interesting metaphor for exploring the role of emotions in learning. Seeing red, feeling blue, as indicated in various headings in this chapter, are one way we try to capture our emotions and what they feel like, but what about a story of a young boy who actually sees and experiences his emotions as colours? In their (2011) research article 'Coloured halos around faces and emotion evoked colours: A new form of synesthesia', neuroscientists Ramachandran et al. relate the story of a twenty-three-year-old man with Asperger's disorder who was encouraged by his mother to use colour to understand emotions as a child and now experiences emotions as colours. For example, when he is feeling happy he would report that he was feeling green:

> TK's synesthesia seems to be a vital aspect of his conscious understanding of emotions. Evidence of this comes from two observations. First, TK claims that recognition of emotion can only occur after he experiences the colour. Second, when TK wishes to express his emotion (e.g. through a facial expression), he must tell himself to 'do green' (in the case of happiness). This not only provides evidence for the necessity of using colour to judge emotions, but also provides preliminary evidence that his synesthesia is embodied.
>
> (Ramachandran et al., 2011: 13)

Returning to our main purpose in this chapter, to begin a sociocultural exploration of the role of emotion in learning, the work of Ramachandran et al. reveals the enmeshed nature of the affective and the bodily in an understanding of emotion in learning and participation. The authors continue:

> We noticed that TK's color for pride was a shade of blue and the color for aggression was pinkish-red. Intriguingly, the color for arrogance is purple, presumably because the combination of blue and red in color space is purple, and the combination of pride and aggression in emotional space is arrogance (TK had not noticed this coincidence until we pointed it out to him). This observation, if further verified would indicate TK's color associations are not random. Instead they are the results of a taxonomy of emotions in TK's brain developed through systematically mapping emotional space represented in the frontal cortices and insula on to color space in V4 and its projection zones.
>
> (Ramachandran et al., 2011: 12–13)

At around the same time that TK began understanding emotion in this way, he also started to see coloured halos around people and the colours of these halos corresponded to his own emotional stance towards the particular individual.

On encountering a new person, they were always surrounded by a blue halo, the colour of which changed over time to signify TK's emotion towards the individual, that developed with repeated exposure.

Ramachandran *et al.* suggest that TK's experiences are a result of increased brain connectivity particularly in the regions involving face processing, vision and emotion, but understood from a sociocultural perspective reveals the centrality of social interaction and relationships in the experience of emotions. TK's colours change as he interacts over time and with different people and, for TK, his emotions, located in the colours he sees, are physically linked to the people with whom he engages in practice every day.

This example from current neuroscientific research aligns with our earlier statement that neuroscientific research is more confirmatory than ground breaking when it comes to theorizing emotion in learning. The authors of this research paper do indicate that neuroscientific research in this area could be employed to develop a novel therapeutic intervention for patients with autism, but what is most interesting here is that, paralleling one of the main themes of this book, the authors relate their neuroscientific research to sociocultural practice, and it is only in this way that it can be useful to an understanding of learning:

> Would it be possible to train the child (initially using cues from social context, situation, overt behavior and people's expressions) to attach color labels to feelings, thereby allowing the child to develop a new internal taxonomy of emotions by mapping them onto his/her color space?
>
> (Ramachandran *et al.*, 2011: 14)

From a neuroscientific perspective, this is where the research finishes but this story is very interesting to help develop a sociocultural understanding of emotion. As previously suggested, TK in his daily practice locates his emotions not in his head but in the people and places around him as, in his interactions with others, he physically sees emotion change and adapt, coloured by and colouring every act of participation in the world. TK's emotions are for him visibly located in his interactions with others and this understanding rather than the neuroscientific description of brain processes allows him to engage in meaningful social interaction.

We conclude this chapter with the story of author Vladimir Nabokov, quoted elsewhere in this text, who writes much on his condition of colour hearing and reveals that his mother and son (and also his wife) experience synesthesia:

> It turned out, we discovered one day, that my son, who was a little boy at the time—I think he was 10 or 11—sees letters in colors too. Quite naturally, he would say 'Oh this isn't that color, this is this color' and so on. Then we asked him to list his colors and we discovered that in one case, one letter which he sees as purple, or perhaps mauve, is pink to me and blue to my

wife. This is the letter M. So, the combination of pink and blue makes lilac in his case. Which is as if genes were painting in aquarelle.

(Nabokov, quoted in Eagleman, 2009)

This image of genes painting experience is central to our argument in this text and the one on which we would like to conclude this chapter. This neuroscientific and deterministic understanding of the role of neurobiology in experience is one that Nabokov himself later abandons in favour of a more sociocultural explanation of his experience. Nabokov suggests that akin to language learning we are in fact all born with the possibility for synesthesia but our capacity for sensory crosstalk is replaced by neural firewalls as over time because of brain plasticity and instructions from parents and others we learn to stop seeing the world in this way. It is interesting that a study presented in *Psychological Science* aligns with this understanding. Wagner and Dobkins (2011) reveal that infants under three months show significant shape–colour associations but by eight months the preference is no longer as pronounced and by adulthood it disappears altogether. Could it be that the practices of Nabokov and his wife encouraged the development of synesthesia in their own son? Though the authors of this text do not claim this, it is interesting to consider this possibility, even more so in light of our discussion of language in the previous chapter and our belief that learning and living are inseparable.

Conclusion

Emotion is highly significant in the maintenance and transformation of identity, it is constitutive of it. Emotion is not a separate thing. More importantly, it is not merely a case of some emotions being good for learning such as 'flow' or enjoyment and others being bad for learning. Pedagogy has to be concerned with the emotional and, as others have argued (Beard et al., 2007), the sociocultural concern for emotion in pedagogy is not about the therapeutic or matters of self-esteem. The point is that affect is always a dimension of learning. Learning is about the process of becoming a member of a community of practice, as we have argued, that becoming can involve marginalization, alienation, and matters of status and legitimation. Thus, feelings of disappointment and not belonging as well as the power of emotion all become relevant to the study of learning as a changing participation in the world.

Some days are yellow.
Some are blue.
On different days I'm different too.
You'd be surprised how many ways.
I change on different colored days.
(Dr Seuss in *My Many Colored Days*, 1998)

Chapter 11

Coming to mind

Telling the story of memory and identity

Introduction

This chapter explores the social processes involved in memory, arguing that remembering is a social activity where both process and product create meaning. Our understanding of memory relates directly to our understanding of mind, previously discussed, and it is central also to our understanding of learning. Individuals sometimes have a tendency to equate memory and learning, but for us, this is not the case. This chapter outlines our understanding of memory and is built around two fundamental questions:

1. What is memory?
2. Why do we remember and forget?

Understanding memory as a complex sociocultural process, this chapter links neurological function, relationships, community, place, identity, meaning, culture, language, history, narratives, past and present, in a story of remembering and forgetting. We explore the functions of memory, why we remember and indeed why we forget, understanding one of the central functions of memory as the perpetuation of knowledge through processes of creation, development, transmission, translation, mediation and distribution. Other functions of memory explored here are the communication and connection of history, and the role of memory in identity and self. Our method is to apply sociocultural theory as a lens to analyse prominent neuroscientific studies on memory, showing how neuroscientific 'findings' convey real meaning only when understood socioculturally.

Once upon a time . . .

I remember where, as a child, I used to swing and I remember the feel of the air rushing by my face. I remember who beat Napoleon at Waterloo, and I remember that eight multiplied by nine is seventy two. I haven't forgotten how to swing a bat; and I remember—no, I feel it again in the weakness in my legs and wrists and in the nausea in my stomach–the terror I felt when the captain made me a 'volunteer' on the first search and destroy mission in the A Shau Valley. I remember the party we had when we got married–the music, the friends, the food, the wine; but (Oh God!) I can't remember any more the face of my dearest friend who died a year ago … There are all sorts of memory and they pervade and define me.

(Brockelman, 1975: 309)

What is a memory? What makes a memory? Where does a memory come from when we remember and where does 'it' go when we forget? Even more interesting, how and why does it suddenly 'come back', coming to mind as though it was never forgotten? Can we ever actually remember anything on our own? What is the relationship between memory and identity? This chapter attempts to address these questions beginning with the understanding that a brain is not built to remember everything. We believe a successful memory is not simply about the truthful preservation of the past. Memories are practices, not just possessions. Remembering is a social activity where process and product create meaning. We believe current memory research fails to provide a satisfactory explanation of memory precisely because theories of memory overlook these understandings and are more concerned with the neurological 'ink and paper' with which memories are made rather than an investigation of the grammar of remembrance (Blakemore, 1977: 101–106).

What does it mean when we say we *gather* our thoughts, *collect* our emotions, *get ourselves together*? Meeting the receptionist of our local health-centre in the supermarket, we *know* we *know* her but we do not know *where* from–we need a moment to *place* her. It is important to remember, as we illustrate throughout this book, that language carries concepts and meaning. Talking about self and memory using the language outlined above, as is common practice in the Western world, for example, assumes that we understand memories as *things*; things to be gathered, collected, kept and stored. Within this discourse we of course need a storehouse, somewhere to *lock away* our most precious moments and experiences so they become a part of ourselves–we need a brain. Identity becomes equated with memory as we become ourselves through our actions alone. We each hold the key to our own experiences, our own memories, our selves. Brain plasticity, from a neuroscientific perspective, allows us to *store* and *own* these memories, fixed in time.

Brain plasticity and neuroscientific definitions alone, however, have difficulties explaining how we can forget something we *know*, remembering it minutes later after much *searching* as we wrack *our brains* in a *hunt* for something that exists within it. From a neuroscientific perspective, we question why and how does that stored memory disappear and reappear? We break one final time the collective voice in this text to tell a story. Last week, sitting in a lecture next to a colleague and friend that I have known for years, I could not remember his surname. I could remember his child's name and his dog's name but this simple piece of information eluded me and it nearly drove me crazy. Over an hour later, as the lecture came to a close, the name returned to me. We have all had experiences like this but the question remains (unanswered by neuroscience), how do we make sense of it?

This chapter challenges a neuroscientific, one-dimensional understanding of memory, exploring the social processes involved in remembering and forgetting. Coming to memory and mind from this different angle we suggest that it is only when we understand memory as a sociocultural process that we can fully make sense of it. Memory is social because it exists only through its relation to what has been shared between individuals, both in terms of experiences, relationships and identities, and also language, symbols and culture. Each memory we experience is made up of lots of other memories from different places and times. Perception at any given moment in time is only meaningful insofar as it fits with our own understandings of identity, time and place. We understand our present in terms of our past. We use past memories as context for future ones. Memories are meaning makers in the present and function not in terms of truth but of belief. Memories cannot be true or false; they are simply validated or denied through social practice. When it comes to memory, what is important is the present, not the past, as memories *come to mind* through the social world of lived experiences.

It is our belief that memory research is overly concerned with how memory works, how individuals remember and where this memory is stored–the categorization and location of a sociocultural process. This chapter takes a different perspective on the debate, arguing that it is more generative to ask instead what a memory is and why it is created in the first place. Answering these questions, we believe, unearths the undeniable sociocultural nature of memory and will also shed light on how memory works in the process. Our story, inevitably, is also the story of others, or versions of it, and so this chapter fills with the voices of others as we collectively attempt to tell the story of memory. We do not own it; it is not ours alone to tell.

Unmaking memory

What happens after repeated injections of serotonin is that the enzyme kinase A, along with another enzyme, called MAP, moves from the outer cytoplasm into its nucleus. There, kinase A activates a protein called CREB-I, which in turn switches on a set of genes that synthesize the proteins the neuron needs to grow new synaptic terminals. At the same time, MAP activates another protein, CREB-2, which switches off a set of genes that inhibit the growth of new terminals. Through a complex chemical process of cellular 'marking' ... involving extensive chemical and genetic signals and changes ... synapses become able to hold memories over the course of days or even years.

(Carr, 2010: 187)

Nicholas Carr's neurological explanation of how we form long-term memories in our brains appears, at first glance, to be a straightforward and matter-of-fact process. What this definition fails to explain, however, is good memory gone bad, so to speak; how memory can become inaccurate, unreliable, influenced by other people or even fail completely. Carr introduces these issues in his book, claiming that memories are formed in the brain thanks to the extreme plasticity of the organ, but more specifically, our experiences, which continually shape our identities and practices. He concludes, quoting Eric Kandel, that the fact that a gene must be switched on to form long-term memory, shows that genes are not simply determinants of behaviour but are also responsive to environmental stimulation, such as learning (Carr, 2010: 187).

The tendency of memory to be at times hopelessly sketchy, while at other times frighteningly accurate, betrays an understanding central to a sociocultural perspective of remembering: that memory is not misrepresented internally but, rather, the social and creative process of remembering is influenced by a number of external relational factors. Throughout this book research reveals that the brain is a deeply social organ. We did not evolve to read but we did evolve to interact. In this way, one of the main functions of memory–the evolutionary ability to interact with others and the capability to predict our future in terms of our past–places memory as a powerful tool for identity and learning. Memory as process is not centred on rote learning and textbooks but in the lived practices of the everyday. Understood in this way, what becomes central to deconstructing memory is not an understanding of how memories are made in the brain but, rather, a question of who is remembering what version of the past to which end (Middleton and Brown, 2005: 14).

The first part of this chapter attempts to answer the question of what a memory is made of. Focusing on belief rather than truth and examining process alongside product, we ask how something becomes to be believed through social action–how something becomes a memory. What people remember is not simply a matter of encoding, but is influenced by pre- and post-experience social interactions. With the aid of neuroscientific research, we explore the set of sociocultural techniques that we believe *make* memories and question the value of memory itself, as its existence and thus power in the present can only be in its relational and social impact. Our sociocultural understanding of memory posits it as an entirely social, cultural and relational process that exists in, for and of social practice. To achieve this, we divide the first half of this chapter into four parts, each discussing one aspect of what, for us, makes a memory.

Down memory lane: relationships to community and place

What is the quickest way from one place to another? Memory. Relationships are central to memory. To remember any significant time in our lives is first and foremost to remember where we were and who we were with. To think back on our childhood, we first see our childhood home, school and community and the people who inhabit these places; then particular experiences emerge but always in the context of community and place. This is because we are a part of these people and places, and they, through social interaction, become a part of us. When it comes to remembrance of these experiences, they can only be remembered and recreated in the context of our family and the way they were originally experienced and remembered. Memories are made up of places and people, which we creatively and jointly reconstruct with others in social interaction when we remember.

Communities of practice in the home, school or community, construct their own images of the world using memory communicatively, establishing an agreed version of the past between the memories of their members, the value of which does not lie in the power or exaltation of the past but in some present action. Memory can thus be used socially to define a community of practice, producing not only a sense of the past but also setting future aspirations and goals. When it comes to memory as a social process, remembering centres on the memory of the intersubjective past, of past time lived in relation to other people (Misztal, 2003: 6). For example, Gould and Dixon's research into the memory of older married couples reveals the shared and social nature of memory as, when asked to jointly recall experiences such as a recent holiday, they are more likely to engage in serial monologues than other ways of retelling. Gould and Dixon suggest that this is because over time they have developed together a more established pattern of joint recall, knowing which part of the shared memory 'belongs' to which partner (Gould and Dixon, 2003).

It is also important to note that much of what we remember we did not experience as individuals. Middleton and Brown (2005) define memory as at the centre of lived experience as a relational process at the intersection of different durations of living. As we endure in time, our rhythm of living is slowed or quickened in relation to the duration of others (Middleton and Brown, 2005: vii). In this way, memory becomes both a public and social activity that is mediated by collective experience and attached to membership of communities of practice. Current research into memory in groups confirms this belief, revealing how social factors such as audience tuning, perceived expertise, narrator role and social contagion, impose on the neurological basis of memory and an experience can be remembered and believed to have occurred differently than what actually took place (see, for example, Brown et al., 2009).

Further, the role individuals take in remembering in group settings differs according to these social constructs. For example, people will contribute more to narrating a shared event (remembering) when they actually participate in an experience, rather than just observe it (Pasupathi et al., 2007). Audience tuning in relation to memory also highlights the importance of not only the community and place to which the memory refers, but also the community and place where the memory is now retold and jointly recreated. This ability of social experiences to influence the neurological basis of memory to such a degree that it actually changes how an event is remembered is powerful evidence indeed for the social construction of memory. Research reveals that even the mere presence of another individual can affect the process of remembrance (Weldon, Blair and Huebsch, 2000).

Place stands alongside people in our shared memories as a reminder that memory already exists in the social world, rather than in our heads. Places, like selves, are produced in social interaction and are never neutral entities. Places are imbued with meaning for individuals as they are a part of our lived experiences. A picture, a person, a sound can take us back in time, but in all these instances remembering occurs from the outside out–an 'external stimulus', to borrow a term from cognitive psychology, points us to a memory of a time outside of ourselves, embodied in the place and community that inhabit it, as per our shared and creative recollections. This memory may also be categorized as happy or sad, depending on the way we remember the place where the memory occurs. We have an embodied relationship with place and this reveals itself in the social process of remembrance.

One of the first and most influential theorizers of social memory, Maurice Halbwachs, argues that in our remembering we develop mutually responsive relationships to place. We fashion our personal spaces but are, in turn, shaped by the structure of place (Halbwachs, 1980: 130). A remembrance of Charles Dickens' famous character, Ebenezer Scrooge, highlights this relationship very nicely: the miserly old man in his threadbare nightgown and cap, counting his pennies by candlelight and a few fire coals in a dark and dusty room. Calling to mind old Ebenezer, we do not remember him in isolation, as the objects, artefacts and even furniture we recreate around him have a profound effect on how we perceive his identity. In our memories, place is manipulated and recreated, almost territorialized (Middleton and Brown, 2005), by shared memory and the performance of identities. In this way, place as a central part of memory becomes a creative tool in recruiting people to memories or specific created versions of the past. As Halbwachs explains:

> There is no point in seeking where ... [memories] are preserved in my brain or in some nook of my mind to which I alone have access for they are recalled by me externally, and the groups of which I am a part at any time give me the means to reconstruct them.
>
> (Halbwachs, 1992: 38)

A sociocultural perspective on the process of memory as outlined here, underscores the central role of community and place in memory, concluding that one of the most important features of memory is the use of people and places by individuals and groups to recruit people and places to certain versions of experience and history–to certain versions of identity.

From dead reckoning to status updates: Identity and meaning in memory

> I walk around with my life right next to me.
> (Jill Price, ABC News in interview with Diane Sawyer: 9 May 2008)

Relationship to place and social groups imbued in all memories allow individuals to tell meaningful stories of identity. From a sociocultural perspective, identity is just another way to describe how we position ourselves and are positioned by our current practices, which, in time, become our previous histories of participation–our memories. A sociocultural reading of memory suggests that it is through memory we develop, make meaningful and validate our performed social identities. Jill Price, famous for her rare condition hyperthymesia, can remember every day of her life since the age of fourteen, and provides a powerful if exaggerated example of the role of identity in memory. She claims 'Give me the day and I see it. I go back to the day and I just see the day and what I was *doing*' (Jill Price, ABC News in interview with Diane Sawyer: 9 May 2008).

Jill's story has been exhaustively pursued in neuroscientific research (see, for example, Parker *et al.*, 2006) but there has been little work exploring Jill's experience from a sociocultural perspective. The memories Jill recalls in relation to any particular day are always memories involving place, people and identity. Her memories are deeply personal and tied to her interests and experiences. They are so powerful for Jill that she is obsessed with writing things down because they would stick in her mind if she *didn't*. With such a good memory, it is surprising, then, that Jill hated school and received mostly Cs and Ds in her classwork. But Jill also has an explanation for this–she could not consciously learn strategies for learning new information. Her memory only applies to her own life experiences. Identity and meaning are central to these memories, as Jill tells her story of self:

> I would get totally stressed out if I had to memorize a poem, or if I had to memorize a monologue for drama class, I would completely freak out. Because I can't do what they do. I can't look at a phone book and memorize names. I don't do that. It's just really my life.
> (Jill Price, ABC News in interview with Diane Sawyer: 9 May 2008)

Identity is a form of social negotiation with the world. For Jill and every other individual, memory serves as a medium for this process of meaningful social negotiation as our stories about ourselves articulate what you can say you are, according to what they say you can be (Johnson, 1973 in Madsen, 1999: 60). In the stories we tell ourselves and others, identity becomes established and maintained through memory. This process is not a straightforward one, however, as the past is a contested site of meaning and it is through the social processes of remembrance and forgetting on these grounds that ongoing battles of identity are fought, lost and won. Invisible unless explored from a sociocultural perspective, these battles are of the utmost importance, as victory means self-continuity and the semblance of a coherent and agentic self.

Returning to the title of this section, 'the dead reckoning' to which we refer is the concept developed by neuroscientist Dr Randy Gallistel, at Rutgers University. He defines dead reckoning as the process of keeping track of where you are by adding up small changes in position. In his co-authored book *Memory and the Computational Brain: Why Cognitive Science will Transform Neuroscience* (King and Gallistel, 2009), he offers a wonderful example from the animal kingdom of how this concept works from a neuroscientific perspective, showing how diverse information is acquired at different times from different experiences and then put into the memory of jay birds through a process of dead reckoning. The jay birds under study can distinguish between thousands of stored food caches and remember not only where they have stored their cache, but also what they have hidden there and when the cache was made. In this way, they learn and remember how long it takes a particular food item to rot and will not return to this cache even if it is a favourite item of food, such as a mealworm, if it is past its sell-by date.

Appropriating the term 'dead reckoning' for our purposes here, and to a sociocultural reading of the process, we argue that the concept can be compared with our own use of social networking sites such as Facebook and Myspace. In these social spaces, by adding up and publicly displaying our small changes in position, birthdays, Christmases, nights out, and so on, we keep track of where we are, creating a meaningful identity for ourselves in cyberspace and by association—in our relationships with our family and friends who access our profiles—our overt publicly displayed memories. Alongside these memories in time our profile pages also transmit a set of cultural meanings and social values around which we collectively build individual understandings of identity and meaning in a social construction of memory. This sociocultural concept can also be likened to the neuroscientific idea of consolidation, the process by which moment-to-moment changes in brain activity are translated into permanent structural changes in the brain.

So, at the same time that memory creates identity, so too identity creates memory. Also important to the development of memory is the fact that the *they* that Johnson refers to encompasses not only other individuals but also cultural practices and assumptions which shape the world around us. And even more challenging in our search for meaning is the fact that these cultural practices and assumptions seem to evolve from minute to minute, forcing us to engage in even more complicated participation, meaning making, identity performance and memory. So next we take a closer look at the role of history and culture in memory making, as it is only now, with the work of identity, place and community realized in memory, that history and the past can find its actual place in remembering.

Letting the actors take their bow: culture and history

> To remember is always to give a reading of the past, a reading which requires linguistic skills derived from the traditions of explanation and storytelling within a culture and which [presents] issues from a narrative that owes its meaning ultimately to the interpretive practices of a community of speakers.... The mental image of the past ... becomes a phenomenon of consciousness only when clothed with words, and these owe their meaning to social practices of communication.
>
> (Bakhurst, 1990: 219f)

A memory is made up of, and cannot be separated from, the cultural tools it employs to make its meaning. Past is also present, but this past is steeped in both present experience and cultural norms and symbols, such as language, ritual, and so on. When we make a memory we need language, artefacts, objects and reifications of culture such as textual documents to make this memory communicative in social interaction. Language is a medium for remembrance and no memory is possible without the employment of some communicative system to imbue meaning on experience. History in memory is only important in terms of what individuals say about the past in social interaction and what it means presently to everyone involved in the process of remembering. Here again, it is belief and not truth that controls what can be remembered and what can be forgotten. The social meaning of memory, similar to its form and the sociocultural tools necessary to its communication, is little affected by its truth—what is important is what is believed (Fentress and Wickham, 1992).

Our memories are structured and communicated through the use of sociocultural techniques and semiotic mediation such as signs, language, culture and experience. As we learn we develop new ways of appropriating the cultural tools available to us as the tools and reified texts of our time become like cultural mediators to the social processes of our remembering. Wertsch develops this idea in his (2002) book *Voices of Collective Remembering*, arguing that memory is distributed between social actors and texts as individuals employ cultural tools which are historically evolved within a social context to remember. In this way, history gives way to memory but this memory is translated, mediated, distributed and loaded with meaning for its participants in the present.

History, as we know it in present memory making is malleable, mediated and distributed in, by and across social interaction. Our understanding of the past changes over time and depends on a wide range of sociocultural factors. As Middleton and Brown (2005) explain, the relation between past and future in memory is not given but depends on human agency as well as on mnemonic tools, techniques and databases. In this way, and as we will discuss in more detail in the second half of this chapter, memory from a sociocultural perspective becomes highly significant for learning because when we can *do* memory correctly, in the sense of the meaningful employment of cultural tools to recreate a particular version of the past, we have learnt competence in the cultural values and tools of our time and can take part in the dynamic and meaningful processes of cultural transmission and transformation.

Memory in this light becomes a meaningful site for learning but the meaning of history lies not in the past but in the present. To understand memory as a sociocultural process is to understand remembrance not as a window to a past but, rather, in the context of the present and what this memory tells us about this present time. That is, the meaning of history for memory. History, as central to memory, does not only mean our own personal histories, but the ability to connect with past experiences of the communities of practice in which we participate that occurred a long time before we joined the community as if they were a part of our own past. This grants meaning and identity to history and allows it to now be used for our own purposes in the present in memory.

This relationship with history changes dramatically from country to country, and generation to generation (see, for example, Schuman and Scott, 1989) and this fact in itself supports the argument for the social construction of memory. It is also important to remember that the social techniques and cultural tools available at any given time, from the Irish oral tradition, to Facebook, change the ways in which individuals both recreate and access their personal histories and memories. The growing popularity of social-networking sites means not only the multiple telling of stories and identities, but also the transmission of a defined set of cultural values soaked in social meaning according to which we must tell our stories. In these instances, what has sometimes been termed 'collective memory' is really new cultural tools in the form of narratives and stories which we can use to develop new meanings and identities under the guise of memory.

Narratives and forgetting

> It's easy. You just remember eight. You see five, eight and four add up to seventeen. You remember eight, subtract it from seventeen and it leaves nine. Divide nine in half and you get four and five, and there you are—five hundred and eighty four. Easy.
>
> (H.M., in Parkin, 1996: 341)

We conclude this half of the chapter with a discussion of what we understand to be the final social constructs involved in the process of memory making—the importance of narratives and forgetting in remembrance. The stories we tell ourselves and each other allow us to make memories. Even where the neurological basis for functioning is severely damaged, as in the famous case of H.M., narratives still allow the remembrance of information, if only for the shortest period of time and to the confusion of those listening to the story. The story of H.M. focusing entirely on the neurological aspects of memory which this chapter argues are secondary to experience and social interaction, has yet to be explored from a sociocultural perspective.

Stories shape our memories into something meaningful by fusing past, present and future together in the creation of an identity. Elsewhere in this chapter, we have highlighted the fact that one of the abilities of a narrator is the ability to reshape history. If this concept is accepted then when it comes to memory there does not exist some unmediated, undistributed and neutral version of history as we only experience history through the narratives of communication and culture. The stories people tell about the past are purposeful, selective and interpreted through social interaction. A sociocultural perspective can make little sense of how H.M. holds in remembrance the number 584 precisely because his narrative has no meaning for us as social beings. Indeed for H.M., it is as if he lives in a world of his own, as his inability to create long-term memories isolates him not just in time, but in place. Since an operation which created bilateral surgical lesions in the hippocampal region, H.M.'s world has been only a few minutes long and each day he meets anew the researchers who are trying to help him remember. In his own words, he claims:

> Every day is alone in itself, whatever enjoyment I've had, and whatever sorrow I've had. Right now, I'm wondering. Have I done or said anything amiss? You see, at this moment everything looks clear to me, but what happened just before? That's what worries me. It's like waking from a dream; I just don't remember.
>
> (H.M., in Milner, 1970: 37)

Waking from a dream is a powerful analogy. We have all experienced what it feels like for H.M. in his daily experiences. Grasping at glimpses of images of ideas we are unable to fasten them in time and place precisely because they have no place in time or place. They are unreal and have no meaning for us because they are not part of our everyday participation in social interaction. Memory always implies a selection as stories retell themselves to us only when they are meaningful to our everyday experiences. In our remembrance of any given thing, our home, our parents, our siblings, we not only recall the past but compose it anew in our narrative of self and also in the ongoing narratives we continually construct of home, family, siblings by borrowing from other places and times to develop a more comprehensive understanding of these things—to create a more detailed story of our pasts. To remember somebody or something in a certain way is a very powerful process indeed, and influences not only present and future but also past interactions and experiences in relation to this person or thing.

This chapter, aligning with the main thesis of our text, suggests that from a sociocultural perspective, H.M.'s inability to selectively produce long-term memory might be due to the loss of social rather than mnemonic processes. Rather than a root cause, H.M.'s inability to remember could be seen as a symptom of a larger problem where H.M. has simply lost touch with the world and cannot create new memories because of this. He is still able to remember older memories and habits because they were a part of his meaningful story of self. Without the ability to develop our narrative of self in social contexts, H.M.'s case reveals that we simply cannot remember precisely because of the social, mediated and cultural nature of memory itself. One interpretation of H.M.'s story could be that he cannot socially construct memory so he is unable to hold new memories on a neurological basis and his story has many important implications for our developing sociocultural perspective on memory.

An essential part of the making of memory is the ability to forget. For our lives to have meaning we must forget most of what we experience. So, in this chapter, we understand forgetting as also central to the social construction of memory. Forgetting allows us to develop our identities in ways that we want to, overlooking and burying certain experiences that we do not want to perform as a part of our selves. Forgetting is also shared and mediated in communities of practice and requires collaboration, perhaps in an even more obvious way than remembering, if it is to be successful. It is also interesting that as Warnock points out in Fentress and Wickham (1992), memory is the only one of our mental functions we accept as working normally when it malfunctions. This may be because on some level we understand that the malfunction of memory occurs somewhere in the out there of lived experience, rather than in the neurology and genetic make-up of our brains.

Memory: a game of two halves . . . but what a second half!

The first half of this chapter has explored what, for us, makes a memory. Our sociocultural understanding of remembering centres on ideas such as relationships, communities, participation, places, identity, meaning, experience, culture, history, narrative and forgetting, and provides us with, if not a grammar of remembrance, then at the very least a new way to talk about and understand memories. In a complex and messy world we sometimes need a steer and remembering and forgetting allows us to, for a time, pin down and make concrete a particular aspect of our participation–our experience and our identity. From this perspective, memory does not have quite the same meaning as it does in psychology or biology and is about developing identity and learning to belong. Having outlined what we believe constitutes memory, and showing these to be socially and relationally constructed, we would like to conclude this chapter with a discussion of the functions of memory–why we remember and forget–unearthing again, the social meaning at the heart of these processes.

Someone needs to know: memory as knowledge

From a sociocultural perspective, one of the main functions of memory can be understood as the perpetuation of knowledge through processes of creation, development, transmission, translation, mediation and distribution. Powerful sociocultural ideas, yet these processes in play at the heart of remembering and forgetting illustrate that memories are first and foremost sources of knowledge, rather than truth, for individuals and communities. This knowledge is both developed through our social interactions and relationships and then also develops these processes as we learn new ways to be in our participation and reification of experiences. This knowledge is not confined to knowledge of literacies and texts. In this way, remembering can be understood as both a mirror and a lamp–a model of and a model for society (Schwartz, 1996). Due to its anachronism and constant and simultaneous negotiation of past, present and future, it is very easy to see memory as out of time with our experiences and interactions and misunderstand its function as personal and persistent internalization rather than an active process where we both learn and teach, articulating and transmitting memories as stories that reconstruct and renegotiate community, identity and place on our terms.

From this point of view, memory becomes a productive and social learning space where many different kinds of knowledge and understanding can be brought to experience to create a veneer of meaning over our shared practices. The knowledge in question here is always a part of relationships and lived experience, and is not concerned with remembering by heart. The remembering by heart that a sociocultural understanding of memory posits is one in which we remember experiences in certain ways because they interest us and speak to our previous memories and identities. An agentive use of memory allows us to recruit a meaning and a version of the past that complements our identities and tasks in the present, and through this mediated action we change who we are.

It is also important to understand that while memory cannot exist outside of the cultural tools that give it form and function, it is also true that no matter how powerful any cultural tool is it can never do the remembering by itself. Wanting to remember the name of the new actor in a movie I have just watched I can turn on my computer, 'Google' the question and have the answer flick up on screen in a matter of seconds. This scenario begs the complicated question of who or what does the remembering in this context? Without Google, I cannot bring to mind the name on the tip of my tongue, but without my mastery of the cultural tool the knowledge cannot come to mind either. This is an interesting dilemma and one in which Wertsch argues what becomes important in the social process of memory is not remembering what (the actor's name), but rather remembering how (the ability to use the cultural tools to hand to remember). Thus, memory also functions to allow people to become competent in cultural values and tools. This example again reveals the process of memory as occurring in the 'out there' of experience rather than the 'in here' of psychology, as memory is understood in terms of a mind that extends beyond the skin (Wertsch, 1991: 90).

The show must go on: connecting and communicating histories in memories

McGaugh asked, 'So if I say the year is 1987, the month is July and the day is the 15th?'

'Well I was working at the radio station at La Crosse and I had already been working on a play, backstage, on a production of "Peter Pan". But that particular date doesn't bring anything specific to mind.'

'You didn't give the day of the week,' said McGaugh.

'It was a Wednesday.'

'So how did you know it was a Wednesday?'

'The Fourth of July was on a Saturday that year.'

'How did you know the Fourth of July was on a Saturday?'

'Because it was two days after "Peter Pan" closed, which was on a Thursday ...'

'December 21st 1984?'

'I was with my older brother. We were driving across Iowa. We alternated saying words, stringing them together, to see if we could remember them later.'

'Fish, book, cheese, duck.'

He rattles off the words–Twenty three years later.

(Ellis, 2007)

Memory functions socially as a process that both communicates and connects diverse experiences of different individuals through time. The extract above from a conversation with another hyperthymestic sufferer, Brad Williams, shows how he uses memory to connect and communicate with and between time and place. Even more than this, as we read about Brad's story we too enter it, as points of recognition connect to our own experiences and we become drawn into his history and identity.

The ability to see the past as connected to present and future as Brad does is essential both in evolutionary terms and in our ability as individuals to learn. Seeing experiences as connected allows us to understand our own participation and make agentic and informed decisions. In a word, it allows us to learn. It communicates a past and by implication multiple presents and futures that become open to us. Thus, memory provides us not only with a source of cultural and community knowledge, but also as we remember we become more capable of using memory itself as a tool for learning. In this way, social memory is not only a mirror and a lamp, a model of and for society, but can be used, appropriated and manipulated by individuals as a cultural tool itself to rebuild the world in which we live.

Along with the idea of connective structure of societies (Assman, 1992: 293) we believe memory can be appropriated by nations as well as individuals to transform versions of the past. In this sense, memory itself becomes embodied as people actively and agentively employ memory to fight hard for their stories. Memory is always a site of contestation, and contestation implies activity and interaction on the social plane. Mosse (1990) highlights one example of the social appropriation of memory as a tool in his work on what he terms the myth of the war experience:

> As war was most brutal the tasks of consolation were made more public than ever. As a result ... the memory of the war was refashioned into a sacred experience which provided the nation with a new depth of religious feeling, putting at its disposal ever present saints and martyrs, places of worship, and a heritage to emulate.
>
> (Mosse, 1990: 7)

This idea of the appropriation of memory as a social tool can be traced back to Foucault, who introduces the dynamic of power relations to memory as he explains that if one controls people's memory, one controls their dynamism (Foucault, 1977). In this light, memory becomes important for cultural change and functions as the mediator through which different groups of people and individuals vie for a place in history and memory. Examples of this are evident in situations where a story or particular version of a past is remembered and recreated through generations, but the story is nothing special or interesting in itself. In these instances, it is the messages and cultural values and prompts that these stories carry with them that are important, rather than the stories themselves.

Alzheimer's disease and studies of forgetting highlight the social functioning of memory as the neuroscientific research stresses over and over that engaging in social interaction reduces the risk of developing Alzheimer's disease. A longitudinal study by Fratiglioni *et al.* (2000) suggests that a poor or limited social network can increase the risk of dementia by sixty per cent. This could be seen to suggest the centrality of social interaction to memory and the brain as normal neural and social functioning may be less likely to occur for individuals with poor social networks. Communication is central to our lives and studies such as these might suggest it is also central to our survival and very existence. We communicate our histories through other histories to become members of certain communities of practice.

Lest we forget: memory and identity ... and they all lived happily ever after

This chapter has presented a sociocultural reading of current memory studies and research in an attempt to tell our own story about how we remember. Seeing memory as a social process that occurs through relationships to community and place, identity and meaning, history and culture, and narratives and forgetting, we foreground the social functions of memory in terms of knowledge, mediation, history and identity. Like the studies we present and reinterpret, we want our story of memory to take its place among other stories of brain, mind and social interaction. To do this we have to use the stories of others, retelling the past for our own purposes in the present. We are acutely aware, however, that our story is one of so very many and so we would like to conclude this chapter with what, for us, are the most salient points for any understanding of memory.

Memory and identity as processes are inseparable. Understanding memory and identity in this way provides us with a new way of talking about our participation and a new theory for understanding our actions. In instances of learning and forgetting, we learn how to be as we construct and reconstruct selves in communities of practice. For us, identity is the main principle of how memory functions. As argued throughout this chapter, memory is a relational process that becomes visible through processes of social action as we search for meaning and identity in our lives.

Our identity as a species is dependent on our survival. The anticipation of the future has long been understood as the ultimate goal of evolution, and memory is central to our ability to do this successfully. Understood from this perspective, memory is something that has fundamentally evolved from outside of ourselves, as a means of protection and safety. Coming from the outside, about the outside, to be used in the outside by sharing with the outside, it is one of the mysteries of our culture as to why this deeply social process becomes in some way internalized for us and we mistake process for product alone.

Remembering is a creative process, but this chapter suggests that this process primarily functions according to external rather than internal factors. The stories that we have appropriated for our purposes and now return to the history of memory take up their previous places in time but are now somewhat different. They have been given new meaning in social processes. Now that you have read this chapter, for example, you will close the book, go to bed or walk the dog–but what you remember from these pages will be entirely dependent on your reasons for reading this chapter and your previous histories of participation and reification. You may be a doctoral student, a doctor, a parent or an educator, but, whatever your reason for reading this chapter, your remembrance of it will be affected by social and relational influences rather than the neurons and synapses in your brain. Neurons and synapses may be the physical building blocks of remembrance but to get from the bricks and mortar to the top of La Tour Eiffel we need more than the raw materials. We need more than the physical brain.

Shipwrecked minds

> They make glorious shipwreck who are lost in seeking worlds.
>
> (Gotthold Ephraim Lessing, 1868)

Returning to the questions posed at the beginning of this chapter, we may now be in a better position to answer them. Memory is a social process. It comes from our experiences with others in the world around us, and remains there as it becomes socially constructed and reconstructed in processes of communal remembering and forgetting. We believe that memories do not reside in our brain; they are a part of our practice and the world around us. We can never remember anything completely on our own, precisely because we are never on our own. Other people, artefacts, cultural tools come together in a process of remembering, which has individuals at its centre but not in isolation. Memory and identity are complex processes that occur simultaneously as we engage with different communities of practice in our day-to-day experiences.

Returning to the individual author story of memory wracking my brain to *place* that receptionist, or remember the name of my colleague, despite the fact I walk past it on his door every day, is a fallacious metaphor. When I see the receptionist in a different context I do not have the same social cues and experiences as when I normally meet her in the health centre. Brain plasticity, though taking into account the ability of the brain to change through experience, still places the brain as centre. We challenge this. Sitting in the lecture trying to remember the surname of my colleague, again in a different building to where we usually meet, I can remember his daughter's name because we have spoken recently about a sad incident where she hurt her arm. I can remember his dog's name because I have recently got the same breed of dog and we have been talking about them. I cannot remember his name because it does not connect in space or time with anything that is meaningful to my present practice—when we meet, I do not need to know his surname. In the lecture hall again, I *wrack my brains* trying to connect everything I can with my colleague so I can remember. I try to visualize the name on his door, I think about previous conversations, documents I have seen with his name on it. I check I know the surnames of everyone else I work with, in case something might jog my memory. In desperation I turn to cultural tools, I begin going through the alphabet to see what sounds right. A very frustrating experience, but one familiar to all of us. In the end I remember the name not because I have finally found it located in my brain, but because I have brought every social and cultural context I can think of to bear on my situation.

Going back in time to look once again at the meaning of the words we use reveals that *wracking my brain* might not be such a bad description after all of what happens as we struggle to remember—memory is not stored, we literally make the memory again and again with the help of the people and tools around us. The word 'wrack' relates to the Old English words 'wraec' meaning 'misery' and 'wrecan' meaning 'to punish'. In the fourteenth century, the word 'wrack' actually referred to a wrecked ship. Over time, it came to mean anything cast upon the shore and a modern dictionary will now define it as any of a number of coarse brown seaweeds. Within this discourse, neuroscience literally punishes and brings misery on our brains, a shipwrecked mind, as it looks for the memories that reside within it, without considering the context, lived experience and social interactions that this shipwrecked mind remains cut off from in a neuroscientific analysis.

> Again she plunges! hark! a second shock
> Bilges the splitting vessel on the rock;
> Down on the vale of death, with dismal cries,
> The fated victims shuddering cast their eyes
> In wild despair; while yet another stroke
> With strong convulsion rends the solid oak:
> Ah Heaven!—behold her crashing ribs divide!
> She loosens, parts, and spreads in ruin o'er the tide.
>
> (William Falconer, 1762:
> *Shipwreck, Canto III*, line 642)

Conclusion

In summary, this chapter has explored the social processes involved in memory, often neglected in neuroscientific research. Taking two very simple questions–What is memory? and Why do we remember and forget?–we reinterpret some well-known and not-so-well-known neuroscientific research on memory from a sociocultural perspective, making some claims about the role external relational factors play in remembering and forgetting.

What is memory?

We locate memory not in the brain, or even the mind, but in daily practice and culture. Quoting a neuroscientific definition of a memory in the making affords us little scope for understanding this complex process. Outlining the role, from a sociocultural perspective, that relationships with other people, communities and place play in the making of memory, we understand identity and meaning as central to memory. Broadening our understanding even further of what happens when we remember, we explore how language, culture, history and narrative all play a role. Alongside the past we understand the present as playing a vital role in the making of memory.

Why do we remember and forget?

Understanding memory as a sociocultural process, which, just like culture, is mediated and distributed by and across communities, remembering and forgetting serves us in our perpetuation or non-perpetuation of knowledge. In a sociocultural analysis, this knowledge is highly questionable as it is of course constructed by those involved in the process. This knowledge is co-created before it is further mediated and distributed. We also understand memory as facilitating communication and further developing a connection with the histories of ourselves and others. In this we explore the role of memory in identity and self.

The neuroscientific research presented in this chapter is very illuminating, but only when understood socioculturally. Jill Price's amazing story, for example, illustrates very well the role identity plays in memory. The famous story of H.M. also shows the importance of meaning, relationships and social experience in remembering.

Chapter 12

Sociocultural and neuroscientific metaphors for understanding learning

Introduction

By way of pulling together the key themes and pertinent points in our chapters thus far, this chapter identifies a range of metaphors associated with the learning process that are relevant in both neuroscientific and sociocultural perspectives. In line with our argument in Chapter Five, one can think of these metaphors as reifications–attempts to project meanings on the world–in this case on learning. Given our understanding that the duality of participation and reification is central to learning, we focus here on the metaphors themselves (the reifications) introduced in the previous chapters, which centred on experience and practices (participation). We do realize that as a duality when we talk about participation and reification, like two sides of the same coin, one essentially implies the other. In living they cannot be separated out and to borrow a classification from Barbara Rogoff are 'mutually constituting' (Rogoff, 1995: 141). Similar to Rogoff's understanding, we focus on the reifications in this chapter to foreground their nature and explore their meaning but that is all the while understanding that both participation and reification exist as a duality in daily practice.

While there are some theoretical features in common, not all are equally explicated in each theoretical perspective. In this chapter, we draw out some of these key features from the various chapters to extend and deepen our conceptualization of how learning is understood in a sociocultural view, and we revisit and connect these ideas with an important neuroscientific theme: that of plasticity. This chapter is both central and pivotal to our main thesis as it puts forward a number of heuristics emanating from both neuro and sociocultural sciences, highlighting their relative usefulness for thinking about human learning. At the end of the chapter, it elaborates on a key difference in the two approaches in relation to the place to look to understand learning.

Figured worlds, reifications and positionality

As we argued in several chapters (especially Chapters 6, 7 and 8), learning in a sociocultural view involves shifts in identity and ways of acting in the world.

Identities are central to learning and are ways of being, doing and participating in the different communities to which an individual belongs. They are made available and chosen through participation in activity and a person's agency or power to act lies in the choices made, the decision to choose one identity or position over another in a given situation. In this sense, identities can be thought of as resources that can be employed in the construal of a self. Identities can also be thought of as reifications that can be recruited in the presentation and representation of a self.

While they can be thought of as resources, identities incorporate the use of cultural tools or reifications which enable navigation between the self and the collective, the social order. James Wertsch talks about 'mediated action', which is a term designed to bridge the gap between the person and the social world or socio-historical context in which the person lives. Mediated action is about how a person's actions and interactions are accomplished by the use of cultural tools and reifications–shaping resources for acting or performing the self, examples being language/words/forms of discourse, cultural scripts and artefacts. What mediational means or tools people appropriate and how they appropriate them are of significance in understanding identity formation, and therefore learning. Such mediational means are acquired through experience, in participation and engagement with others. Hence, the acting subject and the tools used are enmeshed, constitutive, one inseparable from the other.

Similar to Wertsch's mediational means and Wenger's reifications, the anthropologists Dorothy Holland and colleagues use the heuristic device of 'figured worlds' to capture something of the relation between the personal world of the individual and the wider world of social relations. They explain the notion of a figured world by inviting the reader to imagine the world of academia: '[w]hat if there were a world called academia, where books were so significant that people would sit for hours on end, away from friends and family, writing them?' They go on to say: '[p]eople have the propensity to be drawn to, recruited for, and formed in these worlds, and to become active in and passionate about them' (Holland et al., 1998: 49).

So, 'figured worlds' are 'as if' worlds, imaginary versions of ways of being, which individuals may appropriate or are recruited into and which are then reproduced and developed through the practices of their participants. A figured world is populated by the (imagined) characters and types who carry out its business and who have ways of interacting within it as well as orientations towards it. Drama, play and improvisation provide opportunities within education to inhabit virtual worlds and to imagine other possible ways of being.

The figured worlds (e.g. disabled learner, obedient pupil) that were made relevant and available to Daniel, Laura, Adam and Peter in Chapter 7 were central to the kinds of people they did or could become and to the kinds of practices they engaged in. Just as one can display multiple identities, one can inhabit more than one figured world. Figured worlds are meaning systems which mediate our behaviour. Some figured worlds, suggest Holland *et al.* (1998: 41), are denied us and some we deny to others, some we miss by accident while others we learn fully.

As demonstrated in the various vignettes and accounts in earlier chapters, for example the teacher in the example in Chapter 5, Daniel in Chapter 7, and Rory and Patricia in Chapter 10, while an individual may choose an identity in a given situation, such a choice is always constrained, it is never simply a free choice as it depends on the affordances of the situation. Positionality or relationality captures this concept for sociocultural scientists. Positionality is about the way behaviour signals the nature of social relations with others. It has to do with relations of power, prestige, entitlement, influence, affiliation and status, and as such is always imbued with emotion (Chapter 10). Positional identities therefore depend upon who is present in the interaction (Holland *et al.*, 1998; Davies and Harré, 2001). Positional identities refer to a view of oneself in relation to others in a given situation, how one can enter a conversation, what one can say, what emotions one can express, in sum, one's fitness for certain claims and rights (Holland *et al.*, 1998). Day-to-day, moment-by-moment encounters are the stuff of identity formation and relationality is, therefore, inescapable. People are bound by the structures and spaces–the cultural imaginaries–that are created by the collective, but how they inhabit these structures and figured worlds is not predetermined. They can do so in creative and indeed oppositional ways. What is fundamental is that individuals are shaped by their history of participation in different settings and communities. All of this shows the complexity of learning in a sociocultural perspective.

Sedimentation and lamination

Terms like 'sedimentation', 'fossilization' and 'lamination' are used in the sociocultural literature to explain the nature of identity formation (Holland *et al.*, 1998; Holland and Leander, 2004; Wortham, 2006). Vygotsky, for instance, used the word 'fossilization' to mean characteristic ways of acting that have been practised enough to have become stabilized, at least in the short term. While fluid and emergent in the moment-by-moment, the process of identification is also slow as these metaphors imply. The long term happens in the everyday, moment-by-moment. In Daniel's case, for instance, he was not afforded opportunities to demonstrate himself as able in his primary school–his identity was one of not belonging to the learned community and this identity thickened over time. Unsurprisingly, over time he began to distance himself from that community and to figure other worlds for himself. As he slowly (and mostly invisibly) distanced himself and was distanced from the identity of learned boy, as his experiences were interpreted and reflected back to him by those around him, he was evolving and was granted another identity outside of school as a popular, cool teenager, which involved other kinds of learning and becoming (Hall, 2008). This is not to suggest that identities are singular, rather, they are multiple, since individuals belong to several communities of practice (Wenger, 1998). Daniel's identity as 'not learned boy' endured throughout the later years of his primary schooling.

Lamination suggests something of the layering of events over time, whereby an individual's experience and its social interpretation by others shape and feed each other. Identities are layered and multidimensional. It also suggests solidification and how identities become dispositional. Identities build up and bed down through interactional shifts as they are slowly ascribed and endure as experiences and participation and engagement are repeated and reproduced over time (Wortham, 2006). Adam's case is a most interesting example of such ascription. The ethnographies of Adam, Daniel and others make it possible to 'see' the emerging identities and their solidification over time.

Ethnography and longitudinal work also allow one to uncover the traces, to make visible the history of participation along with the repeated practices and the disruption of usual practices. And practices, of course, can be disrupted. This is exactly what happened in Daniel's case when he entered secondary school. Here he was provided with a new space for agency and the authoring of a different self, one that challenged the old identity of restricted competency, and that did align with the community of able person and learner. So, while the process of becoming a particular kind of person, lamination, is largely unconscious, it is not irreversible as evidenced in Daniel's secondary schooling: 'ruptures of the taken for granted can remove . . . aspects of positional identities from automatic performance and recognition to commentary and recognition' (Holland et al., 1998: 157). This disruption or unlayering happens at the collective level as well as the individual level–at the collective level, assumptions shift allowing for transformation on the part of the group. For Daniel, 'alternative figurings' became available in interpreting the moment-by-moment events in his new school with new sets of peers and teachers and with new activities.

Such ethnographies can challenge educators' more purified conceptions of learning as academic, and such conceptions tend to mask the social processes involved in all learning and development. Though he doesn't use either term 'lamination' or 'sedimentation', Gergen (2010b: 79) captures the complexity of the process in a way that links with our previous discussion of meaning, cultural scripts and collective voices in this text:

> We largely derive our coordination from our previous immersion in a range of other relationships. Actions within these relationships typically derive their intelligibility from traditions of long standing. We arrive in the present relationship as extensions of the distant past. And as the current relationship unfolds, it serves to reform the meaning of the past. These interchanges may be supplemented and transformed by still others in the future.

Plasticity and lamination

Neuroscientists' heuristic of plasticity is akin to the sociocultural heuristics of sedimentation and lamination in several respects and it is a trope that is central to a biological notion of learning. The plastic trope in neuroscience extends to road infrastructure. In an interview on Bloomberg TV, the Nobel laureate, Eric Kandell, talked about some genetically-based brain structures as 'highways'; these, he confidently claimed, are the same for all and are part of the hard-wired system; 'smaller roads' are shaped partly by genetics, partly by environment while 'cow paths and local roads' are controlled entirely by experience and environment. Akin to the cultural neuroscientists discussed in Chapter 4, as well as Chapter 2 on defining brain, the key question for him and his colleagues is how experience and environment build on the hardwired system.

Plasticity is a metaphor that seeks to capture the brain's physical ability to change throughout life and specifically refers to the changes in the brain's circuitry as a result of experiences, incorporating associations, memories and feelings (e.g. Greenfield, 2000). It refers to the changes in internal structure of neurons among which the most significant are the area of synapses and the increase in the number of synapses between neurons. Neural connections can be made or honed. In contrast, they can be weakened or actually pruned. The assumption is that changes in the physical brain manifest in changes in our capabilities to do things. As demonstrated in Chapter 6, experience creates the connections which in turn enable learning. It is a deeply personal process, specific to the individual in that experience becomes unique to the individual and memories stored in the brain facilitate an interpretative stance from which to make sense of the world: 'we see the world in terms of what we have seen already' argues Greenfield (2000: 62). Plasticity gets at the idea that the brain is not static but responds to events and circumstances.

The 'plastic' metaphor, alluding to the 'use it or lose it' principle, aligns with the ideas about identity in a sociocultural view. It would appear that experiences that are repeated over time result in extensive neural networks in the brain, while neural connections resulting from few or limited experiences wither and die. The assumption is that the strength of synaptic connections is indicative of learning. A well-known example, arguably, discussed in Chapter 6, is the study of the structure of the hippocampus in London taxi drivers. As we noted earlier in relation to this research, part of the brain associated with memory and learning–the hippocampus–in this group was found to be different from that of non-taxi drivers and it decreased in size on their retirement. Key, from a comparative sociocultural view, is that the new networks are created by experience in the world and are not pre-figured by nature. And, as brought out in the work of Susan Greenfield, individual experience varies because of our histories and contexts, our neural networks are individualized and highly dynamic. As she says, 'we create our own brains'. In neuroscience, consolidation refers to how existing memories are strengthened over time.

The neuroscientific concept of consolidation in memory, introduced in Chapter 11, is akin to lamination as described above and to sedimentation. Recent neuroscientific evidence challenges an idea, previously assumed by the field, that new information is imposed on a tabula rasa. The new evidence suggests instead that new information must be interwoven with the person's earlier stock of memories. Early studies on consolidation had shown that memory could be erased, but new evidence shows that an appropriate experience can reactivate a memory. Thus, an existing memory is reorganized to incorporate new learning–it doesn't just disappear. The neuroscientific notion of consolidation and reconsolidation is about how new information is integrated with older information, and the research suggests that both processes–consolidation and reconsolidation–are in a never-ending cycle of modification and adjustment in line with experience (McKenzie and Eichenbaum, 2011). Neuronal plasticity as a lifelong process parallels the sociocultural heuristic of sedimentation or the thickening of identity and the idea that it is not an irreversible process. Appropriate opportunity to disrupt old identities and taken-for-granted ways of acting and being can transform the person so he or she can, in time, evolve new kinds of relationships with others and with knowledge. The 'old' identity is never quite 'shed', it is part of one's history of participation and it can re-emerge–hence the metaphor of lamination. In Daniel's case, one identity was submerged, overtaken by more (or less) accomplished sets of relations in a new lamination. The ethnography showed a history of participation that was, at the primary level, one of failure and one of finding success outside school, in other pursuits, while the transition to secondary school marked an opportunity afforded to and taken by him to shape a new self that aligned more closely with academic learning and success. The main point for now is the similarity in the metaphors and their apparent suitability to capture elements of the learning process.

Sociocultural research has long shown that the human situation is educative, that learning is ubiquitous and experience is pedagogical. The ordinary, the everyday is important, with every moment an occasion for learning (e.g. Lave, 1996). Perhaps, as Lave advises, learning is not something in itself, it is part of social life. Learning is living and living inevitably involves learning. Both sciences–sociocultural and neuroscientific–challenge the idea that learning is place or time bound. They also highlight the significance of opportunity to learn. These are important alignments in both perspectives that are captured by metaphors such as plasticity and lamination. However, the differences in looking through the two lenses are fundamental.

Fundamental difference: in or beyond the head

A major difference in the two perspectives on development and learning is that in one the processes of thinking and learning are not contained within the head or individual brains but rather are spread over people, things and environments as illustrated in the analyses of the accounts in most chapters. And the environment and the person are enmeshed. One could be described as a mediational perspective on learning where attention has to be focused on the range of tools in the process of that learning. Reification and participation are involved simultaneously. The neuroscientific lens is much narrower, focused exclusively on the physical brain: here the focus is entirely and exclusively in the head, more specifically, in the brain. The person and her or his environment are completely distinct from each other. This is clearly exemplified in the following extract from one of the interviews we conducted at an international conference on neuroscience in 2011:

> For me, learning means updating an internal model generated and maintained by the brain about the world. The brain is distant from the world. All it has are sensory inputs that are ambiguous, noisy and the brain has to make sense of them–any given particular input obtained needs an image encoded by neurons in the brain and then the brain has to interpret–something causing it in the real world. In order to do that it has to have a model. That model is maintained and updated by the brain in light of prediction ... and that updating is learning. Changing of the parameters of the mathematical model by the physiological architecture of the brain.
>
> (Interviewee H, from the International
> Neuroscience Conference, Wicklow, 2011)

We can now offer a more expansive explanation of opportunity to learn in the light of the metaphors highlighted in this and earlier chapters. We suggest that while neuroscientific studies acknowledge the significant role of experience in the shaping of brains, sociocultural researchers offer a more complicated and nuanced understanding of experience that is highly pertinent to extending access to learning and, by definition, identity. This is so because it offers insights into the how of learning. In order to understand opportunity to learn, it is important to look beyond the individual and the individual's particular experiences to the wider system and distributions and to a multifaceted and relational view in which 'agent, activity and world mutually constitute one another' (Lave and Wenger, 1991: 33). In their ethnographies, McDermott, Hall, DePalma and others show the effort, improvisation and ingenuity that go into the identification process, not just on the part of the focused individual, but on the part of all the participants who are part of the process, some of whom who may be distant from the actual context–for example, textbook writers, policy makers–but all are relevant, nevertheless. As Leander et al. (2010) bring out in their research review, a multiplicity of resources are involved in the processes of identification and therefore in an opportunity to learn. Or, as McDermott and Varenne (1995) tellingly put it: in every society, it takes many people–both disablers and their disabled–to mark people as able and disabled.

The notion of sedimentation or lamination is helpful because it calls attention to what is usually an invisible process–it points to the particular events and actions that matter in the stabilizing of identity. In other words, it suggests a history. In Adam's situation for instance, it was not just any old activity that positioned him as 'not learned'. Repetition or opportunity to show himself as 'not learned' was not simply an abstract process but involved a particular kind of occasion when being positioned as disruptive, talkative, and so on, was noticed and marked. This is a relational process. This is pivotal and something a neuroscientific orientation misses, with its biological focus only on the brain.

Having access to the valued practice is not all of a piece, opportunity to learn is not about being in the same environment. Opportunity to learn is not necessarily of the same order in classrooms. Ivinson and Murphy (2007) demonstrate quite starkly in relation to gender that just because all members of a year group are in the same setting does not mean they all have an equal opportunity to access the valued knowledge. McDermott also demonstrates this in the case of Adam and we saw this too in the case of Peter (Chapter 7). The following become pertinent questions: who has the opportunity to learn and what is available to be learned? What resources are deployed in the promotion of learning for different people and how are different people enabled to take advantage of the learning on offer? Who is included and excluded from the valued practice and what are the mechanisms by which inclusion and exclusion occurs? Such questions are at the heart of a socio-cultural view and shift us away from mere epistemological issues such as what is to be known and to what extent has it been achieved, towards historical, political, economic and cultural analyses. If, as socioculturalists argue, identity is something that is done as opposed to something that one has, the enactment, performance, the doing is the focus of attention and this doing is always dependent on the situation and the available resources people bring to the situation.

We acknowledge the contribution of neuroscience to our increased appreciation of the importance of a nurturing environment for (positive) learning to flourish (although, again, this importance is not unique to neuroscience). Such nurturing would bear on the quality of the social environment and available interactions, the nature of nutrition, the role of physical exercise, and the importance of sleep, as summarized in the OECD Report in 2007. In broad terms, neuroscience has confirmed the interdependence of physical and intellectual wellbeing and the close connection of the emotional and cognitive dimensions–themes already well-established by the inseparability of such dimensions by sociocultural science. While, according to the TLRP/ESRC report (2009), neuroscience provides evidence to suggest that impoverished environments inhibit neural development, there is no neuroscientific evidence currently to show that enriched environments enhance it. What counts as impoverished or enriched is left unstated. Yet, the research pertaining to the developing adolescent brain, especially in frontal and parietal cortices where synaptic pruning starts after puberty, suggests that formal schooling along with social experience may be hugely significant in the shaping of the teenage brain.

The complexity of opportunity to learn and the distributed nature of learning itself direct research and professional practice towards the need to trace the relationship between learners and their experiences in the world (see Gee, 2003). Questions about equity and fairness in education become questions about systems, policies, distributions, resources and access to all these. It expands our conception of what counts as a learning environment and the diversity of contexts, situations and peoples. What, for instance, of the diversity of people in a classroom, their histories and geographies and particularly their histories of participation? How is the opportunity to learn organized and accomplished through trajectories connecting places? (Leander *et al.*, 2010). There is a need to go beyond cognitive and neurological perspectives of mind and brain to address these educational questions. Opportunity to learn is not simply about all being in the same environment because environments are personal as well as communal. This would be a profoundly impoverished notion of opportunity to learn (Gee, 2003). While we have alluded to the kinds of issues and questions that need to be taken into account in providing fair and equitable access to learning, space prevents us here in offering a detailed exemplification of the principle of opportunity to learn. Also, while accounts exist (e.g. Roth and Tobin, 2007; Lankshear and Knobel, 2003; Comber *et al.*, 2006), there is a need for far more publications that provide portrayals and cases of the implementation of this principle within a sociocultural interpretivist framework.

Challenging the dominant model in education

While some education researchers are drawing on sociocultural insights in their studies of learning, the dominant paradigm in practice, policy and educational research is not one that recognizes the world as mediated. Rather, the dominant one is actually more akin to a neurocognitive perspective in some, though not all, respects. We end this chapter by noting how both perspectives interface with some dominant thinking about learning.

The hegemony of the boundedness of the person is especially evident in education discourse and practice and sociocultural theorizing has had some, though limited, impact on the thinking of educators. Jean Lave describes and critiques the dominant model of learning where learning or coming to know is viewed as a 'withdrawal from life' with the consequence that what one withdraws from, life itself, is not a space for learning (Lave, 1996; 2008). The result of this thinking is a split between learning and the application of learning with reduced status attributed by society to more applied, vocational activities compared to 'purer, specialist pursuits' involving libraries, laboratories, colleges and universities. For Lave, this conjures up images of religious prophets, philosophers, poets and painters sitting atop mountains and hilltops, dwelling in wildernesses, cells, garrets, logs in forests, islands and pond sides and, of course, academics in ivory towers. It conjures up separation, solitude, withdrawal from the contamination and hurly burly of ordinary life, from society. The problem is that we still tend to think of learning as though it happens at a remove from the everyday, only in the classroom, the seminar room, the lecture theatre, and that learning does not take place in everyday ways (see Chapter 6).

The notion of withdrawing from life in order to learn also results in a split between knowledge and the application of knowledge, with the latter enjoying less prestige than the former. Referring to the production of scientific knowledge in seventeenth-century England, Steven Shapin provides some relevant comments, the legacies of which still linger. He says 'the producers of our most valued knowledge are not in society. At the point of securing their knowledge, they are said to be outside the society to which they mundanely belong. And when they are being most authentically intellectual agents, they are said to be most purely alone' (Shapin, 1991: 192). Once again there is the clear separation of the individual from society and there is also the value attributed to different kinds of knowledge. Brain studies are incapable of generating insights on matters of value and judgements as to what knowledge is of most worth in different situations. A sociocultural perspective is essential for such analysis.

Ways of thinking about learning, not learning itself, bring about the dualisms and false distinction between learning and living, between the individual and society, and between knowledge and applied knowledge (see Chapters 4 and 5). Learning is not just something that happens in particular places at particular times, but is part and parcel of engaging in the world. Undoubtedly there are different opportunities for learning but there is no distinction between learning in one setting (say school) and learning in everyday life (e.g. home)–the process is the same. Learning is potentially everywhere and both sociocultural and neuroscientific perspectives would align in their emphasis on experience as pedagogical. What becomes central, then, is the value placed on the learning in question by the community. It is also of pivotal importance to sociocultural researchers of learning in seeking to understand how humans change, the way they participate in activity, how different practices are valued or not within different communities, what people do and what it is possible to do in different situations and with different people, and how opportunities to learn are extended or denied people, and how people are agentic in this denial and facilitation. Sociocultural science is interested in the nature of those kinds of questions and relations and what they can help us understand about learning, the person and experience. Neuroscience is less about providing or defending the existence of those relations and, in fact, is silent on issues to do with the politics and values of various educational experiences. Yet, these questions are of pivotal importance in education.

Conclusion

Metaphors are important because they help us think. They shape our thinking and if they shape our thinking, they no doubt impact our practice (Sfard, 2009).

If there is one word that signifies neuroscience in relation to education, it surely is 'plasticity'. It is a metaphor that is a source of a new way of speaking about development. A common, intuitive notion, plasticity as a metaphor has the power to link the intuitive and the scientific. Intuitively, plastic conveys a sense of the malleable, but it also conveys a sense of artificiality and lack of depth and authenticity. It's not entirely real. Anna Sfard (2009: 40) observes that 'metaphors enable conceptual osmosis between colloquial and scientific discourses, letting our primary intuition shape scientific ideas and letting the formal conceptions feed back into the intuition'. The choice of the plastic metaphor arguably proved very powerful for neuroscience in that it most definitely captured the imagination with its implications of lifelong potential for learning right into old age. It fits neuroscience's discourse of hope and expectation. However, the rising status of neuroscience and the potential impact on sociocultural theorizing is a theme we take up in our two final chapters.

Chapter 13

Tensions and struggles over explanations for learning

Resisting a neurobiological take over

It is in the brain that everything takes place ... it is in the brain that the poppy is red, that the apple is odorous, that the skylark sings.

Oscar Wilde

And of course, the brain is not responsible for any of the sensations at all. The correct view is that the seat and source of sensation is the region of the heart.

Aristotle

Introduction

In a book aimed at the general reader, one high-profile neuroscientist proclaimed that neuroscience 'is perfectly positioned as a discipline not only to help explain why we are as we are, but to explore how we might change and be changed' (Greenfield, 2008: x of Preface). Given the proclamations of such scholars about the potential of neuroscience to inform how we learn, the project of our book is an entirely reasonable one. We have sought to find connections and disconnections across neuroscience and sociocultural science that are relevant to the broad areas of learning, experience and personhood.

One of the telling messages from our exploration of the claims of neuroscience for learning is that the field is very much in its infancy with very little substantive analyses that can, as yet, inform us about the way people learn or the way learning can be enhanced. Most, if not all, of the neuroscientists whose work we read acknowledge the newness of their discipline and the limited applications to education of the current state of the evidence. Yet, enough claims emphasize the potential of existing neuroscience to impact education, and these claims include agencies and commercial outfits which may profit from products that purport to be based on it (e.g. Kawashima, 2008; Sousa, 2006). There is plenty of misinformation in the popular press, and media reports frequently exaggerate 'breakthroughs' and claim 'paradigm-shifting' work (see Whiteley, 2012 for a review). Several surveys (e.g. TLRP/ESRC, 2009; Dommett et al., 2011) have shown that teachers are eager to learn about what neuroscience has established about the brain and how it works. This applies to educational researchers as well. It is of note that in April/May 2013, the neuroscience parallel sessions at the biggest and best-known educational research conference in the world–the American Educational Research Association (AERA)–had only standing room for delegates such was the interest in the topics being discussed. Yet teachers express disappointment and some surprise when they discover that there are few major implications emerging for their practice in the classroom that they were not aware of from other lines of inquiry (Dommett *et al.*, 2011). Our analysis in this book leads us to the conclusion that one of the interesting and valuable outcomes of the neuroscientific turn is the confirmation it offers for some claims about learning already generated from sociocultural theory.

Compared to neuroscience, sociocultural science and theorizing yields little allure for the general population or many education practitioners, and is not usually acknowledged by education policy makers. The title of some official reports in education, specifically the OECD's (2007a) *The Birth of a Learning Science*, could be interpreted as indicating that we do not already know about learning from other sciences, especially sociocultural work. Indeed, when neuroscience and education are talked about together the assumption usually is that 'education theory' is all of a piece to which neuroscience research can be added.

In this chapter of the book, we try to explain the allure of neuroscience compared to sociocultural science, given that the latter has so many insights for education as demonstrated throughout this book. We show the tensions in operation in the two discourses and, importantly, we argue that sociocultural ways of conceptualizing learning are in danger of being marginalized even further by neuroscience. We believe that the uptake of the neurosciences may undermine, and, at worst, deny the place of more constitutive psychological perspectives on learning, identity formation and selfhood. Undoubtedly, discourses of neuroscience are likely to refashion how we talk about learning and the person. The following themes are developed in this chapter: the quest for a centre; the assumption of an exact science; colonizing discourses and what gets lost; and, epistemological issues.

The centrepiece: it's all in the head?

Sociocultural theorizing, as a constitutive approach, challenges the notion that what happens in the head of the lone individual is adequate as a basis for understanding the person, learning and human action. It challenges the existence of a presence, a core, some one thing that accounts for human selfhood. It contends that a focus only on the individual, without reference to the context and sets of relations, lacks the kind of explanatory power and depth needed (a) to understand human action, consciousness and experience, and (b) to intervene to support people's future behaviour and understanding. Neuroscientific theorizing privileges the individual, separate from context, history and relations, and within the individual, the brain itself is epistemologically privileged. The exclusive focus on an integrative brain as the centrepiece of human intentionality, action and explanation for action raises an important point of difference in the two approaches, and this difference is, we believe, relevant to the intrigue of neuroscience.

The establishment of a centre, a core, an essence, is deeply satisfying, not just to the layperson but to researchers and professionals as well. In offering something that is apparently tangible and real, a focus on the brain simplifies and tidies up an otherwise messy, enactive, centre-less world–the kind of messy world socioculturalists register, speak to and seek to understand in situ. What is interesting in this regard, then, is that neuroscience's search for or assumption of a centre is far from new. Despite its shiny, new feel and innovative technological methods, the search for a centre is an ancient theme that recent brain science has reinvigorated. Clifford Rose's article 'Cerebral localisation in antiquity' in the *Journal of the History of the Neurosciences*, sketches the lineage:

> Fragments of neurology can be found in the oldest medical writings in antiquity. Recognizable cerebral localization is seen in Egyptian medical papyri. Most notably, the Edwin Smith papyrus describes hemiplegia after a head injury. Similar echoes can be seen in Homer, the Bible, and the pre-Hippocratic writer Alcmaeon of Croton. While Biblical writers thought that the heart was the seat of the soul, Hippocratic writers located it in the head. Alexandrian anatomists described the nerves, and Galen developed the ventricular theory of cognition whereby mental functions are classified and localized in one of the cerebral ventricles. Medieval scholars, including the early Church Fathers, modified Galenic ventricular theory so as to make it a dynamic model of cognition. Physicians in antiquity subdivided the brain into separate areas and attributed to them different functions, a phenomenon that connects them with modern neurologists.
>
> (Clifford Rose, 2009: 239)

Clifford Rose goes on to cite evidence of how a cell doctrine of brain function was exercising philosophers and others for more than a thousand years. There is a reference to an eleventh-century manuscript, which seemingly contains the earliest known illustration of the brain in the Western world. In this illustration, the brain is labelled as 'cold and moist', whereas the heart is assumed to be 'warm and dry'. Over time, various body locations competed to be the centrepiece: the brain, the liver, the heart, the entire body, the ventricles, the pineal gland. The eighteenth century saw the brain as central in determining the 'essence of man' (Karenberg, 2009: 252). Kenneth Gergen says how once it became accepted that the source of human activity was interior and natural, exploration of the cortical basis of mental functioning was inevitable. The related fields of evolutionary psychology, behavioural genetics and cognitive psychology with their universal, inherent tendencies pushed towards cortical determination. The arrival of brain-scanning technologies accelerated this development and resulted in the case of a centre being sealed (Gergen, 2010a). Now the cortex is assumed as the point of origin, the preferred location, the location that matters for 'executive' control and decision making. Specifically, the prefrontal cortices are now commonly associated with executive functions such as planning, judgement, imagination, empathy, decision making, memory work and self-regulation (Damasio, 1994; Stuss and Levine, 2002). Activation in the brain is taken to imply awareness and consciousness. It is also assumed to equate with 'the self': in a recent presentation Immordino-Yang (2013) claimed that neuroimaging is a tool 'to see inside and provide a sense of the self' and noted that what she and her colleagues are really studying is the 'neurobiology of the self'. Such claims stem from her own research on brains in scanners that indicate, for instance, that different areas of the brain are activated when the person admires a skill or admires a virtue.

The preoccupation with establishing the site of the soul or the core of the person has endured throughout history. While the site has shifted over time the assumption is that this time, like other times, we've got it right.

Sociocultural scholars are highly dubious about the presumption of some thing being available to be found, some phenomenon that will explain agency and human action. Susan Greenfield's *The Quest for Identity in the Twenty-First Century* (2008) seeks to link identity and neurobiology. Areas of the brain are responsible for certain activity but in the end the network metaphor is drawn on when particular areas are deemed not to be solely responsible for activity. In a deconstructive analysis of texts that were described as 'remarkable' and 'groundbreaking' in the neuroscientific field, van Ommen and van Deventer (2011) challenge the logic of neuroscientific findings and claims in relation to a centre. They conducted an in-depth analysis of two key texts by the renowned neuropsychologist Elkhonon Goldberg, one such being *The Executive Brain: Frontal Lobes and the Civilised Mind* (Goldberg, 2001). In their analysis of Goldberg's oeuvre, they find that the function ascribed to the frontal lobes is that of a 'mental juggler' involving 'working memory': organizing, selecting and engaging in rapid switching between information. They explain Goldberg's claims, citing his words as follows: 'they [the frontal lobes] are the site of the most advanced and complex functions in all the brain, the so-called executive functions', the 'most uniquely "human" of all the components of the brain' (2), which enable 'intentionality, foresight, and planning' (23). The frontal lobes 'know what type of information is stored where, but not the specific information itself' (74) (van Ommen and van Deventer, 2011: 263). According to Goldberg, the frontal lobes 'makes you who you are', 'defines your identity' and 'encapsulates your drives, your ambitions, your personality, your essence' (p. 1, cited in van Ommen and van Deventer, 2011: 263).

These researchers go on to interrogate the logic of Goldberg's metaphor of conductor and orchestra to describe how the frontal lobes work. Their insightful, logical and discursive analysis of Goldberg's text shows that the very concepts that allow Goldberg to ground his conductor–orchestra analogy simultaneously act as the same grounds that undermine his characterization of the frontal lobes as leader. They show how the same argument that claims the frontal lobes as the 'conductor': 'simultaneously subjugates them and exposes the impossibility of the full presence of the leader (as site and as function)' (van Ommen and van Deventer, 2011: 264). As the frontal lobes are both conductor and orchestra, 'neither fully leader nor fully player', the relationship frustrates any clear distinction or location of function. Their deconstruction of Goldberg's 'executive brain' shows that the frontal lobes are always in need of help, in need of some additional backup to carry out various functions: yet, another brain structure has to be brought on board. Thus, they point out, the prefrontal cortex is always decentred and the executive functions are a centre 'on the move, their axis shifting continuously depending on the situation at hand'.

The ambition of neuroscience to pin down a centre, 'a point from which agency can proceed' (van Ommen and van Deventer, 2011: 273), falls apart on the same basis on which it is claimed. The contribution of van Ommen and van Deventer's analysis is not the demonstration that a deconstructive reading of this particular project pinpoints its failure, but rather that any initiative aimed at the location of a centre for agency, and any other human dimension, will inevitably fail. The assumption of a centre is misguided and the search for it a pointless exercise. But, as the historical literature shows, the search for a centre is as old as it is alluring.

It is its historical context that some argue confers on neuroscience its status and popularity. The historian Fernando Vidal (2009), in pointing out that there is nothing novel about understanding selfhood in terms of the brain, says that it is precisely this history that accounts for the close linking of identity with the neurological. He argues that it is the history lineage rather than its newness that makes the brain the location of the 'modern self' (Vidal, 2009: 5). The ferocious critique of neuroscience by the philosopher, Hacker, and the neuroscientist, Bennett, makes a similar point (see Meloni, 2011 and Bennett and Hacker, 2008). Hacker and Bennett imply that the venerable meta-physical tradition reinforces the naturalness and power of neuroscience's explanations.

An exact, all-encompassing science, but with major omissions!

There is no doubt that sociocultural science is far more conceptually complicated, complex and nuanced than its distant neighbour, neuroscience, when it comes to understanding learning. This is not to suggest that neuro-science is not technically complex, because it is extremely so, variously requiring a thorough understanding of such disciplines as biology, physiology and genetics, to name but a few. But what has to be explained is different in each case. If everything begins and ends in the brain, then once we understand the biology of the brain and how the brain reacts in and to the world, we have cracked the problem. If, on the other hand, this is inadequate as a starting point, that there are other complex phenomena that have to be taken into account as well, then human learning is not so easily explained. Nikolas Rose argues that neuroscience establishes not only what has to be explained, but also what counts as an explanation (Rose, 2003) and, simply put, it has to explain what the brain does. Mind is simply reduced to what the biological brain does. The same can be said for learning, experience, selfhood, motivation, emotion, and so on–all are to be reduced to what the brain does.

Accompanying this stance is an optimism and faith in science that is probably unprecedented. It is as if neuroscience has researched and explained all aspects of human existence. Kenneth Gergen (2010a) offers a list, complete with several neuroscience references to empirical studies in each case: aggression, happiness, altruism, social understanding, suicide, emotion, moral, economic and social decision-making, romantic love, empathy, envy, aesthetic judgement, ethics, jealousy, self-injury, personality structure, social values, cultural conflict. The source of all is assumed to be the brain. One of the best-known neuroscientists, Antonio Damasio, who has published several books on emotion and creativity, claims that the 'self' is no more than physiology, an effect caused by the harmonious, simultaneous interaction of different parts of the biological brain (Damasio, 2005). This view is illustrated by one of our neuroscience interviewees when he explained how plasticity and learning are synonymous and how learning can be measured:

> Analogy of plasticity, you will have to challenge patients by learning processes–make them learn something and measure levels of plasticity expressed in the brain, the trick is to identify it. Tricky but doable. The trick is–we can't place electrodes into our patients' brains and measure single cell or channels but we can obtain core brain measures via non-invasive MRI and quantify the collective connectivity. If learning is going on we identify plasticity–we are looking for change of connectivity during learning process. First quantify the learning or connectivity and then relate that to the computational model–that helps us understand what learning goes on.
>
> (Interviewee H, from the International
> Neuroscience Conference, Wicklow, 2011)

This reductivist thrust is to attribute learning, experience, emotion, will and agency to nature, and to study all such phenomena as if they are entirely natural and biological. Moreover, all are assumed to be accessible through this route.

As all life and life's processes get reduced to biological processes but with a high degree of malleability, it follows that, theoretically at least, interventions can optimize functions so the person can reach their full potential. Programmes and drug treatments can be (and are already) targeted to superior performance, while individuals have choices and are in control of their brains and therefore themselves. Nancy Andreasen, whose work we mentioned earlier in relation to neuroscience and genius, describes her field as offering 'enlightenment and knowledge that can conquer pain and suffering, and build healthier, better, braver brains and minds' (2001: 4). Similarly, the Institute for Neuro-Innovation and Translational Neuroscience at Stanford's School of Medicine, on its website, describes its work as follows: 'Technological advances are yielding detailed genetic and molecular details in the rewiring of neural circuits. These details will help explain how we learn and remember' (http://neuroscience.stanford.edu/research/programs/nprpage.html, accessed 12 January 2013). Neuroscience is a discourse of hope and optimism, which partially explains its relative grip on the imagination over a sociocultural perspective. No such claims can be made for sociocultural perspectives on human beings, which completely challenges the notion that the human being is knowable in such absolute terms.

While simplification and reduction are to be expected in most research studies including ethnographies, reduction in neuroscience is much more extreme. The major criticism is that social neuroscience claims to explain phenomena on one scale by means of phenomena on another scale (Gergen, 2010a; Meloni, 2011). For example, phenomena that have a material existence outside the brain, such as social relationships, places, practices and institutions, are explained by means of phenomena in the brain. The neuroscientific assumption is that phenomena at a higher level can be explained by low-level properties. Social practices, deeply embedded in particular histories, which education researchers, anthropologists and cultural psychologists believe are necessary in order to think about social problems, fall out of the account. They become irrelevant. That meanings can be grasped independently of their behavioural criteria or social setting is anathema to most sociocultural researchers, as we elaborated especially in Chapters 3, 6, 7 and 8. As Meloni (2011) exemplifies, 'no amount of neural knowledge would suffice to discriminate between writing one's name, copying one's name, practising one's signature, forging a name, writing an autograph, signing a cheque'. In similar vein, Alain Ehrenberg criticizes the inadequacy of recent works on the neurobiology of empathy and emotions. It is a mistake, he says, to exchange a social value such as 'empathy', for a cognitive mechanism found in our brain. The same can be said for any number of other social constructions, such as ability, talent, success, failure, as we have been arguing throughout this book.

As previous chapters demonstrate, for a socioculturalist, an understanding of human events requires some understanding of the social context, the actors' intentions, assumptions made, and something of the broader social norms relevant to the setting. Undoubtedly, the central criticism of neuroscience for a socioculturalist is the denial of the social. On the basis of our analysis (see especially our discussion of culture in Chapters 4 and 5), we would argue that some of neuroscience's main assumptions are simplistic, shaky and conceptually contradictory.

We have argued that neuroscience and sociocultural theory are seeking to describe the same thing when it comes to learning but are coming at it from fundamentally different sets of assumptions. Others argue that the ascendance of neuroscience results in a narrowing of the range of available metaphors for depicting what it means to be human (Kirschner, 2010; Thornton, 2011). One of the strongest detractors in this regard is Raymond Tallis (2009; 2011) who writes:

> The fundamental assumption is that we are our brains and this ... is not true. But this is not the only reason why neuroscience does not tell us what human beings 'really' are: it does not even tell us how the brain works, how bits of the brain work, or (even if you accept the dubious assumption that human living could be parcelled up into a number of discrete functions) which bit of the brain is responsible for which function. The rationale for thinking of the kind–'This bit of the brain houses that bit of us ...'–is mind-numbingly simplistic.

The simplistic nature of some neuroscience is perhaps more evident in the claims made by non-neuroscientists, than neuroscientists themselves. In a recent special issue of *Scientific American* devoted to the neuroscience of identity, the following headline appeared: 'Forget cramming: Short regular training intervals may work best for learning' (Stix, 2012). The article was based on a study in the lab of Eric Kandel at Columbia University and had nothing to do with humans. Rather, it involved shocking the tail of a sea slug and checking if the animal would remember by overreacting later when receiving a reduced zap. It did. Dealing with relatively easy problems, portrayals from neuroscience seek to convince us that soon the same methods will solve bigger problems. We believe that it is at least partially the responsibility of neuroscientists themselves to provide correctives to exaggerated claims.

The reductionism and unidimensionality are partly the result of the available, new methodologies. And these methodologies are highly persuasive to the layperson and to professionals outside the neuroscience communities. Who could not be intrigued by the following account 'Inside the mind of a psychopath', reported in *Scientific American Mind*:

> Thanks to technology that captures brain activity in real time, experts are no longer limited to examining psychopathic aberrant behavior. We can investigate what is happening inside them as they think, make decisions and react to the world around them. And what we find is that far from being merely selfish, psychopaths suffer from a serious biological defect. Their brains process information differently from those of other people. It's as if they have a learning disability that impairs emotional development.
>
> (Kiehl and Buckholtz, 2010: 22)

Images of the brain render neuroscientific explanations at once appealing and authoritative (McCabe and Castel, 2008). The neuroscientist Richard Restak (2003: 9) enthuses about the power of neuroimaging to portray the structure and function of the brain: 'Thanks to imaging techniques', he says, 'we can now explore what is actually occurring in the brain as we go about our daily lives.' This apparent visibility offers the 'illusion of explanatory depth' (Keil, 2003) communicating the idea to the layperson that every action a person does and every thought that is thought has a corresponding datum in the brain which can be mapped and observed. There is also the criticism that the neuroimaging technology pushes researchers in this field to privilege methods, that the methods drive the research.

The assumption of exactitude is brought about because it is possible to obtain, see and count the data. Images showing the physical basis of learning, experience, feelings, and so on, authorize neuroscience as an exact science. The work on images of the philosopher of science, John Kulvicki (2010), is interesting in this respect. In his article, 'Knowing with images: Medium and message', he suggests that an image like a functional magnetic resonance image delivers a lot of specific information, whereas a prose description by its nature leaves a lot unsaid. He argues that images (including charts, graphs, etc.) make the viewer/reader 'feel more reliably and intimately connected with their contents' (311) regardless of their accuracy. We seem to trust our grasp of the content revealed in an image. The immediacy and extractability of information in an image make it appealing and convincing. A picture would appear to be worth a thousand words! Moreover, the use of experimental designs with their quantitative methodologies along with the language of the brain has the appearance of impartiality, objectivity and truth. Sociocultural thinking, in contrast, is that experimental models of research, though not precluding them, are not usually sufficiently flexible to capture human experience and activity that are seen as in flux and relational. Moreover, the assumption of timelessness, universality and the relatively static state of human activity and intentionality would not fit in a sociocultural frame, as we have argued earlier in the book.

Colonization and the potential demise of sociocultural perspectives

Discussions about the brain within and without the broad field of neuroscience have centred on three key aspects (Callard and Margulies, 2011). The three areas in question are: plasticity (e.g. Rubin, 2009); a reinvigoration of emotion in human action and learning (e.g. Damasio, 2003); and mirror neurons positing neural mechanisms for sharing understanding (e.g. Lieberman, 2007). The dissemination of these ideas was rapid, not just in the academic press, but also in the popular media (Thornton, 2011). Callard and Margulies (2011) suggest that a fourth emergent aspect, only about a decade old, promises equal dissemination, discussion and uptake. This is the brain's resting state and its default mode of function. The so-called default network is apparently active during spontaneous and unprompted behaviours, such as daydreaming, imagining, self-reflection, and in the retrieval of personal events and memories (Immordino-Yang *et al.*, 2012; Kaufman, 2013) and some have argued its importance for learning (Kaufman, 2013).

In this section, we adopt a more critical examination of the underpinnings of some aspects in order to expose the real and potentially negative influence on sociocultural theorizing. At one level, particularly relevant in current times of economic austerity, there is the question of what research gets supported. The popularity of neuroscience means that cultural-oriented study of education, diversity, cultural beliefs and values, and such like, will be marginalized. More importantly, explanations drawing on sociocultural processes of education are likely to disappear from debate and research as the cortical level gains more and more traction and popularity (Gergen, 2010a; 2010b). We already referred to Nikolas Rose's critique that neuroscience not only establishes what counts as an explanation–it establishes what there is to explain. Ehrenberg's 'cerebral subject' (2004) and Rose's 'neurochemical self' (2007a) capture the idea of the formation of new kinds of subjectivity and identity. By default, therefore, much neurocultural theorizing excludes sociocultural ways of knowing and understanding ourselves, thereby impoverishing the diversity and richness of social life. In this sense, neuroscience–and certainly the interpretation of it on the part of policy makers, practitioners, entrepreneurs and many neuroscience scholars–is a colonizing discourse, overtaking important sociocultural dimensions that help us understand ourselves and our relations in the world.

There is now emerging a substantial literature that is acutely aware and critical of this trend to saturate and colonize (e.g. Gergen, 2010b; Rose, 2007b; Slaby, 2010; Meloni, 2011; Tallis, 2011). In the context of the undermining of the authority of other conceptualizations and the potential demise of the ideas and conceptual tools furnished by sociocultural science, it is important to visit the main criticisms here. By discussing the underlying assumptions of neuroscience that are at odds with sociocultural science, we are seeking to do two things: (1) to understand the current intellectual prestige (Meloni, 2011) of neuroscience and to problematize it; and (2) by highlighting the differences between the core assumptions of neuroscience and cultural lines of thought, to demonstrate the potential for loss of understanding of the human sphere.

Given the publicity and uptake of neuroscientific studies compared to sociocultural studies, it is paradoxical that it is the latter and not the former that gives us a handle on the interpretation of neuroscientific evidence itself–a point we argued earlier in the book (see Chapters 3 and 6). The brain scan cannot be read off as self-evident. The move from brain scan to interpretation requires culture, tradition and an assumption about what is valued in a culture and that is entirely ignored by the scanners. Kenneth Gergen confirms our conclusion when he says it is culture that enables any kind of interpretation or inference from such data (Gergen, 2010a). On this, sociocultural science trumps neuroscience every time, hence our reference to the paradox. And inference is crucial as it determines future action–perhaps where to look to resolve a person's 'mental state'. Referring to 'the problem of inference' Gergen (2010a: 804) expresses the need for a cultural take very well in his insightful article 'The acculturated brain', and is worth quoting at some length:

> The vast bulk of brain research relies on the experimental instigation of the brain state . . . researchers must establish a measurable neural condition, said to be responsible for problem solving, decision making, aggression, altruism, trust, and the like. In all such cases, however, various manipulations or instructions are required to bring the state of the brain into its condition. To instigate problem solving as a cortical condition, for example, requires that the subject is enlisted in the task of solving problems. It may thus be asked, on what grounds do we attribute the resulting behavior to the neural condition? It is not the brain that brings about problem solving, but the cultural conditions in which the very idea of solving problems and the kind of behavior defined as problem solving are nurtured. In this case the brain is simply a conduit that carries the cultural tradition.

As we have noted, meaning as emergent, situational and multiple is among the major concepts in sociocultural theory. Given the possibility of multiple meanings in a given situation, the problem of inference in neuroscience is clear. Again Gergen (2010a: 806) explains with an apt example:

> Consider the brief closing and opening of the eyelid. From a biological standpoint, one might roughly call such a movement a 'blink.' However, from a cultural standpoint, the same activity may be viewed as a 'wink.' To understand the winking of the eye, the biologist might explore the functioning of tear ducts, the drying of the cornea, and so on. As a wink, however, the action may bring forth a variety of different activities. For some the action may 'call hither'; for others it may yield a knowing smile; and for still others, it may be repelling. The same form of biological activity may serve many different cultural functions.

Intentionality, purpose, agency are all left unexplained by the neuroscientist. So the interpretation of behaviours that indicate envy, aggression, empathy, learning, and so on, require one to understand the situation, the people in the situation, their assumptions and agendas, inter-relationships, and so on, aspects that are indeed 'cultural in origin' (Gergen, 2010a: 806). The goal of an action is vital in understanding its meaning and in a sociocultural view is a necessary part of any description. The 'in order to motive' is fundamental.

Where does this sociocultural stance leave the place of brain science? Gergen says that the implications here are profound for neuroscience and lead to the conclusion that neural explanation of learning, memory, leadership, love, altruism, and other such aspects, are entirely vacuous. As in his example of a wink or a blink quoted above, behaviours linked to these descriptors are only loosely tied to bodily movements. On this point, Gergen acknowledges the neural mechanisms involved in understanding, say, brain tumours or Parkinson's disease, and here neuroscience is useful. In response to such problems (of inference, cause and effect, interpretation), Gergen proposes that if the brain is viewed as an organ that enables the realization of culturally created forms of life, a more promising domain of research and practice would open up. In our view, the nascent sub-discipline of cultural neuroscience may be the best hope of such a promise since a desire is emerging to acknowledge the complexities of culture, although, as we argued in Chapters 4 and 5, there is a need for much better conceptualizing among cultural neuroscientists before such a hope could be realized.

Epistemological differences

We end this chapter by summarizing the two perspectives in relation to their respective epistemologies. Differences in the epistemology of the two approaches are pivotal in understanding the contributions of each and in explaining the grounds for their claims. Epistemology is the study of what counts as knowledge, where knowledge is located, where it is located in relation to the knower, and how knowledge increases. An examination of the presuppositions and assumptions underlying the approaches affords a more informed and critical stance in interpreting findings, claims and any pedagogic recommendations arising from them. We have already devoted much space to discussing the underpinnings of brain science in this chapter and we have elaborated on socio-cultural underpinnings and assumptions throughout the book. Table 13.1 offers a summary of the main assumptions.

In the first approach, the quest is to establish universals, general truths and theories that pertain to all in a particular group. Mind, self, emotions, personality, memory, and such like, are entities, variables that can be manipulated. The position of one of our interviewees illustrates the point:

> I do hope we will have a truly mechanistic understanding of brain processing, [understanding] how they may become maladaptive with their exchange with the environment. So we can qualify exact causes; understand symptoms and causes of depression, so we are able to make patient-specific assessments of problems, (right now) we are stuck in a trial-and-error approach that is painful for the patient. I hope we will have instruments in a decade's time–to start to progressively dissect, precisely label and provide accurate assessment.
>
> (Interviewee H, from the International
> Neuroscience Conference, Wicklow, 2011)

Table 13.1 Epistemological differences

Neuroscientific approaches to knowledge	Sociocultural approaches to knowledge
Universal and absolute; timeless	Situated and perspectival
Disinterested/objectivist	Interested
Foundational and reductive: search for general truths and laws	Aversion to meta-discourses: general laws of human nature eschewed
Reduced to biological, ahistorical	History and social context inescapable
In the ascendancy: high visibility	Threatened by other approaches: low visibility
Determinism	Indeterminate
Search for centre and essence of self	Constituted by culture and society: inseparability of psychological and sociocultural realms so no essence; relationality
Search for mechanistic cause and effect	Subjectivity emerging out of otherness and permeated by it; rejects cause and effect mechanisms
Variable independence/fixed/pre-existing, decontextualized	Challenges bifurcations such as: self and society; individual and culture; organism and environment
Brains doing things	Basic unit of analysis: persons acting in the world; persons think and act, not their various parts

There is an emphasis on difference from the norm so the assumption of norms is made. In the second perspective, no universals can be claimed or absolute truths discovered since contexts are local, situated and dynamic. Mind and selves emerge in the moment from social, cultural and historical contexts. Referring to the social origins of knowledge, Gergen (2010b: 72) says:

> what we take to be knowledge of the world and self finds its origins in human relationships. What we take to be true as opposed to false, objective as opposed to subjective, scientific as opposed to mythological, rational as opposed to irrational, moral as opposed to immoral is brought into being by communal activity. . . . It is not in the individual mind where knowledge, reason, emotion, and morality reside, but in relationships.

Knowledge is inseparable from the knower in this view. There is always a wider context or enduring structures that shape events and interactions. There are always cultural traditions, norms for the context and structural relations of power which influence and shape events but not in predictable ways.

In the case of neuroscience, selves and minds are pre-existing and acted upon and cause-and-effect relationships are sought. The person or self is assumed to be a natural creature as opposed to socially produced. Knowledge is assumed to be objective, disinterested and discoverable. The unit of analysis can be reduced to brains doing things, attributes of people, abilities expressed, for example, as an IQ score. Variables can be held constant or allowed to fluctuate in order to determine cause and effect. Determinism is valued: there is a desire to predict and control behaviour. It is this deterministic logic that allows neuroscientists like Haier and Jung (2008: 177) to be so confident in the neuroscientific applicability to education:

> neuroscience findings now point to ways of assessing the strengths and weaknesses of individual brains so that education can be more precisely targeted to individual students. . . . Suppose a person can have a 20-minute structural MRI scan to determine his or her pattern of gray and white matter in the areas salient for intelligence . . . Will this pattern predict either the best subjects for this person to focus on or the best educational strategies to help this person learn a specific subject? Research studies to test these ideas are possible today if there was sufficient funding to test large, diverse samples such as that described recently articulating developmental brain processes associated with intelligence.

These same neuroscientists tell us that 'Educators must work with brain researchers to design the proper studies to establish how new neuroscience information can translate into the classroom' (177). At least one article in an educational research journal, looking forward to 'the new science of evidence-based education' suggests that educational research should concern itself with testing hypotheses from neuroscience in the classroom and the provision of behavioural data on children (Tommerdahl, 2010).

In sociocultural science, it is persons, not brains or their various parts, who think and act (Kirschner and Martin, 2010). The emergent quality of action in a sociocultural view means that truth is never absolute–interpretations will never be final or unambiguous. Indeterminacy is inevitable. Also, because persons, environments, structures of power, and so on, are inter-connected and constitutive, it would be meaningless to conceive of mind, emotions, agency as variables that can be tested systematically in a particular environment. They are in no sense 'givens' or prior to their sociocultural surround (Kirschner and Martin, 2010). Moreover, knowledge is not objective, it is 'interested', always perspectival (Magnusson and Marecek, 2010); it cannot be otherwise. Knowledge is interested and as such can never be neutral.

Conclusion

The main message we would wish to draw in this chapter is the potential of neuroscience to colonize and marginalize the messages of sociocultural humanistic science. Because of the embracing of neuroscience by the most influential politicians with the consequent generation of vast funding streams, other ways of thinking about issues and problems in the sphere of learning and education are undermined or even invisible. Neuroscience offers a new, different vocabulary and set of metaphors for conceptualizing ourselves, human learning and personhood. Yet, reflecting back on the various chapters, a constant theme is how neuroscientific research is in its infancy in most areas. At the level of evidence and state of readiness for educational application, one wonders what all the fuss is about. The fact is that the evidential base is limited and the direct implications for education and for the classroom remain sparse. Knowing which brain structures might be involved in various aspects of living and learning is unlikely, at least at this stage, to tell us much about how to organize our classrooms, and what or how to teach. Several published papers seeking to convince the educational community of the significance of the neuroscientific research base (e.g. Fischer, 2009; Immordino-Yang and Fischer, 2009; Immordino-Yang and Damasio, 2007) do not stand up to scrutiny in terms of the evidence provided. The messages from such papers tend to be aspirational rather than evidential and tend to confirm what we have known for some time, for example, that emotion is important for learning.

We conclude that while neuroscience confirms socioculture's emphasis on the significance of experience and the opportunity to learn, it has nothing to say about values and intentionality or what kind of learning is relevant and valued in different situations. While strong on socialization and adaptation, it is weak on furnishing understandings on what is involved in taking responsibility that goes with living in the world. While strong on empirical work, correlates and new technological methodologies, it is weak on conceptualizing and explaining. On the other hand, sociocultural perspectives are brimming with educational implications. The more fundamental problem is that this may be ignored as the biological and neurological continue in the ascendancy and become a hegemonic discourse. The potential loss is in relation to the humanistic and the depiction of the person as a located, cultural being and the depiction of learning as a distributed, value-laden and moral enterprise.

Chapter 14

Conclusion

Claiming science

We have drawn conclusions throughout the book, identifying key messages from each chapter and we have attempted to pull together overarching messages in the last two chapters. In this final chapter, we invite the reader to consider the status of sociocultural theory as a science. While we have referred to it as a science at various points in the book, we have not offered a justification for this nomenclature. On the basis of the analyses offered, we believe attention to its scientific status merits some commentary. In this chapter, we propose that sociocultural theory offers a science of learning. First, our final vignette, which, we suggest, nicely bookends the account we offered in Chapter 1 of the International Neuroscience Conference. This vignette is taken from the notes one of us made having participated, in 2011, in a Parliamentary Research Enquiry in England. It was entitled: 'How do children learn and what does this mean for education policy?'

> I proceeded through Westminster Hall and Central Lobby and followed directions to the Upper Committee Corridor. I entered a packed Committee Room 20 and took my seat peripherally as the focal round table participants made final adjustments to seating and media arrangements. The session was Chaired by Mr. Graham Stuart, MP, Chair of the Education Select Committee, and was jointly organized by Cambridge Assessment, the University of Cambridge's international exams group, and Cambridge University's Centre for Science and Policy. The rationale for the session was to give experts the opportunity to provide policy makers with information about the cognitive processes of students. Acknowledging that rapid strides were being made in this field, the assumption was that policy makers ought to be updated on these changes so that education policies could reflect cutting-edge scientific views of learning. Policy makers were invited to question a number of practices like why national assessments occur at certain ages, whether these reflect cognitive break-points, and whether there was justification for the split between primary and secondary education.
>
> Professor Usha Goswami, Director of the Centre for Neuroscience in Education, Department of Psychology, University of Cambridge

commenced proceedings with the brief, 'how children learn'. According to Goswami environments affect brains. 'Rich environments', she said, 'are the key to supporting learning'. She argued that 'language in the early years is vital. And if rich language models are not available in the home, schools need to provide them'. For Goswami, teachers must be trained to recognize that 'language is key to fostering self regulation'. Language, she said, 'is totally undervalued in teacher training practices and government policy'. Cognitive neuroscience, according to Goswami 'is not currently fed into teaching practices' but ought to be incorporated into teacher training modules, curriculum and government policy. The starting point should be a 'science of learning'. Goswami provided the example of Finland where the Finnish government 'supports scientists and draws on scientific expertise to filter into teacher training modules and classroom practice'. At the end of her presentation, Graham Stuart, MP, Chair of the Education Select Committee asked Goswami 'What area of policy change would you argue for?' She firmly responded 'Dyslexia exists. Get on and help. Embed science into policy, skill-up teachers, and train teachers at a national level'.

The next speaker was Professor Robert Burden, Emeritus Professor, Educational Psychology/Education Studies, University of Exeter. He argued that environment is vital to learning. He stated that no learning occurs in isolation but rather in a range of contexts, including informal learning contexts that are dynamic and flexible. Within a classroom context teachers are the mediators. Motivation, for Burden, is 'crucial especially in adolescent brains'. Asked 'What area of policy change would you argue for?' Burden steadfastly replied 'Change policy on the basis of scientific evidence'.

Professor Trevor Robbins, Professor of Cognitive Neuroscience, University of Cambridge and Head of the Department of Experimental Psychology, delivered the final presentation. He defined learning as 'diverse, multidimensional and mediated by a plastic brain'. He continued, 'learning is optimal when we are young' and ought to be 'active' and 'directed'. He described as 'vital' the exposure to rich language when a child is young. Asked 'What area of policy change would you argue for?' Robbins decisively responded 'Make changes to curriculum in imaginative ways. In the area of language we need feasibility studies'.

Comments from the floor noted that 'teachers need to undergo an extensive period of training akin to the medical profession. They need to become effective practitioners'; 'teacher training needs to be university based'; and 'people in neuroscience need to be motivated to make a difference in this debate'.

As is clear from this vignette, cognitive psychology and neuroscience hold sway among policy makers and politicians when it comes to understanding learning and advising about it. While the situatedness of learning is noted, the reality is that the cognitive psychological model and neuroscience are privileged. We recognize the contribution that different perspectives and different kinds of evidence can make to our understanding of learning. But, as we have argued in this book, sociocultural theory should also have a role to play. Indeed, our argument is that it is extremely well-placed to inform teachers about how to ensure all learners can participate fully in their learning. Much of the remainder of this final chapter is devoted to our proposal that sociocultural theory merits the description of scientific.

By its name, neuroscience is assumed to be a science. It draws on biology, genetics, physiology and other 'physical' or 'life' sciences. The scientific status of sociocultural theory would appear to be more ambiguous. Rarely, if ever, in the literature, have we come across the phrase 'sociocultural science' though we have used it occasionally in this book. There is cognitive science and complexity science but not sociocultural science. One example from an Internet search shows a school at the Radboud University Nijmegen in the Netherlands entitled School of Sociocultural Science, consisting of Communication Science, Anthropology and Development Studies, and Sociology. One explanation for the limited references to science is very likely the intellectual roots of constitutive or sociocultural thinking in classical philosophy, modern traditions of social theory, and more recently, in the work of Bakhtin, Vygotsky and Bruner and many others not associated with the physical sciences. Moreover, the range of disciplines and interdisciplinary areas relevant to the extended family of sociocultural theory include all of the following: psychology, philosophy, sociology, education, history, semiotics, structuralism, phenomenology, hermeneutics, and cultural and discourse studies—and this is not an exhaustive list.

We see sociocultural theory as a humanistic science. Like all sciences, whether 'natural' or human/social, it has a history, an intellectual lineage and associated institutional trappings such as university departments, associations, journals and research centres. Like all sciences, it makes assumptions and is based on particular perspectives. All science, we believe, is perspectival. No amount of technology can change that. Our stance is that values, history, power, people, structures, institutions, all play a constitutive role in the development of science. All scientific knowledge is of our making—of human action in sociohistorical contexts using technologies, materials, methods and arguments to produce findings that either meet or do not meet the definition of knowledge (Fagan, 2010). As sociocultural researchers, we already recognize that people both shape and are shaped by structures and institutions which by their nature are shot through with power. People appropriate the norms, attitudes, characteristics and competences associated with their discipline—people/researchers are part of that history and bound up with it. This has to be thus because there is no such thing as the lone, unitary self, as we have argued throughout this book. The canonical image of the lone and stoic individual is completely challenged by the constitutive position of the socioculturalist. The 'unencumbered self' (Biddle, 2009) is an illusion.

Trying to find better ways of understanding ourselves and the social world, seeking new ways of seeing and interpretation, and evolving new practices of exploration are all part and parcel of what it is to be scientific. Science is constantly trying new ways of exploring the world in order to address the problems that merit our attention. There are many ways in which to 'do science', but regardless of orientation, focus or methodology, a human science, as a quest for better understanding of societal problems and issues, has to be relevant, accountable, ethical and able to be critical of itself while acknowledging that all such criteria are never absolute or fixed. One philosopher and historian of science talks about intelligibility and how science requires this in order to be plausible (Dear, 2006: 173). He highlights the importance of ideas and assumptions 'that seem right, that make sense' while acknowledging that what counts as intelligible is cultural and situated. We would add that much depends too on who is doing the judging and who is empowered to do the judging. Sociocultural theory offers a way of seeing, it offers tools for interpreting human experience—it is appropriate to refer to it, therefore, as a human science and, because it draws on disciplines associated with the humanities, a humanistic science.

Given our argument throughout this book that sociocultural theory is pedagogically compelling and that it has considerable explanatory power for understanding and supporting the learning process, it is appropriate to give some consideration in this final chapter to notions of 'science'. In order to justify our claim that a sociocultural perspective is a human science, it is necessary to note briefly the historical beginnings of social science more generally. The disciplinary divisions of the social sciences (e.g. sociology, psychology) and the view of science endorsed by most social sciences are relatively recent, dating from the First World War (Manicas, 2007). Until around the 1920s, there were no departments of sociology or psychology. However, during what Manicas calls the period of institutionalization of the social sciences at the turn of the last century, a particular conception of what counted as science came to prevail. Essentially, this conception mimicked the physical sciences in rejecting any assumptions that could not be tested empirically in experience. A theory was simply an assumption, a premise, that was deemed value-free and neutral. Metaphysical orientations were deemed inappropriate and had to be eschewed. This thinking privileged positivism and logical empiricism—approaches that valorized experimental and quasi-experimental methods, hypothesis testing, grand theories and ahistorical abstractions. Taken for granted was that there was no great difference between social and physical science.

The point is that what counts as science is a construction dependent on history, context and who happens to have the power to define it so. The notion of a neutral science, a disinterested science, is a fiction. As Bourdieu (2004) observes, the 'purest' science is a social field with its power struggles and strategies, its interests and profits, its claims for 'scientific authority' and its push for recognition and legitimacy. Science and the scientist are historically constituted. Social scientists arguably sought and achieved legitimation and status for their area of study by aligning with the natural sciences. By such alignment, the claim to be a science was justified–the assumption being that the natural sciences had already worked out and determined what constituted 'scientific' practice. By such alignment also, disciplines could command more status and recognition.

So, in claiming the label 'science' for sociocultural theory, are we not making the same case and for the similar reasons as social scientists before us did? Perhaps yes–we can't claim disinterest in the status of the discipline we value. Highly critical of science and referring to 'the science of science', Bourdieu has argued that recognition enables claims and arguments to be noticed and 'scientific capital' to be accumulated and converted into other capitals, for example, funding for research projects. With particular reference to neuroscience, it is noteworthy that the naming of the 1990s as the 'Decade of the Brain' expanded hugely its recognition factor and the more recent endorsement by President Obama will further extend its reach not just in relation to funding for research but in relation to its permeation into our language and the shaping of our subjectivities. As a consequence, knowledge and research in this area is likely to grow and the emergent sub-disciplines, such as cognitive neuroscience, affective neuroscience and cultural neuroscience, are likely to flourish. Related to the expansion since the 1990s, and undoubtedly causal, was the development of the new imaging technologies like fMRI which allowed more powerful and direct representations of brain function. We recognize that we are 'taking sides' when it comes to adjudicating the relative merits of neuroscience and sociocultural science for addressing questions about learning and how it occurs and could be supported. However, as we hope our analysis has demonstrated, our purpose is not to undermine what neuroscience has to offer, rather, it is to recognize how both may contribute to our understanding of human learning even if we are arguing that sociocultural theory is more advanced, nuanced and helpful in this regard and that there is a danger that neuroscience may swamp the important messages from sociocultural science.

The emergence of the social sciences as scientific, as we noted, was achieved by aligning with the methods and assumptions of the physical sciences. In many ways, the positivist assumptions remain a dominant feature of much of the social sciences, and especially psychology. Such assumptions would preclude sociocultural perspectives as scientific. One could point to several examples of this, especially on the part of policy makers who occasionally commission research reviews with such a narrow remit that the outcome is predetermined. A good example of this occurred over a decade ago in relation to the pedagogy of language and literacy. The then US Government commissioned a National Reading Panel (NRP) to review the research evidence on how best to teach literacy in the elementary/primary classroom (National Reading Panel, 2000). Controversially, sociocultural studies based on ethnographic principles and in-depth, qualitative case studies, were deemed inadequately scientific and were not included in the review, thus skewing the findings, conclusions and recommendations for policy and practice. Not surprisingly, there was considerable debate and resistance to the move (e.g. Cunningham, 2001) and at least one panel member expressed her objections to the framing of the study by including a reservation in the final report (Yatvin, 2000). This particular case is interesting in the context of the science of neuroscience, and one can imagine a similar rationale being offered for its definition of science. In justifying its exclusive focus on experimental and quasi-experimental designs in its systematic review of the effectiveness of various approaches in teaching children to read, the NRP aligned education with psychology and medicine. It said:

> The evidence-based methodological standards adopted by the Panel are essentially those normally used in research studies of the efficacy of interventions in psychological and medical research. These include behaviorally based interventions, medications, or medical procedures proposed for use in the fostering of robust health and psychological development and the prevention or treatment of disease.
>
> (National Reading Panel, 2000: 5)

It then went on to say that the efficacy of the methods used in teaching 'should be tested no less rigorously' and added that unfortunately 'only a small fraction of the total reading research literature met the Panel's standards for use' (National Reading Panel, 2000: 5). This meant that the review was based on only a tiny proportion of the research conducted on literacy teaching in schools, the rest failing the NRP's test of what constitutes *scientific* or *rigorous* or *objective* research. Teaching was seen by the NRP in a particular way–as equivalent to interventions where the person administering the treatment or the intervention was not a significant factor in it. The literacy to be taught and its teaching were assumed to be akin to the curing of psychological and physical diseases in the realm of medicine.

Such an approach to science denies or ignores the notion of subjectivity and intersubjectivity, the idea of a constituted, mediated world, and the emergent, performative nature of social interaction, and the meanings implicit and explicit in practice–all central to sociocultural theorizing, and ideas that, for their exploration, require a different kind of methodology, one that would allow access to people's lifeworlds. And lifeworlds implies a focus on both the person as agent, thinking intentional being as well as the structure in which the person is enmeshed. Lave (2008), as noted earlier in the book, was interested in understanding how people make sense of everyday reality, the nature of subjective experience of everyday life, while Schutz (1970) talks about mundane subjectivity. While the neuroscientist is eager to establish links between the neural brain and the person's intentionality and disposition, adopting the classical view of intentional action as an entirely individual and independent process, the socioculturalist recognizes that the world is 'already furnished' (Thévenot, 2001:

71). The constitutive nature of meanings means that meanings are not just in the minds of actors in a way that can be accessed, say, via a questionnaire survey, but are in the practices which are far more than individual actions. Rather, they are 'modes of social relation of mutual action' (Taylor, 1971: 27). When we act, we draw on tacit knowledge, we make assumptions, about the way the world is and how it works. In trying to understand the meanings and assumptions made, sociocultural thinking draws on different practices of exploration from the dominant way of thinking about human learning and development emanating from mainstream psychology. It tries to escape the dualism inherent in actor and structure by acknowledging that one implies the other, they are opposite sides of the same coin, a duality, not a dualism (Wenger, 1998). A good example is language: it is at once the means of our communication with the reader and a means by which we reproduce the written word. Practice constitutes mind and world. Practice makes practice. It is through specific studies of practice, engaging, acting and doing in specific settings at specific times, that insight into the constitutive nature of actor and world emerges, although it can never result in generalizations, universal truths or predictions. Rather, it is about 'how things and people show up' (Packer, 2011: 242). The sociocultural researcher is concerned with narrating the practices of being and living in the world rather than establishing universal truths that can be applied in all contexts. More to the point, though, sociocultural science seeks to deal with the complexity of life denying the easy separation of such phenomena as person and environment, agent and structure, self and other, subject and object, figure and ground, mind and body, fact and value, individual and society, and so on. What is of interest is how these 'live together' and make each other up. Thus, constitution involves dualities, not dualisms, as we have already argued.

What one might ask, then, is the purpose of research in a sociocultural frame, or what contribution it can make. The answer lies in the search for understanding how social life is enacted and understood, how the social order is appropriated, resisted, transformed, and how *inter alia* people transform themselves through their practice. To achieve this, immersion in the practice is pivotal and the focus has to be on emerging practices and processes. While there is no 'gold standard' methodologically, 'fieldwork is necessary to discover not only the order of a form of life but also the work that goes into producing and reproducing this order' (Packer, 2011: 243). While such accounts are always partial and interested they are subject to accountability at the local level–relatability is relevant. The accounts of studies summarized in earlier chapters are examples and they offer accounts that direct our attention to aspects of schooling that are frequently ignored. They also direct our attention to how different kinds of selves are produced by school practices and the power of schools and teachers to shape the kind of person a child may become. We are convinced that educators at all levels would benefit from an understanding of sociocultural theorizing in this regard.

We are arguing that sociocultural science is science as practice or science as activity as opposed to science as only representation. Science involves participation in the making of a reality–the researcher is ever complicit. The knower and the known are entangled. Practices are patterns of human activity and the socioculturalist seeks to develop an account of that array or pattern of human activity, recognizing their own complicity. How are practices maintained, resisted or transformed by actors? How are practices ordered or organized?

We have referred to the social order in earlier chapters, by which we mean arrangements of people and things (Schatzki, 2001: 12), by which we mean not just rules and regulations but 'practical understandings, ways of proceeding and setups of the material environment'. Practices not only involve people doing things but involve people with agency that is the power to do things, the power to perform. Order, therefore, is akin to an arrangement, that which makes sense for people to do. Practices are understood in a sociocultural perspective as involving routine activities as opposed to consciously decided actions. Because practices are noted for their automatic and unconscious character, they need to be observed–the researcher can't always simply ask questions of the participants as to their assumptions because actors are not necessarily aware of the 'pragmatic regimes' or the reifications (see Chapter 5) that guide ways of engaging and participating. Practices take the form of tacit knowledge–'inarticulate competences' (Rouse, 2001: 190). The socioculturalist scientist seeks to explore and understand what anchors cultural practices and takes a pragmatic stance towards the accounts resulting from such explorations. The claim to science stems from the scholarly, disciplined, evidence-based and rigorous approach to research that is evident in such accounts, as well as the value of such accounts for educators.

Our analysis leads us to the conclusion that both sciences offer a perspective on learning, a way of seeing and a way of analysing. Neither is 'true' in any absolute sense. But the metaphors, vocabularies and systems of interpretation in both cases are likely to lead us in different directions and to produce different effects. It is, therefore, vital that these different directions and effects are kept under critical scrutiny and review. In the end, teaching has to be informed by what learning is assumed to be, and what learning is assumed to be will continue to merit investigation and analysis.

Our last point in concluding this book is about what we see as the potential for greater alignment between sociocultural science and neuroscience in the exploration of learning. Inevitably both will continue along their own respective lines of inquiry based on their own sets of assumptions and epistemologies. However, neuroscience is already connecting with most other disciplines from neuroeconomics to neuropolitics. While there is always merit in interdisciplinary dialogue, we believe that no matter what disciplines are brought together, some cultural, interpretivist framework will always be necessary. To explain and understand experience, a sociocultural science will be needed. As we argued already, everything we say and do as individuals, including the language and sign systems we use to express it, are cultural and social constructions. From this basic but powerful premise, all that follows must also be cultural and social in origin. Learning becomes a social construct and a social process.

A brief illustrated guide to the brain

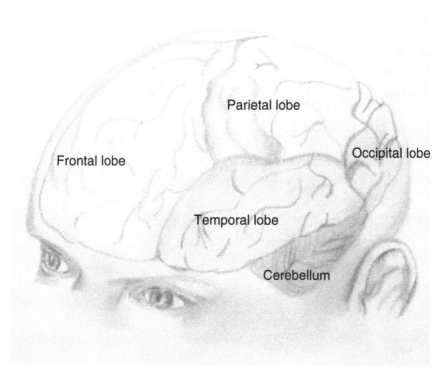

Figure A.1 The major subdivisions of the cerebral cortex

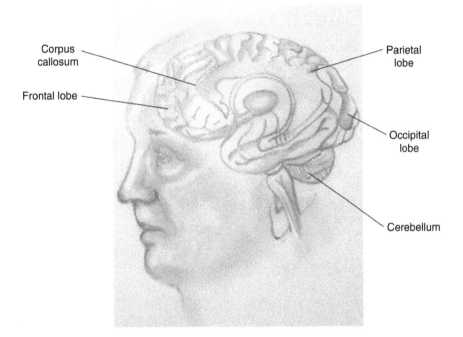

Corpus callosum

Frontal lobe

Parietal lobe

Occipital lobe

Cerebellum

Figure A.2 A sagittal view of the brain

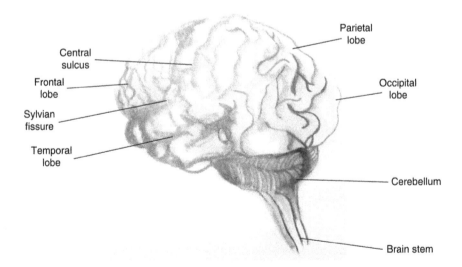

Central sulcus

Frontal lobe

Sylvian fissure

Temporal lobe

Parietal lobe

Occipital lobe

Cerebellum

Brain stem

Figure A.3 A lateral view of the brain

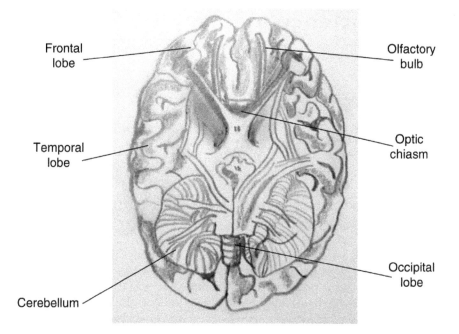

Frontal lobe

Olfactory bulb

Temporal lobe

Optic chiasm

Occipital lobe

Cerebellum

Figure A.4 An inferior view of the brain

Neuroscience glossary

Adapted from OECD (2007) Understanding the Brain: The Birth of a Learning Science. *Paris: OECD, pp. 250–261.*

Amygdala A part of the brain involved in emotions and memory. Each hemisphere contains an almond-shaped amygdale located deep in the brain, near the inner surface of each temporal lobe.

Angular gyrus An area of the cortex in the parietal lobe involved in processing the sound structure of language and in reading.

Anterior cingulated cortex Frontal part of the cingulate cortex. It plays a role in a wide variety of autonomic functions, such as regulating heart rate and blood pressure, and is vital to cognitive functions, such as reward anticipation, decision making, empathy and emotions.

Aphasia Disturbance in language comprehension or production.

Auditory cortex The region of the brain that is responsible for the processing of auditory information.

Auditory nerve A bundle of nerve fibres extending from the cochlea of the ear to the brain, which contains two branches: the cochlear nerve, that transmits sound information; and the vestibular nerve, that relays information related to balance.

Axon The fibre-like extension of a neuron via which the cell sends information to target cells.

Brain stem The major route by which the forebrain sends information to and receives information from the spinal cord and peripheral nerves. It controls, among other things, respiration and regulation of heart rhythms.

Broca's area The brain region located in the frontal lobe of the left hemisphere, involved in the production of speech.

Caudate or caudale nucleus A telencephalic nucleus located within the basal ganglia in the brain. The caudate is an important part of the brain's learning and memory system.

Central sulcus A fold in the cerebral cortex in the brains of vertebrates.

Cerebellum A part of the brain located at the back, and below the principal hemispheres, involved in the regulation of movement.

Cerebral hemispheres The two specialized halves of the brain. The left hemisphere is specialized for speech, writing, language and calculation; the right hemisphere is specialized for spatial abilities, face recognition in vision and some aspects of music perception and production.

Cerebrum Refers to cerebral hemispheres and other, smaller structures within the brain, and is composed of the following sub-regions: limbic system, cerebral cortex, basal ganglia and olfactory bulb.

Cognitive neuroscience The study and development of mind and brain research aimed at investigating the psychological, computational and neuroscientific bases of cognition.

Corpus callosum The large bundle of nerve fibres linking the left and right cerebral hemispheres.

Cortex (cerebral) The outer layer of the brain.

Critical period Concept referring to certain periods when the brain's capacity for adjustment in response to experience is substantially greater than during other periods. In humans, critical periods only exist during prenatal development. Sensitive periods, however, are known to occur in childhood (see *Sensitive period*).

CT (Computed Tomography) Originally known as computed axial tomography (CAT or CT scan) and body section roentgenography. A medical imaging method employing tomography, where digital geometry processing is used to generate a three-dimensional image of the internals of an object from a large series of two-dimensional X-ray images taken around a single axis of rotation.

Dendrite A tree-like extension of the neuron cell body. It receives information from other neurons.

DNA (Deoxyribonucleic acid) A long polymer of nucleotides (polynucleotide) that encodes the sequence of amino-acid residues in proteins using the genetic code.

DTI (Diffusion Tensor Imaging) A magnetic resonance imaging (MRI) technique that enables the measurement of the restricted diffusion of water in tissue. It allows the observation of molecular diffusion in tissues *in vivo* and, therefore, the molecular organization in tissues.

ECG (Electrocardiogram) A recording of the electrical voltage in the heart in the form of a continuous strip graph.

EEG (Electroencephalogram) A measurement of the brain's electrical activity along the scalp via electrodes. EEG is derived from sensors placed in various spots on the scalp, which are sensitive to the summed activity of populations of neurons in a particular region of the brain.

Electrochemical signals These signals are the means by which neurons communicate with one another.

Emotions There is no single, universally accepted definition. The neurobiological explanation of human emotion is that emotion is a pleasant or unpleasant mental state organized mostly in the limbic system of the mammalian brain.

Endorphins Neurotransmitters produced in the brain that generate cellular and behavioural effects similar to those of morphine.

Epigenetic Changes in gene function, often elicited by environmental factors.

ERP (Event-Related Potentials) Electric signals are first recorded with an EEG. Data from this technology is then time locked to the repeated presentation of a stimulus to the subject, in order to see the brain in action. The resulting brain activation (or event-related potentials) can then be related to the stimulus event.

Experience-dependent A property of a functional neural system in which variations in experience lead to variations in function, a property that might persist throughout the lifespan.

Experience-expectant A property of a functional neural system in which the development of the system has evolved to critically depend on stable environmental inputs that are roughly the same for all members of species (i.e. stimulation of both eyes in newborns during development of ocular dominance columns). This property is thought to operate early in life.

fMRI (Functional Magnetic Resonance Imaging) Use of an MRI scanner to view neural activity indirectly through changes in blood chemistry (such as the level of oxygen) and investigate increases in activity within brain areas that are associated with various forms of stimuli and mental tasks.

Forebrain The largest division of the brain, which includes the cerebral cortex and basal ganglia. It is credited with the highest intellectual functions.

Frontal lobe One of the four divisions (parietal, temporal, occipital) of each hemisphere of the cerebral cortex. It has a role in controlling movement and associating the functions of other cortical areas, believed to be involved in planning and higher-order thinking.

Functional imaging Represents a range of measurement techniques in which the aim is to extract quantitative information about physiological function.

Fusiform gyrus A cortical region running along the ventral (bottom) surface of the occipital-temporal lobes associated with visual processes. Functional activity suggests that this area is specialized for visual face-processing and visual word-forms.

Gene The unit of heredity in living organisms. Genes influence the physical development and behaviour of the organism.

Genetics The science of genes, heredity and the variation of organisms.

Glia/glial cells Specialized cells that nourish and support neurons.

Grey matter/gray matter Grey matter consists of neurons' cell bodies and dendrites.

Gyrus/gyri   The circular convolutions of the cortex, each of which has been given an identifying name: middle frontal gyrus, superior frontal gyrus, inferior frontal gyrus, left interior frontal gyrus, posterior middle gyrus, post-central gyrus, supramarginal gyrus, angular gyrus, left angular gyrus, left fusiform gyrus, cingulated gyrus.

Hard-wired   Meaning 'not changeable'. In contrast to concept of plasticity, in which brain is malleable to change.

Hemisphere (cerebral)   One of the two sides of the brain classified as 'left' and 'right'.

Hippocampus   A seahorse-shaped structure located within the brain and considered an important part of the limbic system. It functions in learning, memory and emotions.

Hyperthymesia   A condition in which an individual possesses a superior autobiographical memory, meaning he or she can recall the vast majority of personal experiences and events in his or her life.

Hypothalamus   A complex brain-structure composed of many nuclei with various functions. These include: regulating the activities of internal organs, monitoring information from the autonomic nervous system and controlling the pituitary gland.

Left-brained thinking   A lay term based on the misconception that higher level thought processes are strictly divided into roles that occur independently in different halves of the brain.

Limbic system   Also known as the 'emotional brain'. It borders the thalamus and hypothalamus and is made up of many of the deep brain structures–including the amygdala, hippocampus, septum and basal ganglia–that work to help regulate emotion, memory and certain aspects of movement.

Lobe   Gross areas of the brain sectioned by function.

MEG (Magnetoencephalography)   A non-invasive, functional brain-imaging technique sensitive to rapid changes in brain activity.

Metacognition   Conscious awareness of one's own cognitive and learning processes.

Mind   The mind is what the brain does; it includes intellect and consciousness.

Mirror neuron   A neuron that fires both when a human performs an action and when a human observes the same action being performed by another. Mirror neurons therefore 'mirror' behaviours as if the observer himself was performing the action.

Mnemonic technique   A technique that enhances memory performance.

Motor cortex   Regions of the cerebral cortex involved in the planning, control and execution of voluntary motor functions.

Motor neuron   A neuron that carries information from the central nervous system to the muscle.

MRI (Magnetic Resonance Imaging)   A non-invasive technique used to create images of the structures within a living human brain, through the combination of a strong magnetic field and radio-frequency impulses.

Myelin Compact, fatty material that surrounds and insulates axons of some neurons. The sheath (myelin) around the nerve fibres acts electrically as a conduit in an electrical system, increasing the speed at which messages can be sent.

Myelination Process by which nerves are covered by a protective fatty substance (myelin).

Neurodegenerative diseases Disorders of the brain and nervous system leading to brain dysfunction and degeneration (including Alzheimer's disease, Parkinson's disease and other neurodegenerative disorders) that frequently occur with advancing age.

Neurogenesis The birth of new neurons.

Neuromyth Misconception generated by a misunderstanding, a misreading or misquoting of facts scientifically established (by brain research) to make a case for use of brain research, in education and other contexts.

Neuron A nerve cell. It is specialized for the transmission of information and characterized by long fibrous projections called axons, and shorter, branch-like projections called dendrites. Building-block of the nervous system; a specialized cell for integration and transmission of information.

Neurotransmitter A chemical released by neurons at a synapse for the purpose of relaying information via receptors.

Occipital lobe Posterior region of the cerebral cortex receiving visual information.

Olfactory bulb A structure of the vertebrate forebrain involved in olfaction.

Optic chiasm The part of the brain where the optic nerves partially cross. Located at the bottom of the brain, immediately below the hypothalamus.

OT (Optical Topography) Non-invasive, transcranial imaging method for higher-order brain functions. This method, based on near-infrared spectroscopy, is robust to motion, so that a subject can be tested under natural conditions.

Pallidum/globus pallidus A sub-cortical structure of the brain.

Parietal lobe One of the four subdivisions of the cerebral cortex. It plays a role in sensory processes, attention and language.

PET (Positron Emission Tomography) A variety of techniques that use positron-emitting radionuclides to create an image of brain activity; often blood flow or metabolic activity. PET produces three-dimensional, coloured images of chemicals or substances functioning within the brain.

Pituitary gland An endocrine organ closely linked with the hypothalamus. In humans, it is composed of two lobes and secretes a number of hormones that regulate the activity of other endocrine organs in the body.

Plasticity Also 'brain plasticity'. The phenomenon of how the brain changes and learns in response to experience (see also *Experience-expectant/Experience-dependent*).

Prefrontal cortex The region in front of the frontal cortex, which is involved in planning and other higher-level cognition.

Primary motor cortex Works in association with premotor areas to plan and execute movements.

Primary visual cortex The region of the occipital cortex where most visual information first arrives.

Pruning/synaptic pruning The natural process of eliminating weak synaptic contacts.

'Reptilian' brain (so-called) Refers to the brain stem, which is the oldest region in the evolving human brain.

Right-brained thinking A lay term based on the misconception that higher-level thought processes are strictly divided into roles that occur independently in different halves of the brain. Thought to be based in exaggerations of specific findings of right hemisphere specialization in some limited domains.

Sensitive period Time frame in which a particular biological event is likely to occur best. Scientists have documented sensitive periods for certain types of sensory stimuli (such as vision and speech sounds), and for certain emotional and cognitive experiences (such as attachment and language exposure).

SPECT (Single Photon Emission Computed Tomography) Functional imaging using single photon emission computed tomography.

Stimulus An environmental event capable of being detected by sensory receptors.

Sylvian fissure Divides the frontal lobe and parietal lobe above, from the temporal lobe below.

Synapse A gap between two neurons that functions as the site of information transfer from one neuron to another.

Synaptic density Refers to the number of synapses associated with one neuron. More synapses per neuron are thought to indicate a richer ability of representation and adaption.

Synaptic pruning Process in brain development whereby unused synapses (connections among neurons) are shed. Experience determines which synapses will be shed and which will be preserved.

Synaptogenesis Formation of a synapse.

Temporal lobe One of the four major subdivisions of each hemisphere of the cerebral cortex. It functions in auditory perception, speech and complex visual perceptions.

TMS (Transcranial Magnetic Stimulation) A procedure in which electrical activity in the brain is influenced by a pulsed magnetic field. Recently, TMS has been used to investigate aspects of cortical processing, including sensory and cognitive functions.

Visual cortex Located in the occipital lobe; involved in detection of visual stimuli.

Wernicke's area A brain region involved in the comprehension of language and the production of meaningful speech.

White matter Consists of myelinated axons that connect various grey-matter areas of the brain.

Sociocultural glossary: a social history of sociocultural theory

This short reader presents some of the main concepts of sociocultural theory relevant to our own text and locates them in relevant theory and research; we have emboldened these key themes and terms throughout. We include this section here, though it is in no way an exhaustive list, to acknowledge how our understanding of learning as a social phenomenon developed through and on the understandings of others.

Lev Vygotsky: social cognition

Lev Vygotsky's theory of **Social Cognition** claims that **culture** is the prime determinant of individual development. Because every human child develops in the particular context of his or her own culture, this process affects every individual's learning and development. In Vygotsky's view, culture teaches children what to think and how to think, and because of this and the fact that children can do more with the help of others than they can on their own (**Zone of Proximal Development**), Vygotsky concludes that **mind is a socially mediated phenomenon.**

Etienne Wenger: meaningful participation and reification in communities of practice

Etienne Wenger describes learning as a changing relationship of participation in the world. His core concepts of **practice, meaning** and **identity** offer ways of talking about learning and how it changes who we are as we actively and with agency create personal histories of becoming within shared historical and social practices with the ultimate goal of experiencing the world and our interaction with it as meaningful. Wenger argues that learning occurs socially as the *meanings* of what we do are always social. The practices in which we find meaning, become the practices in which we invest our identities that we share with others in the same community of practice. Living in the world and engaging in practice, we do not individually just make up independent meanings of the world, but neither does the world force external meaning on us. Meanings and our understandings of the world and ourselves are, according to Wenger, always

mediated and develop in the **dual social and historical processes** of participation and reification.

Wenger defines **participation** as the process of taking part in the world, the social experience of living in the world in terms of membership in social communities and active involvement in social enterprises. As such, participation is a source of identity. **Reification**, on the other hand, describes how we impress our meanings onto the world, and then, on meeting them again, perceive them as existing as external facts. Reification provides **communities of practice** with tools and points of focus around which the negotiation of meaning can be organized.

Participation and reification are complementary processes and form a unity in their duality. Each makes up for the shortcomings of the other and Wenger argues that both are necessary to the successful **negotiation of meaning** that is learning. They are not neutral processes, and a change in their relation always enables a change in the possibilities for the negotiation of meaning. Wenger concludes that in life we produce precisely the reification we need in order to proceed with the practices in which we participate. According to Wenger, **learning is the engine of practice** and **practice is the history of that learning**.

Jean Lave: agent, activity and world

Learners are active participants seeking meaning and identity in a social world. Learning occurs through **identity** development, as participants layer meaningful experiences and stories to form a construction of identity; a self. This identity is fluid rather than solid and changes depending on what we are doing, where we are and who we are with. **Agent**, as the power to act, refers to how our performed, mediated and shared plastic identities influence the shared resources we can appropriate to participate in practice. **Activity** relates to the task in question, brings something unique to our participation and prioritizes the importance of developing specific identities. **World** explains that when we act, we act as a historically located individual, creating and created by personal and shared histories of participation and reification—our culture and our world are resources for identity development.

Jean Lave and Etienne Wenger: situated cognition and legitimate peripheral participation

Jean Lave and Etienne Wenger have completed extensive research on how individuals place themselves and are placed on trajectories of learning and identity in communities of practice. In *Situated Learning: Legitimate Peripheral Participation* (Lave and Wenger, 1991), they employ the process of apprenticeship across various jobs and cultures as their research subject so as to achieve a fresh perspective on learning. They understand **learning as situated** and meaning as existing and developing in social situations. Further, as their study of apprenticeship reveals, learning takes place within a community and not an individual mind, thus, they argue, **learning is also distributed**. Within their understanding it is the community, or more specifically its participants, that learn.

Lave argues that on engaging with a community of practice, new members are allowed limited **legitimate peripheral participation** in the practice. Their discussion of apprenticeship learning among midwives in Mexico (Jordan, 1989), tailors in Liberia (Lave and Wenger, 1991), quartermasters in the US (Hutchins, 1995–final publication), American butchers (Marshall, 1972) and non-drinking alcoholics (Cain, 1991) reveals that on encountering a community of practice and making the decision of engagement, an individual's limited peripherality allows them more than mere observation. It offers participation as a way of learning about the group and the world. The social experiences and activities of these individuals within the community of practice facilitates the development of an identity of membership within the group and, over time, legitimate peripheral participation offers opportunities to new members to make its culture of practice their own. In all five cases, Lave and Wenger conclude that there is very little observable teaching–the most basic phenomenon is learning.

Barbara Rogoff: planes of participation and distributed cognition

In her article 'Observing sociocultural activity on three planes: Participatory appropriation, guided participation and apprenticeship', Rogoff conceives of participation in communities as occurring across three interlinked and interdependent planes: apprenticeship, guided participation and participatory appropriation. She defines these cultural, social and personal practices as the multi-layered sites where learning occurs. Central to her theory is that **learning and participation occur simultaneously** on all three planes as they are 'mutually constituting' (Rogoff, 1995: 141).

Rogoff's metaphor of **apprenticeship** means participation on the plane of community, culture and family and includes our shared funds of knowledge (Gonzalez, Moll and Amanti, 2005). In apprenticeship, members of a community of practice increase their skill and understanding through participation with others in culturally organized activities. In relation to learning, the idea of apprenticeship forces acknowledgement of the cultural constraints, values and resources available to communities of practice as well as cultural tools such as language, maths, equipment, and so on. The focus here is on community practices.

Rogoff's concept of **guided participation** refers to the processes of involvement between individuals–conversations, communications, interactions, joint participations–as they go about the process of apprenticeship. It is the social or interpersonal plane which stresses the mutual involvement of individuals and their social partners, communicating and coordinating their involvement as they participate in socioculturally structured collective activity (Rogoff, 1995: 146). It includes both deliberate attempts to instruct and casual conversations that occur between expert and learner or among learners.

Rogoff's final plane, **participatory appropriation**, refers to how individuals transform their understandings of and responsibility for activities through their own participation. This personal plane of learning is the most studied in current education theory and includes many aspects such as cognition, emotion, behaviour, values and beliefs. Rogoff states that the basic idea of participatory appropriation is that through participation people change and become capable of engaging later in similar activities. In our opinion, this idea is only marginally acknowledged in education.

In her (2008b) article 'Thinking with the tools and institutions of culture', Rogoff argues that the wrong understanding of cognition tends to prevail. Cognition does not occur within individual heads, it is distributed across communities of practice, cultural tools and institutions. Thus, while cognition is central to schooling, our conception of cognition needs to be revisited. We need to understand **cognition as distributed and situated within communities of practice.**

James V. Wertsch: memory in mind and culture

Borrowing a vignette from Tharp and Gallimore (1989), James V. Wertsch exemplifies the **social processes** and **cultural tools** involved in **memory** and **practice**. In the story, a six-year-old boy has lost a toy and asks his father to help him find it. His father asks the child a number of probing questions such as 'Do you remember when you last had the toy?', and so on, culminating in the question '[Did you have it] in the car?', to which the boy answers 'Yes' and goes out and retrieves the toy. For Wertsch, this raises the very problematic question of who did the remembering in this experience. He concludes that remembering is itself a **mediated action**, which occurs through the **interaction** of **social actors** and **cultural tools**.

Lewis, Enciso and Moje: agency and power in learning

Lewis, Enciso and Moje define **agency** as the strategic making and remaking of selves within structures of power (Lewis, Enciso and Moje, 2007: 4). Understood from this perspective, agency is not an internal state, rather, it is defined as a way of positioning oneself within communities so as to allow for new identities. **Power**, a result of interactions and relationships, according to the authors is produced and enacted in and through discourses, relationships, activities, spaces and times by people as they compete for access to and control of resources, tools, identities (Lewis, Enciso and Moje, 2007: 17).

A sociocultural understanding of learning

Who learns?

Contrary to popular opinion, cognition, mind and learning do not exist in individual heads. They occur between people in communities of practice. As a result of this, learning and cognition are both situated in group activity (Lave and Wenger, 1991) and distributed across group participation (Rogoff, 1995). In any given activity, it is the group and its participants who learn.

What do they learn?

According to Wenger (1998), learning is a process of identity formation. When something is interesting and meaningful and a part of our identity we are more likely to learn from it. When individuals participate in meaningful practices and are allowed to reify for themselves the necessary abstractions to their practice, they learn (Wenger, 1998). Individuals learn to participate in communities of practice, rather than acquire information. Learning is a change in participation.

Where do they learn?

Learning occurs through participation and reification in communities of practice (Lave and Wenger, 1991). Learning is ubiquitous. It is neither place nor time bound.

When do they learn?

Learning occurs in the everyday (Lave, 1988). As we go about our day-to-day lives, we layer experiences and identities over one another to form histories of participation within different communities of practice. That is the case whether we are participating in formal contexts like schools, or more informal settings like homes and clubs.

How do they learn?

Communities of practice learn as their participants engage in practice through mutual engagement and a joint enterprise using a shared repertoire. Newcomers to a group learn to become full members through legitimate peripheral participation (Lave and Wenger, 1991). Once newcomers have gained member status, they learn to participate in group activity through apprenticeship, guided participation and participatory appropriation (Rogoff, 1995). In their development of identities through their practices, issues of agency and power become central (Moje, 2007). Emotion is also central to learning.

References

Ackerman, D. (2004) *An Alchemy of Mind: The Marvel and Mystery of the Brain*. New York: Scribner.

Adey, W. R. (1968) *The Mind: Biological Approaches To Its Functions*. Michigan: Interscience Publications.

Allman, W. (1990) *Apprentices of Wonder: Inside the Neural Network Revolution*. New York: Bantam.

Ames, D. L. and Fiske, S. T. (2010) Cultural neuroscience. *Asian Journal of Social Psychology*, 13: 72–82.

Andreasen, N. (2001) *Brave New Brain: Conquering Mental Illness in the Era of the Genome*. Oxford: Oxford University Press.

Andreasen, N. (2005) *The Creating Brain: The Neuroscience of Genius*. Oxford: Dana Foundation.

Assman, J. (1992) *Das Kulturelle Gedächtnis: Schrift, Erinnerung und Politische Identität in frühen Hochkulturen*. Munich: C. H. Beck.

Bakhtin, M. (1981) *Diologic Imagination: Four Essays by M.M. Bakhtin* (Trans. C. Emerson and M. Holquist). Austin, TX: University of Texas Press.

Bakhurst, D. (1990) Social memory in Soviet thought. In D. Middleton and D. Edwards (Eds) *Collective Remembering*. London: Sage, pp. 203–226.

Bao, Y. and Pöppal, E. (2012) Anthropological universals and cultural specifics: Conceptual and methodological challenges in cultural neuroscience. *Neuroscience and Behavioral Review*, 36: 2143–2146.

Beard, C., Clegg, S. and Smith, K. (2007) The affective in higher education. *British Educational Research Journal*, 33(2): 235–252.

Bennett, M. and Hacker, P. M. S. (2008) *History of Cognitive Neuroscience*. Oxford: Blackwell.

Biddle, J. B. (2009) Advocates or unencumbered selves? On the role of Mill's political liberalism in Longeno's contextual empiricism. *Philosophy of Science*, 76: 612–623.

Blakemore, C. (1976) *Mechanics of the Mind*, BBC Radio 4 Lectures. http://www.bbc.co.uk/programmes/p00gmw6w (Retrieved 20 April 2013).

Blakemore, C. (1977) *Mechanics of the Mind*. Cambridge: Cambridge University Press.

Bloom, B. (1982) The role of gifts and markers in the development of talent. *Exceptional Children*, 48(6): 510–522.

Bourdieu, P. (2004) *Science of Science and Reflexivity* (Trans. R. Nice). Cambridge: Polity.

Brockelman, P. (1975) Of memory and things past. *International Philosophical Quarterly*, 15: 309–325.

Brodkey, H. (1988) *Stories in an Almost Classical Mode*. London: Knopf.

Brown, A., Coman, A. and Hirst, W. (2009) The role of narratorship and expertise in social remembering. *Social Psychology*, 40(3): 119–129.

Brown, N. and Michael, M. (2003) A sociology of expectations: Retrospecting prospects and prospecting retrospects. *Technology Analysis and Strategic Management*, 15(1): 3–18.

Bruner, J. (1996) *The Culture of Education*. Harvard: Harvard University Press.

Bussis, A., Chittenden, F., Amarel, M. and Klausner, E. (1985) *Inquiry into Meaning: An Investigation of Learning to Read*. Hillsdale, NJ: Lawrence Erlbaum Associates.

Cain, C. (1991) Personal stories: Identity acquisition and self-understanding in Alcoholics Anonymous. *Ethos*, 19(2): 110–134.

Callard, F. and Margulies, D. (2011) The subject at rest: Novel conceptualizations of self and brain from cognitive neuroscience's study of the 'resting state'. *Subjectivity*, 4(3): 227–257.

Carr, N. G. (2010) *The Shallows: What the Internet is Doing to our Brains*. New York: W.W. Norton.

Chabris, C. (2011) *The Invisible Gorilla: How our Intuitions Deceive Us*. New York: Three Rivers Press.

Charness, N., Tuffiash, M., Krampe, R., Reingold, E. and Vasyukova, E. (2005) The role of deliberate practice in chess expertise. *Applied Cognitive Psychology*, 19: 151–165.

Chiao, J. Y. (2010) At the frontier of cultural neuroscience: Introduction to the special issue. *Social, Cognitive and Affective Neuroscience*, 5(2–3):109–110.

Chiao, J. Y., Hariri, A. R., Harada, T., Mano, Y., Sadato, N., Parrish, T. B., *et al.* (2010) Theory and methods in cultural neuroscience. *Social, Cognitive and Affective Neuroscience*, 5(2–3): 356–361.

Christakis, D. A., Gilkerson, J., Richards, J. A., Zimmerman, F. J., Garrison, M. M., Xu, D., Gray, S. and Yapanel, U. (2009) Audible television and decreased adult words, infant vocalizations, and conversational turns: A population-based study. *Archive of Pediatric and Adolescent Medicine*, 163: 554–558.

Christie, A. Quote obtained from http://www.happydyslexic.com/node/14

Claxton, G. (1997) *Hare Brain, Tortoise Mind*. London: Fourth Estate.

Clifford Rose, F. (2009) Cerebral localisation in antiquity. *Journal of the History of the Neurosciences*, 18: 239–247.

Comber, B., Nixon, H., Ashmore, L., Loo, S. and Cook, J. (2006) Urban renewal from the inside out: Spatial and critical literacies in a low socioeconomic school community. *Mind, Culture, and Activity*, 13(3): 228–246.

Conway, P. F., Murphy, R. and Rutherford, V. (2013) 'Learning place' practices and Initial Teacher Education in Ireland: Knowledge generation, partnerships and pedagogy. In M. Jones, O. McNamara and J. Murray (Eds) *Teacher learning in the workplace: Widening perspectives on practice and policy*. Amsterdam: Springer/Verlag.

Cooley, C. H. (1902) *Human Nature and the Social Order*. New York: Scribner.

Cunningham, J. W. (2001) The National Reading Panel Report. *Reading Research Quarterly*, 36(3): 326–335.

Curtin, A. and Hall, K. (2013) Literacy as shared consciousness: A neurocultural analysis. In K. Hall *et al.* (Eds) *The International Handbook of Research on Children's Literacy, Learning and Culture*. Oxford: Wiley Blackwell.

Curtin, A. (2011) *From Exceptions to Exceptional: Choreographing adolescent learning and identity in the everyday*. Unpublished thesis.

Damasio, A. R. (1994) *Descartes' Error: Emotion, Reason and the Human Brain.* New York: Avon Books.

Damasio, A. R. (2003) *Looking for Spinoza: Joy, Sorrow and The Feeling Brain.* Orlando, FL: Harcourt.

Damasio, A. R. (2005) *Descartes' Error: Emotion, Reason and the Human Brain, 2nd Edition.* New York: Avon Books.

Damasio, A. R. (2005) The neurobiological grounding of human values. In J. P. Changeux, A. R. Damasio, W. Singer and Y. Christen (Eds) *Neurobiology of Human Values.* London: Springer Verlag.

Damasio, A. R. (2011) TED Talks – *The Quest to Understand Consciousness.* http://www.ted.com/ (Retrieved 20 April 2013).

Davies, B. and Harré, R. (2001) Positioning: The discursive production of selves. In M. Wetherell, S. Taylor and S. Yates (Eds) *Discourse Theory and Practice.* London: Sage, pp. 261–271.

DCSF (Department for Children, Schools and Families) (2009) Who is gifted and talented? http://www.education.gov.uk/ (Retrieved 13 January 2010).

Dear, P. (2006) *The Intelligibility of Nature: How Science Makes Sense of the World.* Chicago: University of Chicago Press.

Dekker, S., Lee, N. C., Howard-Jones, P. and Jolles, J. (2012) Neuromyths in education: Prevalence and predictors of misconceptions among teachers. *Frontiers in Educational Psychology.* http://www.frontiersin.org/Educational_Psychology/10.3389/fpsyg.2012.00429/full (Retrieved 3 January 2013).

Denkhaus, R. and Bos, M. (2012) How cultural is 'cultural neuroscience'? Some comments on an emerging research paradigm. *BioSocieties,* 7(4): 433–458.

Denzin, N. (1984) *On Understanding Emotion.* San Francisco: Jossey-Bass.

DePalma, R. (2008) When success makes me fail: (De)constructing failure and success in a conventional American classroom. *Mind, Culture, and Activity,* 15(2): 141–164.

Dietrich, A. and Kanso, R. (2010) A review of EEG, ERP, and neuroimaging studies of creativity and insight. *Psychological Bulletin,* 136(5): 822–848.

Doidge, N. (2007) *The Brain That Changes Itself: Stories of Personal Triumph from the Frontiers of Brain Science.* New York: Penguin Books.

Dominguez, D. J. F., Turner, R., Lewis, E. D. and Egan, G. F. (2010) Neuroanthropology: A humanistic science for the study of the culture–brain nexus. *Social Cognitive and Affective Neuroscience,* 5(2–3): 138–147.

Dommett, E. (2012) What our nerves tell us about talent. *Times Educational Supplement,* 'Behaviour' section: 13 January 2012, p. 8.

Dommett, E. J., Devonshire, I. M., Plateau, C. R., Westwell, M. S. and Greenfield, S. A. (2011) From scientific theory to classroom practice. *The Neuroscientist,* 17: 382–388.

Draganski, B., Gaser, C., Kempermann, G., Kuhn, H. G., Winkler, J., Buechel, C. and May, A. (2006) Temporal and spatial dynamics of brain structure changes during extensive learning. *Journal of Neuroscience,* 26: 6314–6317.

Dunbar, R. (2004) *The Human Story.* London: Faber and Faber.

Eagleman, D. M. (2009) *Wednesday is Indigo Blue: Discovering the Brain of Synesthesia.* Cambridge: MIT Press.

Ehrenberg, A. (2004) Le sujet cerebral. *Esprit,* 11: 130–155.

Ellis, A. (2007) *Picturing the Past: How Science is Mapping Memory. Part Two.* http://blog.nj.com/ledgerarchives/2007/12/picturing_the_past_how_science.html (Retrieved 4 November 2012).

Ellis, S. and Coddington, S. (2013) Reading engagement research: Issues and challenges. In K. Hall, T. Cremin, B. Comber and L. Moll (Eds) *International Handbook of Research on Children's Literacy, Learning, and Culture*. Oxford: Wiley Blackwell, pp. 228–240.

Ellison, R. (2013) http://thinkexist.com/quotes/ralph_ellison/ (Retrieved 20 April 2013).

Emerson, R. W. (1876) *Letters and Social Aims*. Boston: Hughton, Osgood and Company.

Emerson, R. W. (1993) *Self Reliance and Other Essays*. New York: Dover Publications.

Ericsson, K. A. and Charness, N. (1994) Expert performance: Its structure and acquisition. *American Psychologist*, 49(8): 725–747.

Eugenides, J. (2003) *Middlesex*. London: Bloomsbury Publishing.

Eyre, D. (Ed) (2009) *Gifted and Talented Education*. London: Routledge.

Fagan, M. B. (2010) Social construction revisited: Epistemology and scientific practice. *Philosophy of Science*, 77: 92–116.

Falconer, W. (1762) *Shipwreck (Fourth Edition)*. Dublin: Printed for H. M. Kenly, 1777.

Feigenson, N. (2006) Brain imaging and courtroom evidence: On the admissibility and persuasiveness of fMRI. *International Journal of Law in Context*, 2: 233–255.

Feinstein, S. (2011) The teenage brain and technology. In L. Butler-Kisber (Ed) *Learning Landscapes: Mind, Brain and Education: Implications for Teachers*. Autumn 2011, 5(1): 71–84.

Fentress, J. and Wickham, C. (1992) *Social Memory*. Oxford: Blackwell.

Ferrari, M. and McBride, H. (2011) Mind, brain, and education: The birth of a new science. In L. Butler-Kisber (Ed) *Learning Landscapes: Mind, Brain and Education: Implications for Teachers*. Autumn 2011, 5(1): 85–100.

Fink, A., Benedek, M., Grabner, R. H., Staudt, B. and Neubauer, A. C. (2007) Creativity meets neuroscience: Experimental tasks for the neuroscientific study of creative thinking. *Methods*, 42(1): 68–76.

Fischer, K. W. (2009) Mind, brain, and education: Building a scientific groundwork for learning and teaching. *Mind, Brain, and Education*, 3(1): 3–16.

Fischer, K. W. and Bidell, T. R. (2006) Dynamic development of action, thought and emotion. In W. Damon and R. M. Lerner (Eds) *Handbook of Child Psychology: Theoretical Models of Human Development*. New York: Wiley.

Florio-Ruane, S. (2001) *Teacher Education and the Cultural Imagination*. New Jersey: LEA.

Foucault, M. (1977) Film and popular memory. *Edinburgh Magazine*, 2: 22.

Fratiglioni, L., Wang, H. X., Ericsson, K., Maytan, M. and Winblad, B. (2000) Influence of social network on occurrence of dementia: A community-based longitudinal study. *The Lancet*, 355(9212): 1315–1319.

Freeman, J. (2005) Permission to be gifted. In R. J. Sternberg and J. H. Davidson (Eds) *Conceptions of Giftedness*. Cambridge: Cambridge University Press.

Freire, P. (2007) *Pedagogy of the Oppressed*. New York: Continuum.

Fuster, J. M. (2003) *Cortex and Mind: Unifying Cognition*. New York: Oxford University Press.

Gardner, H. (1983) *Frames of Mind*. New York: Basic Books.

Geake, J. G. and Gross, M. U. M. (2008) Teachers' negative affect toward academically gifted students. *Gifted Child Quarterly*, 52(3): 217–231.

Gee, J. P. (1996) *Social Linguistics and Literacies: Ideology in Discourses, 2nd Edition*. London: Taylor and Francis.

Gee, J. P. (2000) Discourse and sociocultural studies in reading. In M. Kamil *et al.* (Eds) *Handbook of Reading Research: Volume Three*. London: Routledge, pp. 195–208.

Gee, J. P. (2003) Opportunity to learn: A language-based perspective on assessment. *Assessment in Education*, 10(1): 27–46.

Geertz, C. (1973) *The Interpretations of Culture*. New York: Basic Books.

Gergen, K. (2010a) The acculturated brain. *Theory and Psychology*, 20: 795–816.

Gergen, K. (2010b) Beyond the enlightenment: Relational being. In S. R. Kirschner and J. Martin (Eds) *The Sociocultural Turn in Psychology: The Contextual Emergence of Mind and Self*. New York: Columbia University Press, pp. 68–87.

Gilman, S. L. (1997) *Smart Jews: The Construction of the Image of Jewish Superior Intelligence*. Nebraska USA: University of Nebraska Press.

Goldberg, E. (2001) *The Executive Brain: Frontal Lobes and the Civilised Mind*. New York: Oxford University Press.

Goleman, D. (1995) *Emotional Intelligence: Why It Can Matter More Than IQ*. London: Bloomsbury.

Goleman, D. (2011) *The Brain and Emotional Intelligence: New Insights*. More Than Sound. ebook ISBN 978-1-93444-115-2.

Gonzalez, N. (1999) What will we do when culture does not exist anymore? *Anthropology and Education Quarterly*, 30: 431–435.

Gonzalez, N., Moll, L. C. and Amanti, C. (2005) *Funds of Knowledge: Theorizing Practices in Households and Classrooms*. Mahwah, NJ: Lawrence Erlbaum Associates.

Gopnik, A., Meltzoff, A. N. and Kuhl, P. K. (1999) *The Scientist in the Crib: Minds, Brains, and How Children Learn*. New York: Morrow.

Gould, O. N. and Dixon, R. A. (2003) How we spent our summer vacation: Collaborative storytelling by young and old adults. *Psychology and Aging*, 6: 93–99.

Grant, S. (2012) Madness, genius and the origin of the brain. Public Christmas Lecture: University of Edinburgh.

Green, J. (2008) *Paper Towns*. New York: Dutton Books.

Greenfield, S. (2000) *The Private Life of the Brain*. London: Penguin.

Greenfield, S. (2008) *ID: The Quest for Identity in the 21st Century*. London: Sceptre.

Gutierrez, K. D. (2013) Foreword. In K. Hall, T. Cremin, B. Comber and L. Moll (Eds) *International Handbook of Research on Children's Literacy, Learning and Culture*. Oxford: Wiley-Blackwell, pp. xxix–xxxvii.

Gutierrez, K. D. and Correa-Chavez, M. (2006) What to do about culture? *Lifelong Learning in Europe*, 3: 152–159.

Gutierrez, K. D. and Rogoff, B. (2003) Cultural ways of learning: Individual traits or repertoires of practice. *Educational Researcher*, 32(5): 19–25.

Haier, R. J. and Jung, R. E. (2008) Brain imaging studies of intelligence and creativity: What is the picture for education? *Roeper Review*, 30: 171–180.

Hakuta, K. (2008) Bilingualism. Prepared for *New Encyclopedia of Neuroscience*. http://www.stanford.edu/~hakuta/Publications/(2008)%20%20Encyclopedia%20of%20Neuroscience,%20Hakuta.pdf

Halbwachs, M. (1980) *The Collective Memory*. New York: Harper and Row Colophon Books.

Halbwachs, M. (1992) *On Collective Memory* (Trans. and Ed L. A. Coser). Chicago: University Chicago Press.

Hall, K. (2008) Leaving middle childhood and moving into teenhood: Small stories revealing agency and identity. In K. Hall, P. Murphy and J. Soler (Eds) *Pedagogy and Practice: Culture and Identities*. London: Sage, pp. 87–104.

Hall, K. and Burke, W. (2004) *Making Formative Assessment Work*. Maidenhead: Open University Press.

Hall, K. and Ozerk, K. (2010) Primary curriculum and assessment: England and other countries. In R. Alexander *et al.* (Eds) *The Cambridge Primary Review Research Surveys*. London: Routledge, pp. 375–414.

Hall, K., Collins, J., Benjamin, S., Nind, M. and Sheehy, K. (2004) SATurated models of pupildom: Assessment and inclusion/exclusion. *British Educational Research Journal*, 30(6): 801–817.

Hall, K., Cremin, T., Comber, B. and Moll, L. (2013) *The International Handbook of Research in Children's Literacy, Learning and Culture*. Oxford: Wiley-Blackwell.

Hall, K., Goswami, U., Harrison, C., Ellis, S. and Soler, J. (2010) *Interdisciplinary Perspectives on Learning to Read: Culture, Cognition and Pedagogy*. London: Routledge.

Hall, K., Murphy, P. and Soler, J. (Eds) (2008) *Pedagogy and Practice: Culture and Identities*. London: Sage Publications Ltd.

Hand, M. (2007) The concept of intelligence. *London Review of Education*, 5(1): 35–46.

Hanson, A. (1994) *Testing Testing: Social Consequences of the Examined Life*. California: University of California Press.

Hanson, A. F. (2000) How tests create what they are intended to measure. In A. Filer (Ed) *Assessment: Social Practice and Social Product*. London: Routledge.

Harris, S. J. (2013) http://www.quoteland.com/author/Sydney-J-Harris-Quotes/605/ (Retrieved 20 April 2013).

Hart, B. and Risley, T. R. (1995) *Meaningful Differences in the Everyday Experience of Young American Children*. Baltimore: Paul H. Brookes Publishing Co.

Heath, S. B. (1982) Protean shapes in literacy events: Ever-shifting oral and literate traditions. In D. Tannen (Ed) *Spoken and Written Language: Exploring Orality and Literacy*. Norwood, NJ: Ablex, pp. 91–117.

Hermans, H. J. M. (2001) The dialogical self: Toward a theory of personal and cultural positioning. *Culture and Psychology*, 7(3): 243–281.

Hinton, C., Miyamoto, K. and Della-Chiesa, B. (2008) Brain research, learning and emotions: Implications for education research, policy and practice. *European Journal of Education*, 43(1): 87–103.

Holland, D. and Leander, K. (2004) Ethnographic studies of positioning and subjectivity: An introduction. *Ethos*, 32(2): 127–139.

Holland, D., Lachicotte, W., Skinner, D. and Cain, C. (1998) *Identity and Agency in Cultural Worlds*. Cambridge, MA: Harvard University Press.

Hood, W. (2012) *The Self Illusion: How the Social Brain Creates Identity*. New York: Oxford University Press.

Hutchins, E. (1995) *Cognition in the Wild*. Cambridge, MA: MIT Press.

Immordino-Yang, H. (2013) Embodied brains, social minds: Neurobiological perspectives on inspiration. Paper presented at the American Educational Research Association (AERA) Conference San Francisco, April.

Immordino-Yang, M. H. and Damasio, A. (2007) We feel, therefore we learn: The relevance of affective and social neuroscience to education. *Mind, Brain, and Education*, 1: 3–10.

Immordino-Yang, M. H. and Fischer, K. W. (2009) Neuroscience bases of learning. In V. G. Aukrust (Ed) *International Encyclopedia of Education, 3rd Edition*. Oxford: Elsevier, pp. 310–316.

Immordino-Yang, M. H., Christodoulou, J. A. and Singh, V. (2012) Rest is not idleness: Implications of the brain's default mode for human development and education. *Perspectives on Psychological Science*, 7: 352–364.

Ivinson, G. and Murphy, P. (2007) *Rethinking Single-Sex Teaching: Gender, School Subjects and Learning*. Berkshire: Open University Press McGraw-Hill.

James, W. (2008) *Talks to Teachers on Psychology and to Students on Some of Life's Ideals*. Rockville: Arc Manor LLC.

Jordan, B. (1989) Cosmopolitical obstetrics: Some insights from the training of traditional midwives. *Social Science & Medicine*, 28(9): 925–944.

Kalbfleisch, M. L. (2004) The functional neural anatomy of talent. *The Anatomical Record* (Part B: New Anatomy), 277B, 21–36.

Karenberg, A. (2009) Cerebral localisation in the eighteenth century. *Journal of the History of the Neurosciences*, 18: 248–253.

Kaufman, S. B. (2013) Rethinking intelligence in light of the default network. Paper presented at the American Educational Research Association (AERA) Conference, San Francisco, May.

Kawashima, R. (2008) *Train Your Brain More: Better Brainpower, Better Memory, Better Creativity*. New York: Penguin.

Keil, F. C. (2003) Folkscience: Coarse interpretations of a complex reality. *Trends in Cognitive Sciences*, 8: 368–373.

Kiehl, A. and Buckholtz, J. W. (2010) Inside the mind of a psychopath. *Scientific American Mind*, September/October: 22–29.

King, A. P. and Gallistel, C.R. (2009) *Memory and the Computational Brain: Why Cognitive Science will Transform Neuroscience*. Malden, MA: Wiley Blackwell.

Kirschner, S. R. (2010) Sociocultural subjectivities: Progress, prospects and problems. *Theory and Psychology*, 20(6): 765–780.

Kirschner, S. R. and Martin, J. (Eds) (2010) *The Sociocultural Turn in Psychology: The Contextual Emergence of Mind and Self*. New York: Columbia University Press.

Kitayama, S. and Park, J. (2010) Cultural neuroscience of the self: Understanding the social grounding of the brain. *Social Cognitive and Affective Neuroscience*, 5: 111–129.

Kitayama, S. and Tompson, S. (2010) Envisioning the future of cultural neuroscience. *Asian Journal of Social Psychology*, 12: 92–101.

Kress, G. (2003) *Literacy in the New Media Age*. London: Routledge.

Kuhl, P. K., Tsao, F. -M. and Liu, H. -M. (2003) Foreign-language experience in infancy: Effects of short-term exposure and social interaction on phonetic learning. *Proceedings of the National Academy of Sciences, USA*, 100: 9096–9101.

Kulvicki, J. (2010) Knowing with images: Medium and message. *Philosophy of Science*, 77: 295–313.

Lankshear, C. (1999) Literacy studies in education: Disciplined developments in a post-disciplinary age. In M. Peters (Ed) *After the Discipline: The Emergence of Cultural Studies*. New York: Greenwood Press.

Lankshear, C. and Knobel, M. (Eds) (2003) *New Literacies: Changing Knowledge and Classroom Learning*. Maidenhead: Open University Press.

Latour, B. (1991) *We Have Never Been Modern*. Cambridge, MA: Harvard University Press.

Lave, J. (1988) *Cognition in Practice: Mind, Mathematics, and Culture in Everyday Life*. Cambridge, UK: Cambridge University Press.

Lave, J. (1996) Teaching, as learning, in practice. *Mind, Culture and Activity*, 3(3): 149–164.

Lave, J. (2008) Everyday life and learning. In P. Murphy and R. McCormick (Eds) *Knowledge and Practice: Representations and Identities.* London: Sage.

Lave, J. and Wenger, E. (1991) *Situated Learning: Legitimate Peripheral Participation.* New York: Cambridge University Press.

Le Clézio, J. M. G. (2010) *Mondo et Autres Histoires.* http://www.goodreads.com/work/quotes/872651-mondo-et-autres-histoires (Retrieved 20 April 2013).

Leander, K. M., Phillips, N. C. and Headrick Taylor, K. (2010) The changing social spaces of learning: Mapping new mobilities. *Review of Research in Education*, 34: 329–394.

Lessing, G. E. (1868) *Nathan the Wise* (Trans. E. Frothingham). New York: Leypoldt and Holt.

Lewis, C., Enciso, P. and Moje, E. B. (Eds) (2007) *Reframing Sociocultural Research on Literacy: Identity, Agency and Power.* Mahwah, New Jersey: Lawrence Erlbaum Publishers.

Lieberman, M. D. (2007) Social cognitive neuroscience: A review of core processes. *Annual Review of Psychology*, 58: 259–289.

Madsen, W. (1999) *Collaborative Therapy with Multi-Stressed Families: From Old Problems to New Futures.* Watertown MA: The Guildford Press.

Magnusson, E. and Marecek, J. (2010) Socioculturalist means to feminist ends: Discursive and constructionist psychologies of gender. In S. R. Kirschner and J. Martin (Eds) *The Sociocultural Turn in Psychology: The Contextual Emergence of Mind and Self.* New York: Columbia University Press, pp. 88–112.

Maguire, E. A., Woollett, K. and Spiers, H. J. (2006) London taxi drivers and bus drivers: A structural MRI and neuropsychological analysis. In *Wiley Interscience* (published online 5 October 2006).

Manicas, P. (2007) The social sciences since World War 2: The rise and fall of scientism. In W. Outhwaite and S. Turner (Eds) *The Sage Handbook of Social Science Methodology.* London: Sage, pp. 7–21.

Marshall, H. (1972) Structural constraints on learning: Butchers' apprentices. In B. Geer (Ed) *Learning to Work.* Beverly Hills, CA: Sage Publications, pp. 39–45.

Marshall, P., Reeb, B., Fox, N., Nelson III, C. and Zeanah, C. (2008) Effects of early intervention on EEG power and coherence in previously institutionalized children in Romania. *Development and Psychopathology*, 20: 861–880.

Mateo, M. M., Cabanis, M., de Echeverría Loebell, N. C. and Krach, S. (2012) Concerns about cultural neurosciences: A critical analysis. *Neuroscience and Biobehavioral Reviews*, 36: 152–161.

McCabe, D. P. and Castel, A. (2008) Seeing is believing: The effect of brain images on judgments of scientific reasoning. *Cognition*, 107: 343–352.

McDermott, R. (1996) The acquisition of a child by a learning disability. In S. Chaiklin and J. Lave (Eds) *Understanding Practice: Perspectives on Activity and Context.* Cambridge: Cambridge University Press.

McDermott, R. (2001) The acquisition by a child of a learning disability. In J. Collins and D. Cook (Eds) *Understanding Learning: Influences and Outcomes.* London: Paul Chapman Press, pp. 60–70.

McDermott, R. (2006) Situating genius. In Z. Bekerman, N. Burbules and D. Silberman-Keller (Eds) *Learning in Places.* New York: Peter Lang, pp. 285–302.

McDermott, R. and Hall, K. (2007) Scientifically-debased research on learning, 1854–2006. *Anthropology of Education Quarterly*, 38(1): 9–15.

McDermott, R. and Raley, J. (2009) 'The tell-tale Body': The constitution of disabilities in school. In W. Ayers, T. Quinn and D. Stoval (Eds) *Handbook of Social Justice in Education*. Mahwah, NJ: LEA, pp. 431–445.

McDermott, R. and Varenne, H. (1995) Culture as disability. *Anthropology and Education Quarterly*, 26(3): 324–348.

McKenzie, S. and Eichenbaum, H. (2011) Consolidation and reconsolidation: Two lives of memories? *Neuron*, 71(2): 224–233.

Mechelli, A., Crinion, J. T., Noppeney, U., O'Doherty, J., Ashburner, J., Frackowiak, R. S. and Price, C. J. (2004) Neurolinguistics: Structural plasticity in the bilingual brain. *Nature*, 431: 757.

Meloni, M. (2011) Philosophical implications of neuroscience: The space for a critique. *Subjectivity*, 4: 298–322.

Metzinger, T. (2010a) *Brain Science Podcast Interview*. 10 March 2010. Transcript available at http://brainsciencepodcast.com/bsp/thomas-metzinger-explores-consciousness-bsp-67.html

Metzinger, T. (2010b) *The Ego Tunnel: The Science of the Mind and the Myth of the Self*. New York: Basic Books.

Middleton, D. and Brown, S. (2005) *The Social Psychology of Experience: Studies in Remembrance and Forgetting*. London: Sage.

Mihoces, G. (2011) Rory McIlroy falls apart on Masters' back nine. *USA Today*. http://usatoday30.usatoday.com/sports/golf/masters/2011-04-10-rory-mcilroy-back-nine_N.htm (Retrieved 4 October 2011).

Miller, J. G. and Kinsbourne, M. (2012) Culture and neuroscience in developmental psychology: Contributions and challenges. *Child Development Perspectives*, 6(1): 35–41.

Milner, B. (1970) Memory and the temporal regions of the brain. In K. H. Pribram and D. E. Broadbent (Eds) *Biology of Memory*. New York: Academic Press.

Misztal, B. A. (2003) *Theories of Social Remembering*. Buckingham: Open University Press.

Mitchell, K. (2010) Wiring the Brain. Online blog. http://www.wiringthebrain.com/2010/11/announcing-wiring-brain-conference-2011.html (Retrieved 20 April 2013).

Moje, E. B. (2007) Developing socially just subject-matter instruction: A review of the literature on disciplinary literacy. In L. Parker (Ed) *Review of Research in Education*. Washington, DC: American Educational Research Association, pp. 1–44.

Mosse, G. L. (1990) *Fallen Soldiers: Reshaping the Memory of the World Wars*. New York: Oxford University Press.

Munte, T. F., Eckart, A. and Lutz, J. (2002) The musician's brain as a model of neuroplasticity. *Nature Reviews Neuroscience*, 3: 473–478.

Nabokov, V. (2013) http://www.tumblr.com/tagged/existentialism?before=1318360705 (Retrieved 20 April 2013).

Naik, G. (2009) What's on Jim Fallon's mind? A family secret that has been murder to figure out: nature plays a prank on a scientist looking for traits of a killer in his clan. *The Wall Street Journal* http://online.wsj.com/article/SB125745788725531839.html (Retrieved August 2013).

Nasir, N. S., Hand, V. and Taylor, E. (2008) Culture and mathematics in school: Boundaries between 'cultural' and 'domain' knowledge in the mathematics classroom and beyond. *Review of Research in Education*, 32: 187–240.

National Reading Panel (2000) Teaching Children to Read: An evidence-based assessment of the scientific research literature on reading and its implications for reading instruction. Washington, DC: NICHD. http://www.readingonline.org/critical/shanahan/panel.html

Ng, S. H., Han, S., Mao, L. and Lai, J. C. L. (2010) Dynamic bicultural brains: fMRI study of their flexible neural representation of self and significant others in response to culture primes. *Asian Journal of Social Psychology*, 13(2): 83–91.

Nisbett, R. E. and Miyamoto, Y. (2005) The influence of culture: Holistic versus analytic perception. *Trends in Cognitive Sciences*, 9: 467–473.

O'Boyle, M. (2008) Mathematically gifted children: Developmental brain characteristics and their prognosis for well being. *Roeper Review*, 30(3): 181–186.

O'Connor, J. (2008) *The Cultural Significance of the Child Star*. London: Routledge.

O'Connor, J. (2012) Is it good to be gifted? The social construction of the gifted child. *Children & Society*, 26(4): 293–303.

Obama, B. (2013) Presidential Address. http://www.guardian.co.uk/science/2013/apr/02/obama-brain-initiative-fight-disease (Retrieved 20 April 2013).

OECD (2007a) Organisation for Economic Co-operation and Development, Center for Educational Research and Innovation. *Understanding the Brain: The Birth of a Learning Science (2nd Edition)*. Paris: OECD-CERI.

OECD (2007b) Organisation for Economic Co-operation and Development, Center for Educational Research and Innovation. *Understanding the Brain: The Birth of a Learning Science–New Insights on Learning Through Cognitive and Brain Science*. Paris: OECD-CERI.

Olitsky, S. (2007) Science learning, status, and identity formation in an urban middle school. In W. M. Roth and K. Tobin (Eds) *Science, Learning and Identity: Sociocultural and Cultural-Historical Perspectives*. Rotterdam: Sense Publications, pp. 41–62.

Packer, M. (2011) *The Science of Qualitative Research*. New York: Cambridge University Press.

Packer, M. J. and Goicoechea, J. (2000) Sociocultural and constructivist theories of learning: Ontology, not just epistemology. *Educational Psychologist*, 35(4): 227–241.

Pagel, M. (2012) *Wired for Culture: Origins of the Human Social Mind*. New York: W.W. Norton and Company.

Parker, E. S., Cahill, L. and McGaugh, J. L. (2006) A case of unusual autobiographical remembering. *Neurocase*, 12(1): 35–49.

Parkin, A. H. M. (1996) The medial temporal lobes and memory. In C. Code *et al.* (Eds) *Classical Cases in Neuropsychology, Volume One*. London: Psychology Press.

Pasupathi, M., Alderman, K. and Shaw, D. (2007) Talking the talk: Collaborative remembering and self-perceived expertise. *Discourse Processes*, 43(1): 55–77.

Phillips, N. (2013) Your brain on Jane Austen: An interdisciplinary experiment on literary attention and reading. Carnegie-Mellon University, University Lecture Series.

Quiroga, R.Q. and Panzeri, S. (2013) *Principles of Neural Coding*. Florida: CRC Press.

Ramachandran, V. S. (2003) *Phantoms in the Brain*. BBC Radio 4 Lecture: http://www.bbc.co.uk/programmes/p00gpxk6 (Retrieved 25 November 2011).

Ramachandran, V. S., Miller, L., Livingstone, M. S. and Brang, D. (2011) Coloured halos around faces and emotion evoked colours: A new form of synesthesia. In *Neurocase* epub: 25 November 2011.

Ray, R. D., Shelton, A. L., Hollon, N. G., Matsumoto, D., Frankel, C. B., Gross, J. J. and Gabrieli, J. D. E. (2010) Interdependent self-construal and neural representations of self and mother. *Social Cognitive and Affective Neuroscience*, 5(2–3): 318–323.

Restak, R. (2003) *The New Brain: How the Modern Age is Rewiring Your Mind*. New York: Rodale.

Rizzolatti, G. and Craighero, L. (2004) The mirror-neuron system. *Annual Review of Neuroscience*, 27: 169–192.

Robertson, I. (1981) *Sociology*. New York: Worth Publishers.

Rogoff, B. (1995) Observing sociocultural activity on three planes. In J. V. Wertsch, P. del Rio and A. Alvarez (Eds) *Sociocultural Studies of Mind*. New York: Cambridge University Press.

Rogoff, B. (2003) *The Cultural Nature of Human Development*. New York: Oxford University Press.

Rogoff, B. (2008a) Observing sociocultural activity on three planes: Participatory appropriation, guided participation and apprenticeship. In K. Hall, P. Murphy and J. Soler (Eds) *Pedagogy and Practice: Culture and Identities*. London: Sage, pp. 58–74.

Rogoff, B. (2008b) Thinking with the tools and institutions of culture. In P. Murphy and K. Hall (Eds) *Learning and Practice: Agency and Identities*. London: Sage.

Rose, N. (2007a) Neurochemical selves. *Society*, November/December: 46–59.

Rose, N. (2007b) *The Politics of Life Itself: Biomedicine, Power, and Subjectivity in the Twenty-First Century*. Princeton, NJ: Princeton University.

Roth, W. M. (2010) *Language, Learning, Context*. New York: Routledge.

Roth, W. M. and Lee, R. S. (2004) Science education as/for participation in the community. In P. Murphy and K. Hall (Eds) *Learning and Practice: Agency and Identities*. London: Sage, pp. 173–192.

Roth, W. M. and Tobin, K. (2007) *Science, Learning and Identity: Sociocultural and Cultural-Historical Perspectives*. Rotterdam: Sense Publications, pp. 41–62.

Rouse, J. (2001) Two concepts of practices. In T. R. Schatzki, K. K. Cetina and E. von Savigny (Eds) *The Practice Turn in Contemporary Theory*. London and New York: Routledge, pp. 189–198.

Rubin, B. P. (2009) Changing brains: The emergence of the field of adult neurogenesis. *BioSocieties*, 4(4): 407–424.

Rutherford, V. (2013) The Panopticon: St. Ultan's Infant Hospital, Dublin 1918. In C. Delay and C. Brophy (Eds) *Ordinary and Outcast: Poor Women, Family and Sexuality in Ireland, 1840–1950*. New York: Palgrave.

Samovar, L. A., Porter, R. E. and McDaniel, E. R. (2009) *Communication Between Cultures*. Boston: Wadsworth Cengage Learning.

Sawyer, K. (2011) The cognitive neuroscience of creativity: A critical review. *Creativity Research Journal*, 23(2): 137–154.

Schatzki, T. R. (2001) Introduction: Practice theory. In T. R. Schatzki, K. K. Cetina and E. von Savigny (Eds) *The Practice Turn in Contemporary Theory*. London and New York: Routledge, pp. 1–14.

Schnorr, R. F. (1990) 'Peter? He comes and goes...': First graders' perspectives on a part-time mainstream student. *Journal of the Association for Persons with Severe Handicaps*, 15(4): 231–240.

Schuman, H. and Scott, J. (1989) Generations and collective memories. *American Sociological Review*, 54: 359–381.

Schutz, A. (1970) *On Phenomenology and Social Relations*. Chicago: University of Chicago Press.

Schwartz, B. (1996) Memory as a cultural system: Abraham Lincoln in World War II. *American Sociological Review*, 61(5): 908–927.

Seuss, Dr. (1998) *My Many Colored Days*. New York: Random House Children's Books.

Sfard, A. (1998) On two metaphors for learning and the dangers of choosing just one. *Educational Researcher*, 27(2): 4–13.

Sfard, A. (2009) Metaphors in Education. In H. Daniels, H. Lauder and J. Porter (Eds) with S. Hartshorn *Educational Theories, Cultures and Learning: A Critical Perspective*. London: Routledge, pp. 39–49.

Shapin, S. (1991) A scholar and a gentleman: The problematic identity of the scientific practitioner in early modern England. *History of Science*, 29: 279–327.

Shaw, P., Greenstein, D., Lerch, J., Clasen, L., Lenroot, R., Gogtay, N., Evans, A., Rapoport, J. and Giedd, J. (2006) Intellectual ability and cortical development in children and adolescents. *Nature*, 440(7084): 676–679.

Shaywitz, S. E. (2003) *Overcoming Dyslexia: A New and Complete Science-Based Program for Reading Problems at Any Level*. New York: Knopf.

Sherrington, C. (1942) *Man on His Nature*. New York: New American Library.

Slaby, J. (2010) Steps towards a critical neuroscience. *Phenomenology and the Cognitive Sciences*, 9: 397–416.

Sloboda, J., Davidson, J. and Howe, M. (1994) Is everyone musical? In P. Murphy (Ed) *Learners, Learning and Assessment*. London: Sage, pp. 46–57.

Sommerlund, J. and Strandvad, M. (2012) The promises of talent: Performing potentiality. *Theory Psychology*, 22: 179–195.

Sousa, D. A. (2006) *How the Gifted Brain Learns*. Scottsdale, AZ: Hoagies Gifted Education.

Sousa, D. A. (2011) Mind, brain and education: The impact of educational neuroscience on the science of teaching. In L. Butler-Kisber (Ed) *Learning Landscapes: Mind, Brain and Education: Implications for Teachers*. Autumn 2011, 5(1): 37–43.

Sternberg, R. J. (2008) Abilities are forms of developing expertise. In P. Murphy and R. McCormick (Eds) *Knowledge and Practice: Representations and Identities*. London: Sage, pp. 15–29.

Stix, G. (2012) Forget cramming: Short regular training intervals may work best for learning. *Scientific American*, February 14th, 306(3):12.

Stoppard, T. (2013) http://thinkexist.com/quotes/tom_stoppard/ (Retrieved 20 April 2013).

Stuss, D. T. and Levine, B. (2002) Adult clinical neuropsychology: Lessons from studies of the frontal lobes. *Annual Review of Psychology*, 53: 401–433.

Tallis, R. (2009) Neurotrash. http://newhumanist.org.uk/2172/neurotrash (Retrieved 1 January 2013).

Tallis, R. (2011) *Aping Mankind: Neuromania, Darwinitis and the Misrepresentation of Humanity*. Durham: Acumen Publishing Ltd.

Tang, Y.Y., Zhang, W.T., Chen, K.W., Feng, S. G., Ji, Y., Shen, J. X., *et al.* (2006) Arithmetic processing in the brain shaped by cultures. *Proceedings of the National Academy of Sciences of the United States of America*, 103(28): 10775–10780.

Taylor, C. (1971) Interpretation and the sciences of man. *The Review of Metaphysics*, 34: 3–23.

Tharp, R. G. and Gallimore, R. (1989) Rousing schools to life. *American Educator*, 13(2): 20–25.

Thévenot, L. (2001) Pragmatic regimes governing the engagement with the world. In T. R. Schatzki, K. K. Cetina and E. von Savigny (Eds) *The Practice Turn in Contemporary Theory*. London and New York: Routledge, pp. 56–73.

Thornton, D. J. (2011) *Brain Culture: Neuroscience and Popular Media*. New Brunswick, NJ: Rutgers University Press.

TLRP/ESRC (2009) *Neuroscience and Education: Issues and Opportunities, A Commentary by the Teaching and Learning Research Programme*. London: TLRP/ESRC.

Tommerdahl, J. (2010) A model for bridging the gap between neuroscience and education. *Oxford Review of Education*, 36(1): 97–109.

Trehub, S. E. (2003) The developmental origins of musicality. *Nature Neuroscience*, 6(3): 669–673.

Urton, G. (2003) *Signs of the Inka Khipu: Binary Coding in the Andean Knotted-String Records* (The Linda Schele Series in Maya and Pre-Columbian Studies). Texas: University of Texas Press.

Van Lente, H. (2000) From promises to requirement. In N. Brown, B. Rappert and A. Webster (Eds) *Contested Futures: A Sociology of Prospective Techno-Science*. Aldershot: Ashgate.

van Ommen, C. and van Deventer, V. (2011) The economy of centre within the aneconomy of neurological architecture. *Subjectivity*, 4(3): 258–276.

Vidal, F. (2009) Brainhood, anthropological figure of modernity. *History of the Human Sciences*, 22: 5–36.

Vygotsky, L. S. (1962) *Thought and Language*. Cambridge, MA: MIT Press.

Wagner, K. and Dobkins, K. R. (2011) Synaesthetic associations decrease during infancy. *Psychological Science*, 22(8): 1067–1072.

Weisberg, D. S., Keil, C., Goodstein, J., Rawson, E. and Gray, J. R. (2008) The seductive allure of neuroscience explanations. *Journal of Cognitive Neuroscience*, 20(3): 470–477.

Weldon, M. S., Blair, C. and Huebsch, P. D. (2000) Group remembering: Does social loafing underlie collaborative inhibition? *Journal of Experimental Psychology: Learning, Memory, and Cognition*, 26: 1568–1577.

Wenger, E. (1998) *Communities of Practice: Learning, Meaning and Identity*. Cambridge, MA: Cambridge University Press.

Wenger, E. (2008) Meaning. In P. Murphy and K. Hall (Eds) *Learning and Practice: Agency and Identities*. London: Sage, pp. 31–46.

Wertsch, J. V. (1991) A sociocultural approach to socially shared cognition. In L. B. Resnick, J. M. Levine and S. D. Teasley (Eds) *Perspectives on Socially Shared Cognition*. Washington, DC: American Psychological Association.

Wertsch, J. V. (2002) *Voices of Collective Remembering*. Cambridge: Cambridge University Press.

Wertsch, J. V., Tulviste, P. and Hagstrom, F. (1993) A Sociocultural approach to agency. In E. A. Forman, N. Minick and C. A. Stone (Eds) *Contexts for Learning: Sociocultural Dynamics in Children's Development*. New York: Oxford University Press, pp. 336–356.

Whiteley, L. (2012) Resisting the revelatory scanner? Critical engagements with fMRI in popular media. *BioSocieties*, 7(3): 245–272.

Wolf, M. (2008) *Proust and the Squid: The Story and Science of the Reading Brain*. New York: Harper Collins.

Wortham, S. (2006) *Learning Identity: The Joint Emergence of Social Identification and Academic Learning*. Cambridge: Cambridge University Press.

Yatvin, J. (2000) Minority View. In National Reading Panel: Teaching Children to Read: An evidence-based assessment of the scientific research literature on reading and its implications for reading instruction. Washington, DC: NICHD. http://www.readingonline.org/critical/shanahan/panel.html (Retrieved 17 May 2011).

Yeung, K.-T. and Martin, J. L. (2003) The looking glass self: An empirical test and elaboration. *Social Forces*, 81(3): 843–879.

Zhu, Y., Zhang, L., Fan, J. and Han, S. (2007) Neural basis of cultural influence on self-representation. *NeuroImage*, 34(3): 1310–1316.

Index